From Philippe to Margaret

August

This Bo
Belongs to

Margaret A
Howard.

PRIMROSES and CATKINS © Gay Corran 1986

HELENA SANDERS
&
THE CATS OF VENICE

HELENA SANDERS
&
THE CATS OF VENICE

THE STORY OF A REMARKABLE WOMAN

Frank Wintle

SOUVENIR PRESS

For Helena, of course,
and for Mollie and Juliet
(Bookends)

First published 1989 by Souvenir Press Ltd,
43 Great Russell Street, London WC1B 3PA
and simultaneously in Canada

ISBN 0 285 62895 X

Photoset in Great Britain by
Rowland Phototypesetting Ltd,
Bury St Edmunds, Suffolk
Printed in Great Britain by
BAS Printers Ltd, Over Wallop, Hampshire

ACKNOWLEDGEMENTS

Extracts from the Authorised King James Version of the Bible, the rights of which are vested in the Crown in perpetuity within the United Kingdom, are reproduced by permission of Eyre & Spottiswoode Publishers, Her Majesty's Printers, London.

Thanks also to Messrs Chatto and Windus and the author Jack Clemo for permission to quote from *The Marriage of a Rebel*; to Tessa Harrow, my editor at Souvenir Press; and to helpful and patient friends and colleagues.

FRANK WINTLE

CONTENTS

CHAPTER ONE

A KNIGHT OF ST MARK

The Doge of Venice was a plump man in a grey suit, with a head of hair which fifty years or more had been steadily shaving towards his nape. He looked as if, on either side of a comfortable lunch, he spent his hours at the desk of an important but unglamorous municipal office. As I recall, there were two cats defying his dignity and sharing the ledge on which he sat beneath the chestnut trees, and both were inclined to yawn and stretch and read the pads of their paws during the Doge's speech; a third cat was sitting on a nearby wall, picking at some remnants of spaghetti which had once been involved in a Neapolitan sauce.

As the Doge shifted on his ledge, and tried to keep creases and earth and cats from his suit, the words of a childhood picture-book came incongruously to mind: 'At the Porto di Lido the Doge, standing on the poop of the *Bucentaur*, cast a golden ring into the waters, declaring "O sea, we wed thee in sign of our true and everlasting dominion."' Venice could still sustain such a ceremony, if the *Bucentaur*, the crimson and gold state barge, could have been retrieved from the ash and ingots to which Napoleon's vanity had reduced it, but this Doge looked as if he might lack a certain stability on that or any other poop.

The Doge, meanwhile, was renewing an acquaintance. He and his companion, Mrs Helena Sanders, were both wearing elaborate gold pendants bearing the insignia of the *Cavalieri di San Marco*, the Knights of St Mark, and the Doge was explaining with ample gesture how the order of knights had been instituted centuries before, when the *Serenissima*, the Most Serene Republic of Venice, had been at the zenith of her European influence: a small body of aristocrats from inside and outside the islands had bound themselves together with vows to be 'forever faithful soldiers' of the Republic. The order had lapsed as Venice herself declined, enfeebled by internal corruption and fraught by external attacks, launched on the unhappy journey which had transformed her from a sumptuous and pugnacious empire into a sort of watery pleasure ground, devoid of any power beyond the gift of perennial enchantment. But the *Cavalieri di*

San Marco had been revived in 1976 by a group of leading citizens who felt there should be some means of recognising the exceptional contributions which certain individuals made to the life and culture of Venice.

'It is something which many people covet, many people would like to have,' said the Doge. 'We receive thousands and thousands of applications, and we go through them very carefully. We collect references from civil sources, from religious sources, from the police, the local councils, and we only accept people who are considered to be very serious and very positive. An acceptance isn't a very frequent occurrence; it's really quite rare. It's a serious and moving occasion, and I have seen many people cry when they come to collect their knighthood and be invested in the order.'

The sun shone and the audience of cats continued to eavesdrop casually as Mrs Sanders asked how many British people had been admitted to the order. Four or five, the Doge told her. And why me? Mrs Sanders wondered.

'Your name was given to us by a knight of quite exceptional merit. It was passed to the Council of Ten who gathered references from different sources, and on the basis of those and, of course, what you had been doing in Venice, you were accepted as a Knight, because, you see, we all appreciated what you had done here for the stray cats and the stray dogs. You have performed a very humanitarian action which is, you know, appreciated by all of us.'

Tour Venice in any direction and for any purpose—cultural, culinary, spendthrift, or simply sybaritic—and the cats will impinge somehow or other on your consciousness. There are baroque cats spun from Murano glass, carnival masks with feline lineaments, *papier mâché* cats and cats embossed on writing paper, sketched in charcoal, and languid in watercolour. Just when you thought you had left them behind, a cat squints at you from its comfortable lodging near the feet of Our Lord on the vast canvas of a wedding feast in the Accademia Gallery. And outside, in the city itself, cats move with the presumptuous ease of secure tenants among alleys, canals, bridges and squares. Whole colonies are basking, fornicating, scavenging and fighting in certain favoured neighbourhoods: the churchyard at San Zaccaria, the garden of a civic office near the San Marcuola *vaporetto* stage, and round the Rialto market.

And yet, and yet . . . would you really single out the cats of Venice in any chronicle of a first trip to the glistening remnants of the Serene Republic? Wouldn't it be rather like visiting London for the first time and deciding that the pigeons were the most significant phenomenon in the city? The Palaces that line the Grand Canal sparkle with mosaics; the interior of San Marco's basilica glows like a beehive with its golden

A contented cat licks its chops after a titbit by the Grand Canal. Twenty years ago, as likely as not, a swift kick would have sent it to a watery grave.

tesserae; some of the chapels in the city's churches offer so many fragments of so many saints in silvered and crystal reliquaries that you feel you might assemble an entire apostle from the venerated bits and pieces; and the play of natural or artificial light makes the waterways an entertainment unsurpassed by any laser show. Here is a city which has never made any modifications to accommodate the internal combustion engine, so that it remains a constant visual index of its own historic treasures: paintings, frescos, murals and engravings stretching back over more than five centuries. To walk in Venice is to encounter a kind of giddy dissolution of time itself.

So why should an Englishwoman of 53, holidaying in Venice in 1964, have become so obsessed with the city's cats that she embarked on a twenty-year campaign to improve their lives, enduring, in the early stages, harassment and vilification from the local population, finding herself lampooned in the international press, but managing despite it all to transform Venetian attitudes and successfully to create a thriving Anglo-Venetian society dedicated to the protection of all stray animals?

As I walked back along the Zattere, the southern quay that leads to the city's customs house, I watched a man draw up from the water a sort of net that looked like a rectangular sieve. Inside there were little fish that danced and sparkled like shillings in the afternoon sunlight. A couple of cats dropped indolently from a balcony and began to wind themselves around the man's legs. He caught a few fish from his net and tossed them to the cats. Twenty years before, would his boot have sent the cats squalling on their own last dance into the lagoon? Certainly there was sufficient evidence to show that Helena Sanders' devotion to animal welfare had achieved something of a behavioural revolution in Venice. But it was too simple, perhaps too chauvinistic, to argue that Helena was some kind of veterinary Mary Poppins, crusading with British pluck and zeal against a band of habitually cruel foreigners. One had to burrow deeper into her psyche, and that of the Venetians, to excavate the real cause of her confrontation with the city, and its happy result.

* * *

Months later, browsing through some documents Helena had sent me, I came across a little yellow booklet: *Rapporto Annuale Primo del Gruppo Anglo-Veneziano per la Protezione degli Animali Randagi*—the first annual report of her Anglo-Venetian Society, published in October 1970. The chairman, Helena Sanders herself, wrote as follows:

> After five years, it is still not easy to understand, much less to

City of illusions. The views of palaces along the Grand Canal are not glimpsed through wrought iron gates, but cast back by mirrored glass.

explain, the atmosphere of distrust, ridicule and hostility in which Venetian animal lovers work, often encountering organised opposition, not to mention sadistic vandalism, where they might most naturally look for help. It is not easy to be an animal-lover in Venice. One Venetian member of Dingo was told, when she asked her friends for a contribution, that it is shameful even to speak of animals . . .

Shameful even to speak of animals? The more one explored the literature of Helena's campaign, the more one became aware that there were complex moral dimensions to unfold—elements of directly religious propaganda which suggested that she and her helpers had encountered far greater resistance to the very concept of animal welfare than they might at first have expected. It was not merely a question of persuading the Venetians that it was more decent to be kind to animals than to be cruel. Time and again the dual-language texts which were published in Britain and Venice raided the dogma of Roman Catholicism on behalf of Italian cats, seeking to borrow authority from the Church's fathers to provide a loudly answering 'yes' to the question they offered for debate: *'Gli Animale Hanno Un'Anima?'*—Do animals have souls? Here is one of Helena's helpers, Mary Collier, writing in 1971:

> It has been a dogma of the Roman Catholic Church that animals have no souls, that man alone is a spiritual being. This dogma of convenience has been primarily responsible for the terribly cruel treatment meted out in Latin countries to domestic animals, food animals, birds and livestock of all kinds. Today we are witnessing a retreat from that dogmatic position, which was certainly not in accordance with the teachings of the early Fathers of the Christian Church. St Francis was by no means alone in his faith embracing all creation, an admission of the one-ness of life, whatever that life, that spirit, that 'anima' may be . . .

Helena Sanders and her friends found themselves marshalling arguments from St Francis, St Paul, St Ambrose and St Augustine, and at times their pamphlets had more of the flavour of a dispute between medieval theologians than contemporary tracts designed to banish cruelty. But unless they could convince Italians that, despite an innate prejudice and because of the cat near the feet of their Saviour in Veronese's masterpiece, animals occupied a place on the ladder of creation nearer to men and women than stones or vegetables, the Anglo-Venetian mission would never succeed.

All of which left other questions about Helena Sanders herself, who could so easily and carelessly be stereotyped as the kind of middle-aged

A city of stone and water offers little vegetation to shelter or camouflage a cat. So the gardens of San Marcuola have a thriving—and well tended— colony. Even so, you sometimes have to look quite hard to spot them.

Englishwoman whose characteristic energy is for benign interference in the affairs of others. But what did I really know about her? I had worked out that she was probably born in 1911, and I knew that she had not married until 1959. She had moved from Cornwall to Ely after the death of her husband Guy in 1985. The couple had no children, but when I visited them at their home outside Truro I had found the place populated with cats and guarded by geese and peacocks. In a shed across the road was the gondola which Guy had bought in Venice and transported to England, and which he occasionally rowed along the River Lemon to the evident confusion of passing tourists, and sometimes plied for hire to raise funds for animal welfare work. Another shed was a studio which contained Guy's sculpture. As I reviewed the scraps of evidence, the memories and impressions, it seemed that I knew more about Guy than about Helena. A vast era of her life leading up to that moment of confrontation in 1964, when she holidayed in Venice and determined to crusade for the cats, was an absolute blank. We began to exchange letters, and her replies kept opening and quickly closing windows that offered tantalising glimpses of a rich personal history.

There were allusions to pre-war social and religious campaigns among the slums of Bermondsey; to her own and her friends' efforts to help Jews escape from the Third Reich, which in turn led to battles to retrieve Jewish refugees from internment camps in Britain—battles which were waged with such ferocity that at one stage Helena was threatened with imprisonment herself. Then the letters would skip decades and offer sketches of, say, the eccentric menagerie in Cornwall:

> The peafowl were Guy's, kept solely because he loved their beauty. The male was noisy for about six weeks in the summer, but he was always shut in at night, and usually in the afternoon as well. The goats were kept to eat the weeds in the orchard where Guy kept his gondola. The geese were kept to keep away scrumpers, which the gander did very effectively. He was a magnificent half-Chinese, and very fierce. He hated everyone, especially men. But he loved me and used to display to me. Once, he leapt at me uttering the union cry. I told him I was not Leda and he was not a swan . . .

Another note offered a brief political insight:

> I have had various opinions, ranging from being extremely right wing, under the influence of an aunt, to being a left-wing agnostic. For many years I was active in the Liberal party, and at one time I had hopes of the Alliance. Now I am more inclined to G. K. Chesterton's view of 'God's scorn for all men governing' . . .

But before Helena began to share the Almighty's supposed contempt for Westminster and Washington she was, according to a sudden cameo, more than a passive politician. In 1931 she was invited to undertake a lecture tour on behalf of the League of Nations with a group of fellow undergraduates from St Hugh's College, Oxford. At the time, Helena was cherishing an ambition to become Britain's first woman Prime Minister. The journey was shared with 'an atheistic, socialistic, pacifistic friend', Barbara Betts. 'On one occasion we drove into Rugby with Barbara singing *The Red Flag* leaning out of one window, and me singing *Rule Britannia* leaning out of the other.' Barbara Betts? Wasn't she the woman who came nearest, before a certain daughter of Grantham, to fulfilling Helena's political fantasy?

Dear Frank Wintle,

I am afraid my memory of Helena Sanders is a little hazy, though I do remember doing a tour for the League of Nations with a fellow student whom I assume was she. We took a caravan round some of the English villages: the sleeping accommodation was pretty rough! We would stop on village greens and hold little open-air meetings and I remember doing calls on the local vicar, squire, and so on to try to win support for the League. The fact that Helena was obviously decorous (and probably Conservative) made a great impression on them, though I don't think we won many converts. It was jolly good training for us both and good fun.

I hope this tiny bit of information will be of some help.

Yours sincerely,

Barbara Castle.

No doubt it was all good training for Mrs Castle (*née* Betts). But for what precisely was the young Helena Sanders preparing herself? It could hardly have been the seat she contested and occupied more than twenty years later on a local Cornish council.

Sometimes a story would seem to swim in with no obvious connection to any previous question or answer:

> I once had a boyfriend, Leo, a Russian Jew whose family went to Latvia after the revolution. His grandfather was a rabbi. They had no contact at all with Christianity, and knew nothing of its trappings. Leo's aunt in Latvia awoke one night to find a monk in her room, endlessly repeating a Latin prayer. He said it so often that she learnt it by heart, although she did not understand Latin. She asked the local priest about it, and he said there was no such prayer. She later went to Paris, and asked a more learned priest about her experience. He said: 'That is a prayer of the Baltic Knights, used by the Templars. It has been banned since the fourteenth century.'
>
> Leo came to England in the 1930s, but I haven't heard anything about or from him since he went to Israel in 1946. His aunt perished in the holocaust . . .

Then a large oblong parcel arrived. Helena explained in a note that it contained a series of tapes she had made for her half-niece and godchild, cataloguing the leading events and people in her life. It seemed strange to have seventy or so years of somebody's ambitions, achievements, failures, emotions, friendships, loves, hopes and hates, all done up with brown paper and sticky tape and sitting on the living room floor. I can't explain exactly why, but it was several weeks before I felt able, as it were, to break the seals, and in the meantime I was chasing up a book, for Helena had written in the same note that there was 'quite a lot about me in Jack Clemo's *The Marriage of a Rebel*', adding a characteristic rider—'not always accurate.'

Clemo, who moved some years after his marriage to Dorset, was for decades the visionary poet of Cornwall's claylands. His progressive blindness and deafness left him communicating with the rest of the human world first through his mother, and then through his wife, both of whom became scribes of a sort, scratching the shape of words on his palm, and then constructing statements of piercing lucidity from the apparently incoherent mumbles which issued from his mouth. At that time *The Marriage of a Rebel* was out of print, but a copy still existed in a Cornish library. And there was Helena, moving through the pages under her maiden name, as 'Helena Charles, an Anglo-Catholic social worker and journalist who lived near Redruth in Cornwall.' Clemo continued: 'She was to become a good and generous friend to me and my mother during the next few years, and to help me clarify and modify my attitude to churchy religion. A cultured lady, she had met T. S. Eliot while living in London, where she had written a novel that was destroyed in the blitz.'

Clemo's description of his encounter with Helena provided a significant portrait—a more complete figure than my fragmentary gleanings from letters and conversation had yet supplied. 'She was anxious,' he noted, 'that I should write more prose books, and was therefore troubled because of my handicaps, which she knew were beginning to hinder me as a prose writer.' Clemo had already submitted himself to whatever routines of medical treatment were available at the time and within the reach of his income. Helena's solution was to involve the poet in her Church's ministry of healing.

> She took me and my mother to a morning Mass at her parish church near Redruth. As mother and I were heretics we had to sit well back from the mysteries of the altar, mere spectators of the rites . . . I felt the hush of sanctity, the continuity of rituals unchanged by the veerings of secular thought and history, yet there seemed to be no kinship between this specialised, boxed-in religion and the rugged open-air faith that had grown in me as I read my Bible on tank walls and gravel peaks . . .

As I read this passage, it revived for some reason memories of my own first visit to Venice with Helena and Guy. I—the heathen—had been the one who dived through every church door and exulted in the antiquity and solemnity of each interior, deriving not just an aesthetic and emotional pleasure from frescos and tombs, but unspecified and macabre delights

Light and shadow in Cannaregio.

from various reliquaries. Mr and Mrs Sanders (Guy puffing slightly ahead, tense against the invisible tether of his wife's rather more amiable pottering) had seemed devoutly prosaic in their attitude to the city's monumental and artistic treasures. Perhaps they had drunk the wellsprings of Venetian novelty dry while I was still a schoolboy. When I later asked Helena to think about the special qualities of the place, she looked at me rather sharply, thought for a moment, and decided aloud that there was nothing much to distinguish it from mainland examples of Italian municipality except, of course, its intolerable cruelty to cats, which, on reflection, was only more evident because it was concentrated by a singular geography.

Before leaving Clemo behind and returning the library book, I reread his description of Miss Charles:

> A tall, dark-haired lady, not fashionably dressed but with an air of refinement and a pleasant, serious face . . . when she had gone my mother commented, 'A nice woman, but she eddn jolly—she dun't never what I call laugh' . . . She had no taste for poetry or anything musical. It was as if she had been so hurt by the break-up of her youthful romance that she avoided everything that would remind her of the soft, illusory spell . . .

'Not always accurate,' Helena had warned. I was taller than Jack Clemo, which would explain my impression that Helena was rather more slight than lofty. But wasn't she fair rather than dark? And surely we had laughed a lot on our travels and, perhaps inevitably in Venice, discussed the poetry and argued the politics of Ezra Pound, whose fascism was at least partly redeemed in Helena's evaluation by his devotion to stray cats across two continents and four nations. As we had sat over supper in the Trattoria Cugnai, discussing Pound and his notions of Paradise, Helena had reached back through more than half a century of memories. 'Very early on during my days at Oxford,' she said, 'we had a visit from the Reverend W. G. Peck, who was director of clergy studies at the Industrial Christian Fellowship. He said something that has always stayed with me. It seemed to rub itself right into my mind. "The purpose of all work is the beatific vision".'

At the time, on a warm October evening after a certain quantity of good red wine, Father Peck's maxim had a pleasing ring of archaic moral virtue. It would be some years before I understood that Helena's interpretation of the 'beatific vision' had taken her down into the lowest slums and through the meanest factory gates; that she had expounded it at public meetings and banged its virtues on the tables of private boardrooms, using its absence from the production goals of the workplace as a reason to attack a creeping selfishness she identified in the government of British industry and of Britain itself. Much as she despised Ezra Pound's antisemitism, the two of them had this in common: her 'beatific vision' and his paradise had both been blown to fragments—or so they insisted—by greed masquerading as economic necessity.

Pound's labyrinthine work furnishes a gallery in which to exhibit and to test other people's energies. And I am intrigued, as he was, by the meaning of the 'nostos', the difficult homecoming. Home, to paraphrase Eliot, whom Helena disliked, is never where you set out from, and certainly not the place where other people want to fix you. Helena, whom I thought was at home by the tidal races on the estuary below Truro, fled her cottage when her husband died, complaining of 'vultures', and settled in Haddenham, near Ely. As far as I can work out from the facts of her history, Haddenham was quite literally a strange place to come home to in her widowhood.

The Helena Sanders of Clemo's book almost wastes away from the page. It was true that I would find in her story those pale colours of melancholy heartbreak and religious wistfulness, sometimes colliding with and weakening each other, but there were also to be the vivid stripes of a crusader's livery. All the same, the very impossibility of unanimous recollection—my own, Helena's, Clemo's—becomes the most mischievous issue as one attempts to track down and separate genuine from fictitious elements in a personal history; to discover how the known episodes of the present or recent past may in some way be seen as a preparation for more distant experiences of which a biographer has no direct knowledge. What unfinished business, what dissatisfactions, frustrations and sensations of impotence in her earlier life or lives, were closed and reconciled when Helena Sanders won her battles on behalf of the cats of Venice? It was time to undo the brown paper and listen to the tapes.

Beside me as a guide was a rough chronology which I had asked Helena to sketch, and it had already struck me that if you were to unravel the mileage of her journeys across England and Europe and fling it at the sky she would probably have been the first woman on the moon. In a corner of the box that contained the tapes was a dedication to her goddaughter with a barely legible phrase written (almost etched) in ballpoint on the cardboard. It simply said: 'The Eyes of a Fool'.

That evening I searched the Old Testament to find *Proverbs* XVII, verses 22–24:

> A merry heart doeth good like medicine: but a broken spirit drieth the bones.

> A wicked man taketh a gift out of the bosom to pervert the ways of judgement.
>
> Wisdom is before him that hath understanding: but the eyes of a fool are in the ends of the earth.

Helena later insisted these verses would be apt if I needed an epigraph for her life. Guy had sometimes taunted her gently for her overseas obsessions. Mrs Jellaby, he called her, after the lady in Dickens who constantly worries about distant affairs and neglects the tragedies that neighbour her. When I had listened to all the tapes, and unwoven the tangle of anecdotes that often caused scarcely discernible short-circuits between years and sometimes whole decades, I once again found layer after layer of resonance in a quotation that had seemed at first to be superficially appropriate.

Yes, the eyes had often been cast to the ends of the earth and the mind had incessantly bothered itself (and every nearby mind as well) with obscure and decidedly foreign problems that had baffled senior statesmen. And most of us would say, 'Don't be a fool, have some more bread and butter, switch over and watch *Coronation Street*.' But Helena's was also a merry heart that kept its cheer through astonishing adversity, and though she would say again and again that almost every cause she had championed (with the exception of the fortunate cats of Venice) had 'gone into the sand', her phrase for the kind of total erasure that seemed to render years of effort sterile, there was surely, even the modest dose of medicine one woman could administer among slums or refugees, a potency of lasting goodness, a light that could never have been totally extinguished. The record contained a formidable body of work for charity, and the story was hardly devoid of romance. There were, perhaps, no 'wicked' men, but a gift proffered from the bosom had been twisted and discarded cruelly several times (at least once causing a sort of nervous collapse), and it must have taken every resource of judgement to restore a productive cheerfulness. Much had gone into the sand, but more remained as a lasting testament to her bravery.

CHAPTER TWO

HORTUS CONCLUSUS

Helena and I have talked now and then about the secret garden, or to use its grander name, the *hortus conclusus*, the closed garden. That overtone of 'conclusion' is valid, because the secret garden of literature, painting and music is also a lost garden, an experience that ends with the end of innocence, leaving a crumbling mosaic haunting the memory; and though one might later find the high wall, the gate is locked and the key has gone, or if the gate is open, you turn ecstatically inside—and find a car park or a builders' yard.

Helena, at least, gained a sort of readmission. Her *hortus conclusus* will always be Tenderah, the house near Helston where her grandmother and maternal aunts lived. And when, on the August Bank Holiday of 1959, the Helston Town Band struck up the Flora Dance to celebrate the marriage of Guy Sanders and Helena Charles, the music resounded with a triumphant symmetry, for it was on a Flora Day, more than fifty years before, with lily-of-the-valley in his buttonhole, that Helena's father had first gone to Tenderah and met and swiftly fallen in love with her mother. And after the dance was played, as Guy and Helena walked through three fields and three kissing gates, at each of which they kissed, to a reception in the grounds of Tenderah, I imagine that certain ghosts were being laid to rest, certain sceptics routed, and certain mental scores finally settled.

Her father, Frank Charles, had been born at Simla on 23 September, 1872. Grandfather Charles was known as the Deliverer of Bengal, which is to say that he was the leading obstetrician in that city and officiated in most of what the British community there referred to delicately as 'ladies' cases'. He was previously an Army Surgeon, and his brother officers, sensitive to the fact that his duties among the wounded prevented him getting a share of the spoils of war, used to provide him with trophies from their booty. Among the souvenirs of India which Helena remembers from her youth was a little cannon which had been confiscated from a Rajah during the mutiny of 1856. When Dr Charles retired he took his four sons and two daughters first to Cannes, then decided to divide the year between winters in Rome and summers in Switzerland, and finally, as the century turned, moved to Flushing in Cornwall. He became a passionate archaeologist, and a cameo among Helena's recollections shows the venerable old man pelting down a hill on his bicycle, his great white beard blown to wings on either side of his chest.

The order of the world before the First World War is alien to our modern way of life and yet, thanks to film and television, it is still deceitfully familiar. It does not help that the courtship which united the families Charles and Tyacke took place in late spring and early summer. You have the scene, as they say, entire in your mind. Sunlight; boaters and flannels, dropped waists in creamy poplin swishing to unveil a scintilla of calf; thorn bushes snowed with blossom, lilacs loosening their fragrance across terrace and lawn as the breeze mingles coolness with warmth, laughter with the sighing of the newly fledged trees. In Helena's secret garden at Tenderah the escallonia is always in bloom, and there are hidden places where a child may sculpt a happy and a safe dominion, where a young man and a young woman are perpetually falling in love.

'Daddy saw my mother looking out of a window and fell for her on the spot, even though she was wearing glasses. He was quite determined that he was going to marry her—I think it was love at first sight, and he used to travel over from Flushing to do his courting, on a dreadful old machine

From Helena's 'Baby Book'. Portraits of her father, Frank Charles, born in Simla in 1872, and her mother, Constance Tyacke, born in Helston in 1881.

that was half a pushbike and half a motorcycle. Somehow he managed to get consent. Grandfather Tyacke was an awful old tyrant, and some of his family didn't approve because Daddy was going into trade. When he was introduced to Granny Tyacke's mother her only comment was, "Poor Connie, she never had a chance."

'At the time there was a rule in his firm which didn't permit members of staff to marry until they became partners. Later on I used to have awful rows with my father about this. He said it was sensible because it meant young men didn't saddle themselves with the responsibility of a wife and family until they could afford it. I thought it just encouraged them to take mistresses. Anyway, that's the way things were, and since Daddy's firm wanted him to work in India he went back there, and he didn't become a partner until 1905.'

Another law or custom which now strikes an incongruous note forbade white women to travel to India alone unless they were going to visit their parents or their husbands. Its hidden text, perhaps, was an attempt to prevent prostitution becoming a thriving part of the colonial import and export business. Its effect, in any event, was to preclude an Indian courtship to echo the Cornish romance: Connie Tyacke stepped straight off the boat into a Bombay Church, where her marriage was solemnised. Helena had just three years in which to know her mother, but the memories formed in her infancy were indelible.

Constance was a Helston girl, nine years younger than her husband —their birthdays were but a day apart. 'She was a very vital person, beautifully dressed and very much integrated into the community. She learned first aid—I remember her putting a dressing on the foot of one of our servants and sending him to the doctor, who diagnosed the sore as leprosy, which caused a small alarm. Mother also founded the Indian Society, the Indian version of the Girl Guides Association, and she used to have ecumenical tea parties which included Jesuit priests, and members of the Salvation Army, and social workers, and missionaries of all kinds.

'I think it was from my mother that I inherited my intense hatred of suffering either among people or among animals. I remember we went to see some Pathans dancing and I was extremely worried because the Europeans were throwing their cigarette ends under the bare feet of the Pathans, and I thought they were going to tread on them, so I went round stamping on all the cigarettes. Another thing I remember is the frightful row—this was in Calcutta—when it transpired that I had been with my governess to the Eden Gardens and encouraged her to steal some flowers. The fact that I kept saying nobody would have noticed cut no ice at all with my parents.'

The marriage had been followed by a succession of miscarriages. Small wonder that huge rejoicing greeted the birth of a small wonder, Helena Trevelyan Edmonstone Charles, at 11.50 pm on Easter Day, 16 April, 1911, at 14b, Chowringhee Mansions, Calcutta. Constance Charles' exuberant hand recorded every detail of Helena's infancy in a lavish 'Baby Book': her christening at St Paul's Church, Calcutta ('pearl and diamond pendant from Uncle Ronald, pearl and turquoise brooch from Cousin Evelyn Charles, hymn and prayer book from Cousin Lena, £10 from Great Aunt

Helena at seven months, photographed in Calcutta on November 16, 1912.

Mable Charles . . .'); her diet ('a boiled egg for breakfast early in 1912 . . . very soon she was promoted to gravy and consumed large quantities of bread and butter . . .'); the first evidence of a somewhat iconoclastic sense of humour ('when she saw the King on his way to church on Sunday, December 31, 1911, she laughed with the best of them and said "ta-ta". The Queen was there too . . .'); her quaint sayings ('pip pip, ca ca, high in ky . . . pass me dat fumb dish mummie . . .'); and her travels.

Helena's first grand tour began before she was one, and is recorded in copious and loving detail.

> She left Calcutta on February 7, 1912, and went by railway with Father, Mother, and Nanny to Bombay. On Saturday, February 10, she went on board the SS *China*, and sailed for Marseilles that afternoon. She made many friends on board, including the Chief Officers. She received a teddy bear from Lady Londesborough, a Chinaman from Lord Londesborough, and a doll from Lady Alice Stewart.
>
> She reached Marseilles on Saturday, February 24, having been stranded outside Aden when people said she ran a great risk. But Father said, 'Tell that to the Marines . . .'
>
> She stayed one night at the Hotel Terminus at Marseilles. At Territer she stayed at the Hotel Bonivard, where she again made many friends. She cut three teeth during March, and had chicken pox slightly, when she was attended by Doctor Tucker Wise . . . On Monday, April 15, she arrived in Camberley, having been met at Victoria by Aunt Bessie and Grannie Augusta Wilson. At Camberley Grannie Charles and Aunt Ethel met her, and escorted her to Silverthorne, where she had lodgings.
>
> She spent her first birthday at 18, Heatherdale Road with her adoring relations, and mustered fourteen strong at tea, when she had a cake with one candle and 'Helena, aged 1' written on it. She stayed in Camberley for a fortnight and cut her eighth tooth there. Father saw her and Mummie off to Helston on Wednesday, May 1, and Grannie Tyacke met her at Truro. Aunt Kitty appeared at Gwinear Road and Aunt Gwen at Helston.

The procession of proud parents and first child continued to circulate among its Cornish and Camberley relations until the end of October, when, after 'an awful crossing' to Boulogne, a night in Paris and a train journey to Marseilles, the Charles trio and their Nanny embarked for India in the SS *Medina*. Helena 'was ill with teething and seasickness all the way out.'

Constance Charles' last entry in the Baby Book is a list of the presents

On her first trip to England: Helena with her mother in the gardens of Tenderah, and her two maternal aunts, Kit (on the left) and Gwen.

received on Helena's second birthday ('nursery furniture, toy elephant, tea-set . . .'). After that, photographs seem to be fixed to the pages at random, and where someone has bothered to fill in a page which requires specific information—academic achievements, for example, or engagement and marriage—the only handwriting to be seen is in the mature style of Helena Charles.

* * *

In 1914, as the world itself prepared for the traumatic and irretrievable changes of war and revolution, the transformation of the Charles family was begun. Connie gave birth to Gerard, in February, and within a very few weeks contracted diabetes. She died the day after Helena's third birthday. It was a loss, of course, that made no sense to a small child, though understandably she connected the fact of her brother's existence with the fact of her mother's death, and that was another source of alienation. The catastrophe was ubiquitous, chaotic, unintelligible.

'My mother's going coincided with Gerard's arrival, and I think that accounts for a good deal of the irritation I felt for him when we were young. Actually he nearly died himself. Because of the fear of infection the milk to feed him had to be boiled and that took all the nourishment out of it. He was a miserable baby. Aunt Kit had come out from Cornwall to help with the birth, and she and Daddy brought us home in the April of 1914. It was by no means certain that Gerard would survive the voyage. It was terribly hot, and he was terribly ill and I was very, very jealous. Aunt Kit told me later that when he was crying I said, "Put him out of the porthole, put him out of the porthole." We were on a P & O boat, I think it was called the *Orestes*, and it seemed impossible to get out of the heat. But one morning Aunt Kit got up very early and found the one place where there was a little bit of a breeze to cool the air; she sat there with the baby in his cot, and a woman who'd been sitting there on previous days complained to the Captain that her place had been taken—and he said she should be ashamed of herself for begrudging the coolness to a dying baby.

'What else do I remember about the voyage? Not much, except hitting a little girl on the head with a croquet mallet because she wouldn't speak English, only Hindustani . . .'

Though no doubt the family at Tenderah was grateful that two small children had survived bereavement, sickness, and a voyage in a travelling furnace, the homecoming itself was, to begin with, a sorrowful affair. Grandfather Tyacke, a shy and laconic man, was unable to face the two grandchildren whose lives were associated, however loosely, with the death of his daughter, and removed himself on a fishing expedition to

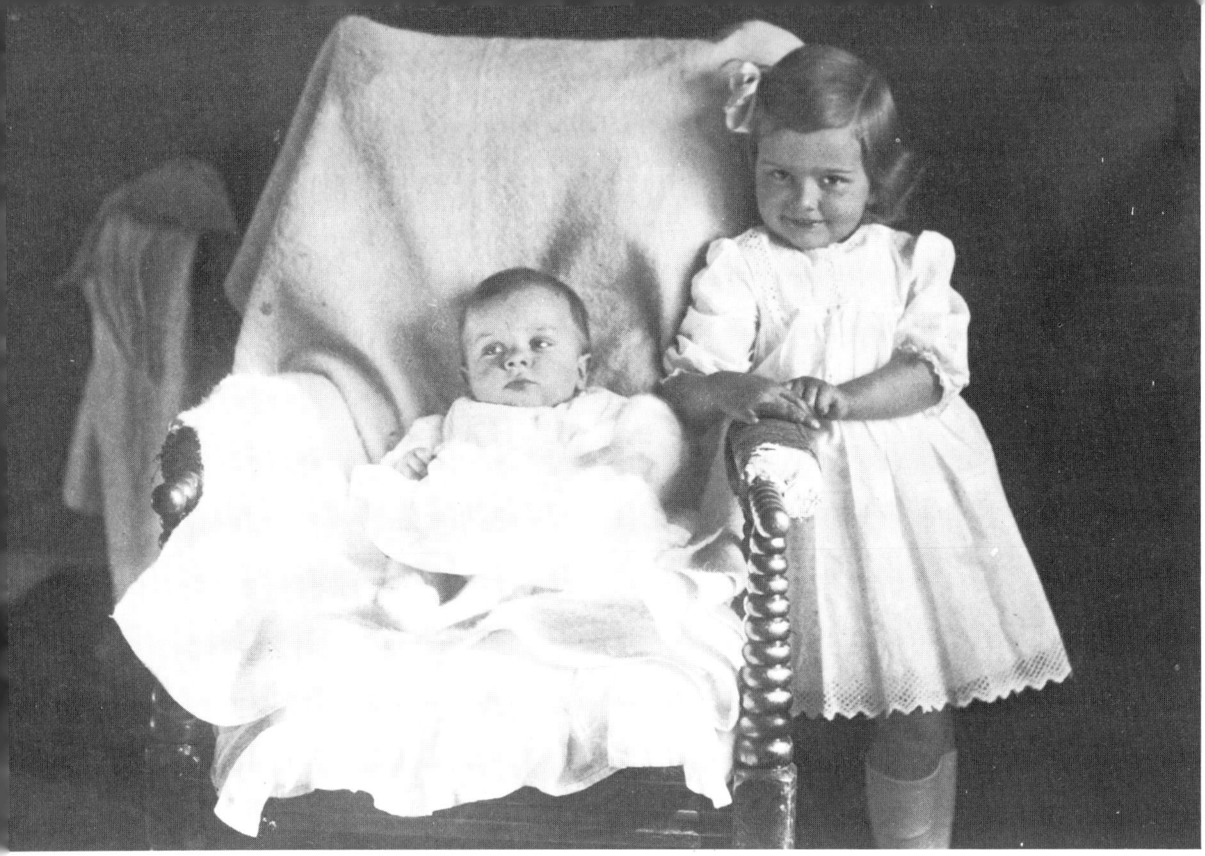

Helena at three, with her younger brother, Gerard.

Ireland before their arrival. But the two aunts and Grandmother Tyacke were more resolute and more practical, and fussed around the children, taking especial care that they felt loved and wanted when their father returned to Calcutta.

Paradoxically, the three years of World War that followed were the happiest and most balanced of Helena's childhood. In the fourth year the children were moved to their paternal grandparents, and in January of 1918 they rejoined their father on his second marriage; but in the meantime, among Cornish hills, Helena and Gerard romped with the stately and bewildered figure of Nanny Bartholomew, imported from Essex, whose verdict on Cornwall was that the county was 'nothing but cows', and whose opinion of members of the bovine species veered from contempt towards paranoia whenever they threatened to intrude on her personal space. 'There was a stray dog we'd adopted, which the three of us took for a walk one afternoon: Nanny pushing Gerard in his pram and me trotting along beside. We met a cow and calf on their way to market, and the cow went for the dog because of the calf, so Nanny plonked me into the pram and took off down the road as fast as she could go. Maybe it's because of that—because I think it really must have been a dream—that I seem to recall a whole herd of bullocks leaping over a hedge and galloping down the road to Tenderah.

'I used to be told the Christmas story, and of course the stable was always the stable at Tenderah, and if you came out through the gate and went up the road, the first house was the house that the three Kings came to, seeking the Baby Christ. I still have a vivid picture in my mind of three wise men and their camels coming up that very road towards the house. And Calvary was a little grave in the garden where Granny's cat was buried. I've always associated that mound with Calvary and the Holy Tomb.'

If any one of us were asked to locate a personal setting for the Nativity story, and then to fix our dislocation from the scene, something might be said about innocence, and the moment when its joys begin to ebb away. Innocence, perhaps, is on the edge of eclipse just when it seems at its brightest, and that point was reached for Helena in 1917 when her grandmother, in a loaded question which curiously but less cunningly prefigured a later inquisition about a kitten and a baby sister, asked her what she'd like most in the world. 'I hesitated over whether I should say a holiday at Carbis Bay, which was our idea of Heaven, or for Daddy to come home, and finally I decided that I'd really better say for Daddy to come home, and Granny said well, he's coming home tomorrow. And I remember him coming down the road in a taxi, and jumping out before it had stopped. Gerard and I were waiting on the doorstep, and then we both sat on his knee, and I made a terrible effort not to be jealous of Gerard, although I always did feel jealous of him, and we used to quarrel most terribly.'

These quarrels would not abate in the coming years, even when brother and sister might seem to have reason for a common cause. But for now the jealousy was bitten down for a period of respite and excitement. I cannot work out whether Helena's father was already engaged to his second wife, but I presume that since their marriage was only a few months away, she must already have been a figure in his life, although for the while she was a presence unannounced and absent from a landscape which was moving towards late summer. Helena and Gerard and their father went jaunting in a dog-cart drawn by an ungratefully bad-tempered cab horse called Wingfield, who had been rescued by the Tyackes from Torquay. They travelled with their picnics all over the countryside and down to the best beaches, and managed to get themselves investigated by the suspicious crew of an airship on anti-submarine patrol. This was, after all, the time when D. H. Lawrence and his ménage were being expelled from a cottage not many miles away for bohemian behaviour which the Cornish construed as sufficiently Teutonic to count as espionage. The Charles family was better anchored in local connections. Very shortly it was to expel itself and condemn Helena to what would always be a kind of exile in the Home Counties.

I once asked Helena to list the most evocative smells, sights, tastes and sounds of her life. After a little time to think, she wrote back, mentioning the scent of escallonia in her grandmother's garden, which she adored and still adores, and the stench of privet, which she hates, because someone once killed a snake beneath a privet bush in a house where she was holidaying as a child. And she continued:

> Sights? I'm not sure. Japanese anemones, perhaps, recalling the ones that used to surround the sandpit where I played with my toy soldiers, again in Granny's garden—which may be why I still let so many of those invasive flowers flourish in my little patch here in Haddenham. Tastes? Cornish cream and Cadbury's Dairy Milk chocolate. I'm not allowed cream now, nor any animal fat, and I've had to cut out chocolate almost entirely, or I'd be a chocolaholic.
>
> Sounds? The Helston Flora Dance. And when I'm emptying my cat litter trays, I often hear my stepmother's voice: 'an interesting and intellectual occupation for a lady'.
>
> Incidentally, I've underplayed her unkindness to us, out of deference to her daughters, of whom I'm very fond. She improved in later life, helped me with my trousseau, and came to our wedding, which is more than can be said of Guy's mother. She stayed at home for the wedding and came to tea a few days after the ceremony, in the little Cornish cottage along the towpath where we'd gone to live. I had my usual pile of crockery to be washed up, and while I was getting the house ready for her visit, I hid it under the bed. Guy and I got into the bed, in the early part of the afternoon, and suddenly there was a terrible crash, as the whole frame gave way under our combined weight.

Both Guy and Helena's earlier boyfriend, Leo, acknowledged Helena's aggressive—or should I say assertive?—temperament, and they attributed it to her relationship with her stepmother. Helena disputes the argument, and none of my entreaties could persuade her to be indiscreet. The lady was, we're told, 'a typical stepmother', and I suppose the hope is that we have read deeply enough among the brothers Grimm and Hans Andersen to flesh out the archetype for ourselves. 'She was pathologically selfish and never thought about anyone except herself, but I think the reason was that in her own childhood she never had any love. Her own mother, whom I knew as Granny Meredith, was the really unpleasant person in her life. She was a tragedy of a person who never loved or made

The *hortus conclusus* of Helena's childhood: Tenderah, near Helston in Cornwall.

herself loved by anyone. Her children were brought up without affection in a condition of total snobbishness and contempt for the people they called "the lower orders", all of which was amply illustrated by Granny Meredith's extreme unkindness to her servants.

'When we were children my half-sister Anne, who was my stepmother's own child, used to ask me why my Granny was so nice and hers was so horrid. I vividly remember the story that was told in the family of her son Jack returning from World War One, after suffering all the horrors of the trenches and nearly dying of typhoid. He arrived at the front door and Granny Meredith's greeting was simply: "Have you no other boots?"

'She was an old beast.'

If, as Helena did, you lose your one real mother in such bitter circumstances, will every other version seem a travesty? Maybe so, but in Helena's very silence, not just on whatever negligent or thoughtless acts took place, but on the subject of any single gesture of affection which might have sweetened her relationship with her stepmother, there is, it seems, a case to be answered. Here are the only public words I can find:

'I never got on with Anne's mother. I didn't like her and she didn't like me. And she very soon got rid of Nanny Bartholomew, which was a great grief.'

The family, if such it really was, would eventually settle together at Camberley in Surrey, but after the marriage, while Helena's father discharged the remainder of his duties in India over a period of a year or more, Helena, Gerard, and the woman who became 'Anne's mother' lived in a succession of lodgings. Nanny Bartholomew was replaced by 'a strange Russian aristocrat', the first refugee whom Helena would encounter, and clearly the one with whom she felt the least empathy. 'She wasn't a great success and she didn't stay for long. She had no proper clothes when she arrived, and so she was taken to Reading and bought a coat and skirt and some other garments as well, and I remember she used to go to bed in the coat and skirt. She was terribly vague and terribly Russian, and very keen on eating what I'd always been told were highly dangerous and poisonous toadstools. She was a good natured creature but not a great success with small children.'

I find no great warmth in Helena's description of Clarewood, the house where Frank Charles and Nancy, *née* Meredith, eventually settled, but nevertheless, to review her description of the property reminds me that this was a family of quality, and these were very different days. The house was a little way from Camberley, and occupied a seven acre estate. It had eleven bedrooms, a drawing room, a dining room, a study, a sitting room and verandah ('to call it a lounge was considered vulgar'), an attached single-storey building which was used as a billiard room ('where we danced to the music of a wind-up gramophone'), the usual utilities (I think that's the estate agents' phrase for the parts of a demesne staffed owners have no need to penetrate) and a servants' hall. The establishment consisted of an eccentric cook called Elizabeth, who was so delighted with a bedspread she was given for Christmas that she swore she would use it as her winding sheet, two housemaids, a kitchen maid, and two, or sometimes three gardeners. Outside there was a tennis lawn—'where when I was young I had to spend endless Sunday afternoons playing with the boneheaded Sandhurst cadets who came to tea'—another sloping lawn that led to a rough grass meadow, and a third lawn which eventually arrived at a wood. 'We also had two acres of allotments, which Daddy bought to stop them being built over, and they had a lovers' walk around the edge. There was a gardener's cottage where Coombe the chauffeur lived, and a stable block—but we weren't allowed to have horses, although I would have given my eyes for a pony.'

Clarewood emerges as a neat and clinical place, and for no reason I can fathom I imagine it sparsely furnished and often cold, while Helena's portrayal of Tenderah evokes a crowded, chaotic, and cordial home. And yet surprisingly, when Helena's developing convictions are investigated, the transition from the joviality of Cornwall to the relative bleakness of Camberley produced not a dreamer, but a very pragmatic woman. How easy it would have been for the displaced Eden near Helston to become the key to a mystical act of self-deception, or more fairly, self-protection: to the sort of Christianity which believes that the here and now is an illusion, a 'vale of sorrows' merely shadowing and travestying life's proper beauties.

The clue to Helena's real attitudes can be found in the books and pamphlets about sociology which she wrote years later for the Youth Committee of the Industrial Christian Fellowship. Here was a woman laying down the principles of her faith for young people, and relating them, unfashionably, to the works of St Thomas Aquinas, whose insist-

Clarewood in Camberley, the eleven-bedroom mansion where Helena spent much of her childhood and adolescence.

ence was always on the unity of body and soul, and the importance of apprehending the very signature of life on the things that we see and touch and feel and hear. All of us, when we begin to worry about the matter of existence, have a choice between Plato and Aristotle, the one arguing that our experiences are no more than phantoms of the ideal, vague shapes cast on the wall of a cave by the fire of life, the other doggedly urging, as Hugh Kenner puts it, that 'perceiver, thing perceived, and perception belong alike to a world of irreducible existences'. You cannot separate a madman from his madness or a sad woman from her sorrow and demonstrate that here is the essence of a sane man apart from an essence of lunacy, here the essence of an equable woman apart from an essence of sorrow. Helena, when there seemed almost to be a conspiracy to force her onto the Platonic path, and to seek in her private Christianity the solace of rejecting the authenticity of her circumstances, chose instead the way of Aristotle and Aquinas, and turned square to confront reality.

I can see Helena as a child staring out of the window at Camberley and beginning to piece together the elements of her sociology in the cold winter of 1921, when the family had just moved to Clarewood. Her father had secured his fortune as senior partner with George Henderson and Son of Calcutta, jute merchants. Frank Charles and his family were prosperous. Others, in the aftermath of the First World War, were less happily placed. So here was a new enigma for Helena Charles to examine: why so many men, so roughly dressed and so subdued in manner, trooped up the drive at Clarewood and banged on the door to ask for work. Any work. A bit of decorating? Plumbing? Gardening? In truth, the only real skill they had ever learned was to duck at the right moment and to use a bayonet. But they would pledge their lives that they could turn their hand to any little job that Mr and Mrs Charles could offer, for any little sum that might help to hold their homes together. Like the man who was taken on to cut down some of the trees in the garden—who within a very little while had driven the axe into his foot and departed for hospital.

It isn't hard to see why, as a child, Helena Sanders found solace and friendship among animals, or why, years later she could say, I think without a trace of irony or misanthropy, 'I don't think that there's any sensual experience to compare with riding a slow canter with a side-saddle.' As a stepchild who sensed, as children invariably will sense, that her new mother disliked her, she was outside the first circle of the family, a part of the group but separated from it, just as cats and dogs and horses are

Her wardrobe adjusted to an English winter, the six-year-old Helena poses for a Camberley photographer.

Helena aged 6

both inside and outside the intimacy of their owners. As Howard Spring made one of his characters say, there are some activities for which animals are fit companions, and others from which they are necessarily excluded, and as a young girl Helena began to exclude herself from activities which would have expressed unanimity with relatives and friends. I do not think it was a consciously symbolic gesture, but it is intriguing that, just as she was beginning to discover in animals a perfect instrument for the measurement of human worth, she developed a vehement dislike for those pursuits which demonstrated the herd-instincts of her own species.

'Looking back, it has come to me that the only thing that really interests me fundamentally is the struggle between good and evil. I think that explains my extreme boredom and dislike of all sports, whether as a spectator or as a very unwilling participant. Tennis, for example, was looked on as a social grace, although there was precious little grace on my part because I was so bad at it, and it was not unusual for my partner to lose his temper with me because I couldn't see any point in what I was being made to do. Cricket was absolutely terrifying. Enormous boys used to bowl at us and I used to try to jump out of the way. I remember once what I suppose was a perfectly easy catch coming towards me and I held out my hands and it bounced off my thumb. Extremely painful. And all for what? It didn't alter anything; whoever won the match nothing was improved in the world.'

Any sort of adversarial play which did not somehow articulate the battle between good and evil was both tedious and meaningless. 'And I'm much more conscious of the evil than I am of the good. Some people may think I'm an extremely compassionate person, but I'm also an extremely violent person with quite a filthy temper, quite prepared to demolish opponents, if not with my fists then with words. I will confess that when the tourist season in Cornwall was over, for many years I had a sense of great relief that I hadn't kicked anybody. The tourists come in their myriads and cause a water shortage despite the heavy rainfall. They clog up the pavements so you can't walk along without stepping into the road and risking being run over. I very often had to go home and not do my shopping because there was nowhere to park the car. I think the only thing that really stopped me from kicking them was the thought of the row and the newspaper headlines.

'During the war I used to have awful fantasies about finding a wounded German pilot and killing him. I used to try to combat them. I know I was wrong but they were there all the same and it would be quite wrong not to admit them. And I used to spend quite a lot of time inventing a human cinch to put on the men who used cinches on horses in rodeos, and all sorts of horrible things of that kind, which I think is why, of all the doctrines of the Creed, the one I find it hardest to believe is the forgiveness of sins.'

Helena, quietly striving to forgive, her orbit an ellipse of the family circle. Helena, a child on or beyond the margin, bestowing her love on a stray kitten, a grey Persian, the most beautiful creature she had ever known, while family love enveloped her new half-sister, Anne.

'That kitten jumped in the pram again.'

'Supposing she smothers the baby?'

'Which do you want, a baby sister or a baby kitten?'

Silence.

'Which would you rather have?'

('And I was longing to say I'd rather have a baby kitten.')

'Well?'

Sullen, tremulous. Not even a sentence, merely a phrase of death. 'A baby sister.'

And the kitten disappears.

* * *

The memories we retain of childhood often re-enact negative events which conveyed a positive importance. By which I mean that the guilt they so vividly describe fixes a moment when an aspect of character was irreversibly defined, a truth explained and locked into the self.

'For a short time my brother Gerard and I went to the local Knowle School. They were nearly all girls, but Gerard was so small that he was allowed to go along and attend the classes. There was a mentally defective girl there whom we all made fun of. We told Daddy how we'd been baiting this poor girl, and he said he hoped neither of his children had taken part. And I said rather shamefacedly that I didn't take any notice of her, and Gerard said, "I just hit her." To this day I can remember Daddy's distress—and how ashamed I felt. He told us that the girl needed help, not neglect or violence, because she was being bullied, and one of his children ignored her, and the other hit her. I've never forgotten the sense of shame that conversation produced.'

To be ashamed for more than sixty years of a sin not of commission, but of omission, suggests that a pretty formidable sense of moral discrimination was evolving in Helena's mind. Hindsight might easily have excused her neglect of, and even her contempt for her disadvantaged schoolfellow on the grounds that it solaced her own vague apprehension of herself as an outsider to find someone who was placed even further from the centre, though for entirely different reasons, and by winking at and even enjoying those taunts in classroom and playground Helena was bonding herself to the group, losing herself in its more malicious camouflage. But it was a false and dangerous manoeuvre, and even as a young child Helena was able to reject it, at whatever cost of being accused of piety and again isolated from the rest of the children. Strangely enough, the next move her parents made in steering her education could hardly have been better designed to reinforce all the wrong ingredients in the virtuous broth that was now being stirred in the girl's personality.

'I've never understood why my parents then switched me to Heathfield School. It was quite unlike Daddy, who was anything but a snob. Heathfield was the most incredibly snobbish place, even though quite a number of the girls who went there were the children of *nouveau riche* manufacturing families from the North and the Midlands. In retrospect, I realise that the woman who ran the place was a complete charlatan. She was supposed to be an invalid, and I daresay she was, because she was pretty old by this time. She wore a comb with a black mantilla stuck into her hair, and her clothes were completely black, and she was terribly effusive. On the occasions when she came to the school she had to be treated like royalty. She had one or two schools in London, and she had then opened this house in Surrey with its magnificent grounds, a fantastic white building with steps leading up to the entrance, and we eighty or ninety girls who lived there were like birds in beautiful golden cages. The whole regime completely lacked any kind of freedom. It was terribly pious and religious and High Church, and the way all this was administered was really enough to put anybody off religion for life: frightfully strict, with all kinds of mad rules about when you could and couldn't speak. For example, there was one part of the house where you could speak on Saturdays but not on weekdays, and on Sundays you could only speak somewhere completely different again.

'You were honour-bound to take an order mark if you spoke inadvertently in the wrong place, or if you had one foot on the asphalt outside the building and you uttered a single word. You weren't allowed to talk on the asphalt because it ran along beside the chapel, and I dare say if there was a service taking place that would have been a very good reason to keep quiet, but to give you an example of the absurdity to which the system stretched, one girl was told by the matron to go out in break time and call out "scarves", because it was a cold day and we were all to come in and put our scarves on. So the girl went out and ran down the asphalt and called "scarves"—and then realised that because she had touched the sacred place while uttering the fatal word she would have to take an order mark for herself.

'Needless to say, it was absolute silence when we went to bed, but some of us discovered that some of the girls were getting together after lights-out for some sort of harmless amusement, probably just telling stories and

Family group, 1926. Grandfather and Grandmother Tyacke with cousins David and Stephanie. Helena, at fifteen, dominates the sextet, and her brother Gerard is on the extreme right.

having a good giggle. Two of my friends and I discussed this, although it was really no business of ours at all, and after a great deal of agonising we decided that it was our duty to tell the head girl in strict confidence. So we did, and that was by no means the end of it, because she felt obliged by the atmosphere to tell one of the mistresses, and of course there was a most unholy row. We made ourselves extremely unpopular and thought that we were martyrs for the cause of morality, and had a pretty nasty time afterwards. The more I think of it, the more totally wrong I know it to be, but I don't blame the children that we were, I blame the general mood in the school which made us feel that it was our duty to go and interfere in something that didn't concern us and to get these girls into very serious trouble.'

Poor Helena, sitting alone from lights-out to dawn in her single room with the hip bath under the bed which a maid filled each day—yes, it was that kind of segregation—sitting alone, honour-bound not even to talk to herself through the night; not even to mutter a gentle profanity when the pillow fell in the hip bath and came out soaking wet. It was a sourly-sugared atmosphere, an other-worldly confection of rules and loud unctions. And the teachers were duffers. As far as the pupils could work out, only the history mistress had actually been to a university and managed to study her subject hard enough to win a degree. Helena's subsequent career at other schools and at university in Oxford redeemed her own academic performance and mark her out as an outstandingly adept pupil. And indeed her parents knew she was bright before she went to Heathfield; she had a governess, Catherine Carse, who had formerly looked after Prince John, the epileptic son of King George V and Queen Mary. Carsie, as the Clarewood children called her, coached Helena's precocious talent for languages, and proved by her good sense and loyalty to be a lasting influence on her pupils. Indeed, she indirectly gave a lesson in sticking to a job in the face of adversity by her decision to remain at Clarewood: 'She realised very fully the problems which Gerard and I were having to face, and although she wasn't at all happy with the position she decided it was her duty to stay on and do what she could to relieve the situation.'

But when academic results were finally wrung from Heathfield, Helena's early promise and her successes with Catherine Carse might have been dismissed as a flash in the pan, a freak spark of prodigy that had almost been extinguished as she moved into her early teens—although other parents must have begun to entertain the same worries about their children, and finally to compare notes, because the Heathfield staff and their remote and pseudo-aristocratic headmistress had to be coerced, at last, by parental pressure, into entering groups of pupils for the School Certificate. 'After we'd worked at it for five terms the majority of girls failed. I did too, in arithmetic and geometry. It was the first time I'd ever failed at anything. And then we worked for another four terms, and we mostly failed again. This time I flunked in arithmetic and algebra. I think it was around then that my father began to spot the danger signs.'

Really the signs had been there from the start, not least in the school's manic obsession with games. There were compulsory games six afternoons a week, all good stuff with hard balls and sticks and bats to bruise life's natural non-combatants—lacrosse in winter, cricket in summer. 'As for the school matches, you can't imagine the awful gloom if we lost one. There was a cup match once a year with a place called Briarsfield, and if we won, the Captain was carried in on the shoulders of the team with a laurel wreath around her shoulders, which she took off and put around the cup while we all sang the Heathfield cup song which went to the tune of "John Peel", and if we lost there was the deepest despondency all round the place, which even at that relatively early age struck me as being extremely stupid.'

On top of all that, there were sessions in the gymnasium each day of the week. 'I was rather good at climbing ropes and all the stupid exercises we had to do—bend, stretch and all that sort of thing—but I just couldn't do the vaulting. There were exercises called tiger-leaps and long-flies that I knew I would never, ever be able to do. I used to rush up to the horse and put my hands on it and grind to a stop and feel thoroughly humiliated, and it happened every day.'

Out of the gym, into the chapel. This was muscular Christianity working itself out in cycles of dizzy lunacy to circumscribe the hollowness at the academic core of Heathfield's life. If one wanted to capture the corporate stupidity and pretentiousness of the place, one might describe the moment in the Headmistress's study when that impeccable woman inferred that Helena was guilty of pride in wanting to wear a gold cross, a present from her father, in the days leading to her Confirmation at the age of 15, instead of a silver cross with a white ribbon which the Headmistress was graciously giving to all the candidates. The price of a silver cross (with white ribbon), and the cost of a presentation Prayer Book or Bible, was subsequently added to the parents' bill for each child. And then came the day itself: 'Everything we wore had to be white—white underclothes as well as white dresses, and we had white food, chicken with a white sauce and a white pudding, and we were marched into the gymnasium and onto a platform to sing "Holy Ghost, Come Down Upon Thy Children".'

And back again to the playing fields, the blue knees and chapped noses of unfortunate girls trapped in a seemingly endless game of lacrosse, like innocents caught by mistake in one of Dante's more punitive imaginings. Frank Charles marches thoughtfully up those grand steps to terminate his daughter's association with the school.

One might add Helena's footnote: 'When the headmistress died all the old girls were circulated and we were told that the best memorial we could possibly give this wonderful foundress of our school would be not a plaque in the chapel or a new building, but to discharge her debts. She'd paid herself an enormous salary and been a shareholder in the enterprise, and she still managed to finish her days deeply in debt. I did not subscribe.'

That staccato final sentence, rapid and conclusive as a guillotine, is something of a signature in Helena's conversation, her writing, and her tape recordings, a reminder that although the years may have softened her temper, the wasp still has its sting. Acquaintances whose behaviour fails to reach the standards she sets can still be summarily lopped from the order of the blessed. Only recently she wrote me an encyclical which excommunicated a villain in Europe who had sought her advice on animal welfare and rescue, and through indolence or squeamishness had shrunk from some of the harsher tasks involved—sterilisation and euthanasia—and abandoned the project. 'A Failure,' she began the letter, and underlined the word as well. All of us who know Mrs Sanders palpitate occasionally for fear that she might burst literally or metaphorically into our lives and discover that our feet are up on the sofa.

But the young Helena took a while to separate the defects of which we are guilty from those which are inflicted on us, and Heathfield had been no help. She used to return exasperated from its term-time pomposities to a household which was loveless when her father was on business abroad, and exorcise her frustration on brother Gerard. 'I think that our stepmother was even more unkind to him than she was to me, but I never seemed to be able to lose that very early instinct of jealousy I had of him. He was a late developer because he'd had such an unpromising beginning to his life, and he had rickets, partly because of the various food shortages. He was slow and he was overweight, and we used to have terrible quarrels and fights. I was the stronger of the two, and I remember Daddy coming into the schoolroom at Clarewood on the last day before we went back to school and finding me sitting on Gerard's chest and banging his head on the floor. He was terribly unhappy, it was his birthday as well. I think that was the last fight we ever had.'

Gerard went to Winchester School while Helena was in her last days at Heathfield, and the staff managed to mend his body and fire up his mind. Afterwards he refused to go to Oxford, preferring to join the family firm. Years later he and Helena shared digs while she was preparing for her career as a social worker. Although their relationship was periodically uneasy, as time passed they became closer.

CHAPTER THREE

STUDENT WITH A MISSION

St Mark's Square, Venice, 1980. A woman bustles across the piazza carrying a cat in a wicker basket, diving through the tourists, for whom she provides a momentary diversion from the glitter of the mosaics on the basilica, the purchase of ice-creams, and the pigeons. The cat, perhaps, utters an irascible screech, and the woman increases her speed, knowing that any Venetians who spot her cargo are likely to harangue her for the sin—that is how they see it—of taking an animal to undergo the snip and stitch which will bring its prodigious fertility to an end. You might say, if you must make personal remarks, that the woman is shabbily clothed and shod, and that there are some rather dubious stains on her dress. But then, the kind of catwalk the woman treads is not the sort a fashion designer knows: it may plunge into all sorts of unsavoury alleys and gutters; it might require a rapid snatch beneath a warehouse door to produce a squalling parcel of kittenhood to be appraised and despatched to the vet for inoculation and sterilisation.

St Mark's Square, Venice, 1930. A girl is parading on her father's arm along the open quadrangle of cloisters where the wealthy take tea, flourishing their wealth by chasing exorbitant bills with extravagant tips. The girl is happy, her father proud. I like to think the Venetians look at them with approval and admiration, because they have honoured a city which rates appearances by dressing for dinner. It is the girl's first visit to the Serenissima, and if she seems more than usually serene, it is because she has her father to herself, and because she had fulfilled his faith in her abilities by winning a place at Oxford.

Helena Sanders; Helena Charles. Fifty years apart. Why do we never see even a flicker of a prefiguring ghost to announce that some place will become, perhaps decades later, the centre of our physical and intellectual lives? Absurd to suppose that the phantom of a blue plaque might appear on a casual journey to give just a hint of an unsuspected and as yet unseeded significance.

Not that Helena's journey was merely a casual holiday. It was a reward for a successful school career of which, certainly, there had been no prefiguring ghost at Heathfield. And after a few days at the Danielli Hotel in Venice, Frank Charles took his daughter on a particular route through the Alps to Switzerland, up among the Lakes, where at a particular hotel they leafed through the guests' register together and found the twenty-year-old signatures of Frank and Connie Charles.

Three years earlier, Helena had left Heathfield and transferred to St Stephen's College in Folkestone. The vacuous gilded cage was replaced by a more spartan, more exacting, and more fulfilling environment. 'There was none of the luxury, the satin cushions and posh furniture and that sort of thing. It was really quite rough. There was one Common Room where the senior school sat on benches round the edge with just a few tables and chairs.' The minds of the staff, however, were richly furnished. They were all of graduate status or its equivalent, and some held double-firsts from Oxford or Cambridge. Helena was assessed, and her tutors agreed that her grasp of mathematics was so poor that she would never pass the London matriculation. So they pared away algebra and geometry from her syllabus, and concentrated on coaching her with the arithmetic she would need to support her English, history, and French if she was to get into Oxford. Macaulay was her historian, and in English the field of study was narrowed to the first two books of Milton's *Paradise Lost*, and two plays by Shakespeare: *Macbeth*, which she quickly learned by heart, and *As You Like It*, which she did not.

The French mistress, of course, was French, and the girls called her Old Fido, although I'm unable to discover whether that was a lampoon on her looks or simply a play on her name. She clung to a remarkable disesteem of the English, and in particular their tortured and torturing efforts to get some sort of purchase on a foreign language. 'I cannot stand your face, you are so deadly English,' was her favourite way of enlivening a conversation with one or other of her pupils. Except, that is, '*petite* Charles'. French was a convention of the Clarewood household, and although Helena and Gerard had initially found the campaign to make the household bilingual something of a bore, Helena surprised herself by her skill; by the time she reached St Stephen's College, despite the numbing hand of Heathfield, which might have been enough to make her forget the use of English, she was approaching fluency. '*Petite* Charles', Old Fido told the other girls, in interludes during her abuse of their faces, was the sunbeam among the stormclouds of her daily tutelage. She was better, she was nicer, she was prettier, she was, in every way, more clever. Surprisingly, the others did not peel onions and put them in Helena's pudding and knickers. Perhaps they were relieved that there was someone whose competence distracted Old Fido and cheered her up, which she certainly needed, since a favourite theme she asked her classes to investigate and expound (with quotations) explored the similarities between Molière's *Le Misanthrope* and Shakespeare's unendearing and unorthodox chef, *Timon of Athens*.

During her three years at St Stephen's College Helena spent a considerable time in the lavatory. She was not the victim of a persistent stomach disorder, but a student in search of solitude, and the other girls would hear, as they passed by, a resonant treble voice chanting extracts from Corneille, Racine, or Molière while the cisterns gurgled applause. It was the only quiet place she could find to learn the swathes of French her teacher insisted she would have to memorise for her Oxford entrance examination. If it was a consolation, in Old Fido she had an ally in her crusade against the pitch battles that schools call sport. 'I liked the teachers and I liked the other girls. They were all accessible human beings and pleasant people. But there were the inevitable games and gymnastics which were thrust down my throat again. More lacrosse and more tennis. We didn't have cricket, which was a boon, but tennis, which I suppose is slightly less dangerous. On one gorgeous occasion the Captain of Tennis, who was called Phyllis and was a very stupid girl—except with a tennis racquet—was put in detention by Old Fido because she'd made such a mess of her French, but the Games Mistress came and took her out so she could practise before a match. And the whole of the next lesson was taken up by Old Fido's anger. There was a piece of chalk on her desk which kept rolling out of the little depression on top, and every time Fido caught it and put it back as she muttered, "I will tell her, I will tell that woman. I will tell her what I think of her." I never found out whether she did or not.'

Ultimately, Helena became a sort of conscripted assistant French mistress, head of a dining room table which was supposed to talk French throughout meals. Her task consisted mainly of the weary correction of grammar and case in a dialogue whose lines ranged from 'pass the salt' to 'may I have the water?' only leavened by occasional observations on the climate, which was either doing well or badly, and on the important issue of whether the hour lacked or possessed a quarter or a half. It was hardly Molière, and after a while Helena dreaded the duty, almost beginning herself to hate the sight of English faces contorting themselves in the massacre of foreign sounds.

She passed her exams, of course, and the interviews that followed secured her a place at St Hugh's College. Celebrations at school were cut short by an outbreak of mumps, and Helena was moved to an aunt's house until it was clear that she had not been infected, and there was no danger of her father falling ill. Her degree was still more than three years away, but she had already enjoyed an early and perhaps more significant sort of graduation. Heathfield's confusions were dissipated; the teachers at St

'I made a terrible effort not to be jealous of Gerard . . . we used to quarrel most terribly.' A temporary ceasefire between brother and sister in 1930.

Classic Venice: A gondolier sweeps his tourist cargo towards the Rialto Bridge . . .

. . . and by the bridge a woman waits. 'La donna e mobile' – by boat, of course.

Most Venetian strays are tabbies, descendants of the original brigades brought from Syria by a Doge in the Middle Ages, to fight the city's rats. Since then their numbers have been augmented by domestic rejects and their offspring.

Opposite: Although the health of the feral cat population has improved beyond measure since Helena's campaign began in the 1960s, some, like the ginger tom in the foreground, still betray symptoms of disease and neglect.

Enjoying the spring sunshine near the Strada Nova.

Washday near the Campo di Ghetto Nuovo.

Stephen's had instilled a sense of confidence and clarity, a rigour of thought and a grasp of the essential qualities that distinguished Helena Charles from her schoolfriends and, more importantly, from the other members of her family. She moved to the centre of her own circle, no longer dithering between anger and melancholy on the circumference of the misunderstood and misunderstanding circle of the rest of known humanity.

It was her father's choice, in the holiday that followed her examination successes, to travel to Switzerland and pay a series of sentimental visits to the scenes of his childhood and first marriage. For Helena, an entirely backward-looking journey was interesting, but insufficient. She added Venice to the itinerary, and when the Swiss portion of the trip was over, she and Frank Charles moved on to Paris, and then to Brittany, where he left her staying with a French family and performing acrobatics in the language without the safety harness of teachers or translators around her. 'I came back speaking French really as well as I could speak English. I've never spoken French as well as that before or since. And then in the autumn of 1930, I went up to Oxford.'

* * *

I do not know what the weather was like in Oxford at the beginning of October 1930, but in my imagination Helena arrived to enrol at St Hugh's during a succession of those cool, fine days with which autumn clarifies the landscape before surrendering to winter greys. The city itself, if you subtract the traffic, would not be very different except, perhaps, for the complete absence of denim in the undergraduate wardrobe. The same imperial heads would have glared and grimaced from the Sheldonian as Helena entered Blackwell's and began to browse the shelves with her booklist in her hand; and found by chance, and read at one session, standing there among the other customers, a book by Leslie Weatherhead called *The Mastery of Sex through Psychology and Religion*.

It was, she recalls, 'very informative' for a girl who had been brought up in total ignorance of the facts of life, or at least those facts and imperatives that pertain to its continuation. 'When I was a very small girl we had a cat we called Old Snowy. One day when she was on heat a tom came into the garden and began to stalk her, making the most alarming noises. I thought he was going to attack Old Snowy so I picked him up. He gave an almighty shriek and sank his teeth into my hand and just hung there. I was in agony, but all the sympathy I got was a terrible row and a telling off for thinking too much about animals. The next day the tom attacked our gardener, who shot him, and I got blamed for that as well. They said if I

Helena (on the right, standing at the back) with the family Champenors in Brittany, 1930.
'I came back speaking French really as well as I could speak English.'

hadn't interfered the previous day the tom would still be alive. My left hand was almost dead for nearly a year, but the injustice hurt for much longer, and I've felt increasingly as the years have gone by, if they'd only explained sex to me none of it would have happened.'

Weatherhead's book poured facts into the vacant spaces that Camberley, Heathfield and St Stephen's had prudishly left in Helena's education. But some of the authorities he quoted might have been chosen to provoke a chill and premonitory tremor in the young reader—the Reverend Doctor Herbert Gray, for example:

> In the districts in which I have worked, there have always been at least a few unmarried women who were spending with lavish generosity their whole life in practical service and sympathy for needy children, harassed mothers, wayward men and the sufferers of the district in general . . . No other women are called blessed with greater effect.

Helena did not want to be reminded that spinsterhood was an emotional option. 'I had a terrible inferiority complex when I was at Oxford,' she says. 'I was convinced that I was unattractive and that no man would ever love me or want to marry me.'

She quickly formed an inseparable team with four friends: Barbara Waley ('she was fearfully pretty'), Freda Troup, a South African who was ferociously anti-apartheid, another South African, Dorothea Jeudwine, and Mary Milner, a scholar who later became a nun, then converted to Roman Catholicism and extricated herself from an Anglican convent.

'We did everything together. We took all our meals as a group, and scarcely ever talked to anybody else. We used to watch the handsome young men rowing in the eights, or go to Kemps Hall where they served delicious cakes and fudge. But mostly we worked, attending our lectures and tutorials.'

'I was convinced that I was unattractive and that no man would ever love me or want to marry me . . .' Helena in her rooms at St Hugh's College, Oxford.

There was time to be found for one flirtation, the innocence of which can be judged by the fact that the couple exchanged not love letters, but limericks. 'His name was Edgar Tomlin, and he rowed for Oxford in the boat race. He would see me home occasionally, and because he spent most of his time reading in the Radcliffe Camera, I'd go there as well, more to see him than to study. When my old headmistress, Sister Jean Marion, visited me in Oxford, she told my tutor how pleased she was that I seemed to be always among the books at the Radcliffe.'

The rules of social conduct at Oxford in the 1930s might be described as 'modified monastic'. On the one hand it was perfectly proper for Helena and her friends to dance with young men until six in the morning at a commemoration ball, and then to spend the day with their beaux punting on the Cherwell. On the other, unchaperoned visits to the men's rooms were strictly proscribed. Naturally enough, the ban was widely ignored, and Helena Charles was among the welcome trespassers, but her conscience troubled her, because she was conceiving strong notions of an individual's duty to abide by the conventions of the society that supports him—notions derived from a close reading of Rousseau, in the original French, of course.

School and university set no limit to Helena's capacity to take new languages into her mind. Throughout her life she would continue to submit to the discipline of a personal maxim which asserts that the only way to understand the fundamentals of a foreign culture is to get inside its native tongue and read in it, speak in it, think in it—even dream in it. One by one she mastered German, Italian, and Spanish. When her post-war enthusiasms involved her in the cause of the Jewish homeland, she plunged into the obscurities of Hebrew. When she finally moved back to Cornwall and tried to understand its industrial depression in terms of the historical subjugation of a Celtic people first by Anglo-Saxon and then by Norman-French conquerors, she tackled the Cornish language and became a founder member of *Mebyon Kernow*, 'the sons of Cornwall', a quasi-militant, quasi-academic group which still nourishes a hope that the Duchy (another piece of colonialist nomenclature) might achieve independence from England.

So why didn't this brilliant language scholar pursue a career as a linguist? The answer, perhaps, would have been more comprehensible in the late nineteen-sixties than it is in the late nineteen-eighties. Rather austere, they seem, the universities of the 'eighties, factory farming facts and theories for students who are pinioned to their books and bunsen burners by economic and vocational uncertainties. The years of the 'sixties rose on a vector of prosperity. Those of the 'eighties and the 'thirties did not. Yet the universities of the 'thirties and 'sixties were cauldrons of controversy, where students sincerely believed their ideas could tap into the body politic and influence its dynamics. The 'sixties believed that European and American prosperity was a sham when beyond those countries' windows lay a vista of international stress and poverty upon which local wealth seemed to depend. The young intellectuals of the 'thirties felt more simply but as keenly that tracts of the nation were deprived, and that the apparatus of the State stood indicted for selfishness on the one hand, and irresponsible failure on the other. Helena has often remarked that the solutions which were proposed by her student generation seem more than apt for today. But curiously, the effect of contemporary deprivation has been largely to silence the student voice.

Be that as it may, political notions were raging around Oxford when Helena Charles arrived, and with that frame of reference to the fore (and bearing in mind how many of her later adventures into foreign or forgotten languages were motivated by political issues, whether their subjects were Jews, cats, or Cornishmen), it helps to understand the decision she made in her first year to abandon French—the course she had elected to take—and change instead to History, where Oxford offered a strong bias towards political philosophy.

Her acknowledged ambition to be Britain's first woman Prime Minister—and with her equally acknowledged right-wing views, and her determination 'to do politics to stop communism', she seems to have had the right qualifications—was fired within a year of her arrival at Oxford when she joined Barbara Betts (later, as we've seen, to come within a hand's breadth of the top of the greasy pole as Barbara Castle) on that three-week League of Nations tour of the Midlands. In addition to furnishing some 'extremely good practice in public speaking', it also reinforced the insights provided by Leslie Weatherhead's *Mastery of Sex through Psychology and Religion*, when Barbara, observing Helena's discomfiture as they passed a bull being taken to the cows, asked her, 'What is it that's embarrassing about a biological fact?'

But these were the nineteen-thirties, not the nineteen-sixties, and although some 'rather aggressive logical positivists' at Oxford were attacking the connections between Church and State, religion was as firmly joined to politics in the search for solutions to the problems of human and social suffering as it was joined by Mr Weatherhead to psychology to achieve the mastery of sex. Then, as now, students wove alarmingly through the traffic on bicycles with one or both eyes fixed on a book, kept in place along the handlebars by agile thumbs. But then, unlike now, the book was very often a Bible, and the student would be battling with a passage of scripture, for Divinity was a compulsory subject. As well as her academic tutor, Helena had a 'moral tutor', and she became ever more deeply convinced that to amputate religion from the political equation would be to liberate a dubious materialism whose concern for the plight of the unfortunate would be at best capricious, at worst hypocritical.

Two events in Helena's life confirmed the trend of her thoughts and dished, for her at least, the notion that politics could be isolated as a science or provide a self-supporting creed. Firstly, she saw the monster that was created when anti-communism sought the symmetry of a position on the extreme right wing. Fascism was trying to find root-space in England, and the spectacle of Mosley's blackshirted lieutenants beating up hecklers and throwing them down staircases, reckless of the injury caused, horrified Helena and inspired her, she says, 'with a profound mistrust of politics'. Perhaps she perceived a potential for violence and intolerance under the respectable veneer of all political parties? Certainly her contempt for politicians of all hues dates from this period, but its birth was the result of her simultaneous experience of fascist cruelty—and of Archbishop Temple's mission to Oxford in 1932.

It is curious how, in a little over half a century, the popular concept of a religious 'mission' has undergone so unsubtle a change. Today, I suppose, it evokes the idea of a Bible-waving demagogue astride his podium, trying to engender the fear of damnation among an audience of twentieth-century sophisticates watching in a hall or, via television, in their living rooms. The appeal is feral, emotional, pitched at those who are either sated with the excesses of the consumer society, or envious because, through accident or default, they've been excluded from its bounties. And some succumb, and there are Press photographs of a crocodile of shining-eyed and possibly temporary converts making their way to the front of the hall to sign on with cash or credit card for their entrance to the New Jerusalem.

But the sort of mission William Temple launched in 1932 buttressed its spiritual pitch with an elaborate intellectual architecture. What do we remember of the man? Born in Exeter in 1881, he was educated at Rugby and Oxford, and became Headmaster of Repton before entering the Church. At the time of his mission he was Archbishop of York, and was to rise to the Primacy ten years later. A moral leader of his day, he campaigned strongly for social reform, speaking out against the evils of the time.

From the moment when Helena heard him preach, through all her campaigns for slumdwellers, refugees, exiled Jews and abused animals, the central principle of her life has hardly ever varied. It was captured, I think, in a sharp cameo, in 1962 when, at odds with the local clergy over approach and method, she and her husband Guy designed and constructed a freelance religious stand for the Royal Cornwall Show at Wadebridge. Its theme was 'Behold, and See', its message very simple: 'Because God became man, and a working man at that, all work should be able to be done to the glory of God. Can yours?' Does that sound preposterous? Naïve? Behind it, in Helena's mind, is a body of evidence grounded in the arguments of the first Fathers of the Church, dislocated during the burgeoning of Europe's great empires, rediscovered in remorse and nostalgia by certain enlightened Victorians, and lost, irrecoverably, she sometimes seems to believe, in the nation that forged a new shape for itself after the Second World War. Let me try to set out the Temple–Sanders argument in her own words.

'In the Middle Ages there was no distinction between life and religion. Everyone assumed that the Christian message applied to every part of life. But then, in the Renaissance, there was a fracture. Usury, for example, was still officially banned by the Church, but capital was needed to finance the merchant venturers, and banks emerged to lend money on interest to explorers and settlers. And because religion remained paramount in England, say, or Spain, while merchant venture enriched the State and added to its stature and strength, the Church found itself in the contradictory position of prohibiting and condoning usury. The priesthood as an institution was internalising an hypocrisy which became worse and worse as the centuries passed, and reached a climax in the Industrial Revolution, when labourers were forced to live in unspeakable and immoral conditions. But the expedience of profit led clergymen to turn somersaults to justify postures and circumstances which the scriptures condemned outright. Men like Shaftesbury and Wilberforce tried to mitigate industrialisation's most tragic effects, but they were on the outside, and although some parts of the establishment applauded their crusades, they never really became part of an official policy.

'The Victorian Oxford Movement was one reaction, an attempt by Manning and Newman and their followers first to purge the Church of England, and then to oppose it by abandoning it and joining the Church of Rome; that has to be seen as an attempt to get back to the original and purer principles of Christianity, and I think it should be taken in conjunction with the Pre-Raphaelite movement. Although theirs was primarily an artistic school, the Pre-Raphaelites' eyes were also turned to the ideals from the past. There were muddled and fanciful allusions to an imaginary lost world of chivalry, but at the core was a progressive force, which William Morris realised and separated into his own form of socialism, which indirectly gave birth to the Christian Social Movement.

'At the same time Elizabeth Garnett began her Navvy Mission to those hundreds of poor and outcast men who were building the railways, who slept in the waterpipes they were laying, and whose social position was scarcely one rung up from slavery. She forced legislation through Parliament to have them properly housed, she distributed literature for those who could read, and she trained some of them to preach the gospel. After the First World War the Christian Social Movement and the Navvy Mission merged to form the Industrial Christian Fellowship, for which I later worked. Its message was that Christ was "the Lord of all life", that there was no aspect of life which was outside Christianity. Nowadays there doesn't seem to be anybody doing what the ICF was doing: questioning the whole purpose of work, asking what it is for. I used to be quite an authority on the purposes of industry and on the principles which ought to govern the relations between management and the workforce.

'Everything that we tried to do from Archbishop Temple's mission onwards has run into the sand. It's very difficult to find any trace of that energy in the contemporary Church, although perhaps I am being unduly pessimistic. On several occasions recently the Church of England Board for Social Responsibility has stated its concern about housing and employment. And, true to form, the politicians reject the very idea that the Church has a role to play in any of these issues. Just as the Minister of Food furiously rejected our proposals during the Second World War to make a fairer distribution of what foodstuffs were available. Just as Baldwin angrily told Archbishop Temple to mind his own business when he begged him to use a budget surplus to restore dole cuts. The cry was the same then as it is now: "These left-wing clergymen should keep their noses out of government—it's none of their business."

'It infuriates me that I can't answer them back. I want to tell the politicians how stupid they are, and that because a bishop or a priest is concerned about the fact that people are hungry, or workers aren't getting a fair deal, or are living in conditions that are bad for them, it doesn't mean that bishop or that clergyman has to be left-wing. There are no words I can safely use to describe the rubbish politicians talk on these issues.'

Temple and his allies were trying to annul the divorce between mind and matter, to reconcile the essential and actual elements which God had brought together in the creation, and man in his sophistry had put asunder. For too long, Christians who were disgusted by the state of society had chosen the path of renunciation, walling themselves up in a life of contemplation which would, they hoped, lay up riches in Heaven. But was that, perhaps, a sort of pious usury? The Oxford mission demanded that the scrolls of the law should be taken out of the sanctuary, out of their dusty, mystical silken wrappers, and unrolled and declaimed on the factory floor, in the farmyard, down mineshafts, on fishing smacks and merchant ships, in slums and tenements—wherever men and women were gathered in the modern communion of uncertain and ill-paid work, weak tea, stale bread, beer, gin and misery.

We have already seen how an instinct in Helena refused to allow sweet memories of Tenderah to turn her into a dreamer: how the anger boiled, spitting at first irrationally at any target, defending itself in an acute and satirical awareness of the nonsenses at Heathfield, refining itself at last at St Stephen's College into a will to succeed. The tenets of Temple's theory had already existed for some time in outline in her mind. A cocktail of his lectures, her academic and divine studies, and the encouragement of sympathetic companions soldered together a personal philosophy which would prove invincible, in spite of every reverse, heartbreak, and cynical shift of fashion in the ensuing years.

Seventy students were so fired by Temple's visits in 1932 that they agreed to undertake their own mission, and chose to go to Streatham. They trained for a term in teams of either eight or ten, and then launched themselves at the London borough 'with great trepidation', banging on doors, talking, preaching, leafleting and, perhaps most importantly, seeing for themselves—many for the first time—the kind of conditions which thus far they had only heard about in their lectures, or read about in sociological literature. It must certainly have been on this pilgrimage to squalor that Helena Charles began to resolve that her life's work would be governed by the triumvirate of social action, political agitation and religious conviction.

> To be a Christian (she wrote in 1946) is to believe in Christ. But this involves more than believing a certain set of truths and living according to certain rules. It is a personal relationship with the living Christ and an acceptance of Him as Saviour and God. This new relationship with Christ is brought about through repentance, and turning away from sin to God, and the realisation that human nature is incapable of standing alone. There is nothing in this that is contrary to reason, but through reason alone we cannot find God (neither can we fall in love, nor write a poem through reason alone). Any human relationship implies response from two or more persons. In the relation of man to God which is brought about by conversion, nothing is possible without God's action towards us, to which we give the name Grace. This sounds fantastic and incomprehensible to those who have not experienced it: but so are being in love and many other forms of human experience incomprehensible to those who have not experienced them.

Both eyes, in this affirmation, are wide open, challenging the reader to call the faith blind. And although the words were written fourteen years after Archbishop Temple's mission, they encapsulate beliefs that Helena thenceforward hoped workers and managers and proprietors would incorporate in the business of the workplace until they became as reflexive as a firedrill. It was a tough order, and one can imagine in various locations its polite and maybe impolite reception, and plot the sniggers that followed the young missionary's departure. 'All gone into the sand'.

And love—that frail human analogy of God's robust grace? How many times did Helena's campaigns find a curious echo, almost a parody, in a melancholy personal relationship? As Temple's 1932 audience prepared for the crusades of 1933, a young curate was finding lodgings in Helena's heart.

'By the time we launched our mission to Southampton in 1933 I had fallen for Bernard in a big way. But it had been absolutely drummed into me when I was young that you never in any circumstances let a man know that you were interested in him. Certainly you should never make the first move, or he would immediately cease to respect you. So I kept Bernard at arm's length and had a persona of being a frightfully sophisticated and very much sought after young woman who really had little time for him, and he was terrified of being snubbed by this Gorgon, so he did nothing about it either. It was an absurd situation. Quite a few people actually thought we were sweethearts when we weren't, but we kept each other at arm's length for ages. Then on New Year's Eve he came to stay with us.'

There was a dance nearby. Helena and Bernard waltzed and foxtrotted with the elegant facility of two familiar partners. Afterwards, the couple returned to Clarewood, and sat by the fire in the study, talking. There must have been plenty to talk about: after all, they were fellow students, both inspired by and following the new bearings set by William Temple. What differences there were between them maybe involved Helena's more sociological, Bernard's more theological approach to the tasks the crusaders had imposed upon themselves. Perhaps they talked and disagreed about an implausible future date when women might be ordained to the priesthood. But they were also talking, talking, in an unspoken conspiracy to effect a domestic filibuster: to weary and bore young brother Gerard to bed. More logs on the fire, more talk, the clocks chiming, and still he sat there stuck to his chair like a barnacle.

'It just slipped out from me. My defences cracked. "Oh, Gerard," I said, "Please do go to bed!" And that was it—I'd given the whole game away.'

It did the trick, however, and Gerard did go to bed. And now a different and more intimate talk began, rehearsing and releasing emotions and tensions that had been shaping themselves for two years. The conversation did not stop until five in the morning. 'I went upstairs and found my hot water bottle had leaked and my bed was soaking wet. But I didn't care a damn. There was just this wonderful feeling of peace and fulfilment. I just couldn't believe it was happening to me.'

Peace and fulfilment. Less than two years would elapse before they withered away to bitterness and sorrow. The clocks had already rung in 1934 and ticked five hours away.

CHAPTER FOUR

PAGES FROM VENETIAN NOTEBOOKS

You have to remember that between the cigarette and the denim cap, behind the unshaven mask, lodged in the mind of the young man who slouches in the pilot's seat, gassing to his friend while he steers the boat with a bare foot on the wheel, something like one and a half thousand years of knowledge and instinct have been accumulated, transmitted, inherited, enabling one foot and two indolent eyes to navigate a lagoon which, through the centuries, has defeated and destroyed some of Europe's most powerful navies. The first Venetian towers sharpen into amber focus as the boat threads a passage among the shallows, among reefs that were once inhabited islands, drowned long since by the insidious and iridescent waters, among islands fenced and Alsatian-patrolled, each with a single landing stage and villa, among islands abandoned, rubbled with fallen masonry, testament to the cruelties that fog and marsh and mosquito can work between them.

City of exiles, in exile. Neither inside Italy nor outside Italy. You next have to wish away the airport, the railway and the road to understand the otherness of Venice, remember that you couldn't see her when the boat left the mainland, but then she suddenly and swiftly materialised, moving from ghostliness to gold and terracotta glory as you approached. 'To glory?' says a friend. 'To gaudiness, more like. Venice is a whore. Her painted eyes enchant you while her hand is in your pocket.' Marinetti and the futurists published a manifesto, *Contra La Venezia*, in 1910. They wanted to blow the place up; the gondola they called 'a ship for cretins'. Mussolini, the futurists' hands in his gloves, yoked the city to his fascist state with rail and road connections. Ruskin found exemplars of decadence and immorality; Wagner and Browning and Pound found peace.

The waterbuses, the gondolas, and four hundred bridges give an illusion of coherence to the one hundred and eighteen islands which make up the city, once the Serene Republic, of Venice. At first, they were an asylum for Roman citizens, fugitives from the invading Visigoths and their

A gondolier prepares to cast off. Behind him, a view across the lagoon to the island of San Giorgio Maggiore.

leader Alaric, whose emblem, says Gibbon, was a raven, because ravens circled above his armies, waiting to scavenge the carrion of his defeated enemies. The ravens might have hovered above the coast at Mestre, but the labyrinthine waterways of the lagoon held the barbarians at bay, and besides, who would want to conquer a cluster of swampy, misty, salty islands where a dog couldn't live, let alone a man?

By the time four centuries had elapsed, the hut dwellers in the lagoon commanded the Mediterranean's pre-eminent naval force; had plundered the treasures of Europe and Africa—including the bones of St Mark, smuggled from Alexandria, round which holy relics the great basilica was raised—to make theirs the richest nation in Europe; and had set in train a policy of trade and conquest without rival in the world. The Venetian empire eventually reached from the Alps to Yugoslavia, and Venice beautified herself with painting, architecture, and sculpture by Titian, Giorgione, Lombardo, da Ponte, Veronese, Tintoretto, Longhena, Tiepolo, Canaletto, Sansovino and Scamozzi, while listening to or reading the works of Monteverdi, Gabrieli, Cesti, Vivaldi, Goldoni and Gozzi.

On alighting in St Mark's Square, as the guide books say, the visitor's curiosity is straightway excited by a plethora of architectural and ornamental effect. He scarcely knows where to look first (but in his confusion he had better keep a hand on his wallet and passport, and she should keep her handbag buttoned up). Possibly a single lens reflex will swing his eye towards the soaring redbrick Campanile, a 310-foot bell tower which dominates the piazza and piazzetta. The first of many Venetian deceptions. In 1902, after eight hundred years, the original fell down. There was only one fatality: a cat.

City of cats, for here they come again, arguing for a place on mantelpiece or wall: glass cats, ceramic cats, *papier mâché* cats, engraved cats, embossed cats, oil cats, watercolour cats, tempera cats, wooden cats, enamel cats . . . and, merely arguing for a scrap of food and a quiet berth, several thousand genuine, one hundred per cent authenticated Venetian stray cats, in different states of plumpness, scrawniness, concupiscence or pregnancy.

A gondola passes beneath the hotel window. The singer and accordionist are dressed not in traditional straw hats and striped vests, but cloth caps and anoraks. Sitting opposite them, a group of tourists nervously applaud the serenade when it stops, and don't seem to want an encore. In Cornwall, the dialect word 'hobbler' describes one who acts as a guide or a ferryman, but it has a derisive undertone poised somewhere between touting and pimping. A lot of graceful hobbling goes on in Venice.

Opposite the hotel, a dozen Japanese tourists, their arms stuck with tripods and their necks heavy with lenses, are photographing a bleached Italian model. She wears a fur coat and underclothes, and her smile is a function only of the muscles round her mouth. She is persuaded to drape a leg over a parapet, to squat beneath a bridge, to perch on a windowsill, to straddle some railings, to embrace a waiting gondolier (attired in the proper livery), to bite a nectarine, to toast the pack with a glass of sparkling water, and, finally, to remove her fur coat and essay some rather more desperate poses.

City more photographed than real. A billion shutterclicks a year? And now the videotape as well. This afternoon in the basilica, in the chapel reserved for prayer only, where the overarching mosaics suffuse the building with the light of an autumn dusk, where the candles burn in silvered cases of red Murano glass to indicate the presence of the consecrated Host, which is, they say, the living flesh of Christ, a party of children burst in, squint their cameras one by one at the altar, and depart within half a minute. Outside in the piazza, the same few square feet of the great square are tenanted each day by hundreds of delegates of a dozen nationalities, each of whose husbands, wives, lovers, mothers, fathers, teachers or friends use the same unblinking lions, apostles, doges or popes as celluloid props and companions.

This afternoon on the *vaporetto*: a teacher loudly, pleadingly offers his

Before the tourists rise: grocery rounds, Venetian style.

pupils a biographical sketch of the Virgin St Lucia of Syracuse as we pass her church. The girls scream *'Ciao!'* at two suave *carbonieri* who are overtaking in their launch. *'Pace e Luce al Mondo,'* whispers St Lucia's wall in sable letters on white stone. St Lucia is in there, looking a little weatherbeaten in her glass case. Elsewhere in the city repose St Athanasius, St Zaccaria, and a few other saints, each looking as benign as a few hundred years of transformation from flesh and blood to parchment and bone allows. I wouldn't care to be in Venice on Judgement Day, when the blessed and the butchered try to sort out the bits and pieces of their bodies to reclothe their immortal souls.

Look at the lions' mouths in the wall of the Doge's palace. Their inscriptions invite public-spirited citizens to denounce, anonymously, those of their fellows they suspect of tax-dodging, conspiracy, smuggling, theft, murder, fraud or any other malefaction. A real dead letterbox. A knock in the night, a rope round the neck. At one time a certain section of the lagoon was reserved for strangled victims of the Council of Ten. Fishing prohibited, by order. If the victim had been particularly wicked, he might live until daylight to be publicly cut to pieces, with joints of him despatched around the city to act as bloody and eloquent mementoes. Or buried upside down in St Mark's Square. The lucky ones went across the Bridge of Sighs and into prison and thence, perhaps, to the galleys with which Venice dominated Europe. It was the cruelty, said Helena, which often made her dislike the city. Its odour seemed to cling to the opulent palaces and rise from the canals like the mists which can suddenly invade the sunniest evening. You feel the cruelty as soon as you see the lions' mouths and the Bridge of Sighs, the metal slaves who strike the hours in the Piazza, and the metal slaves who are burdened with the world itself, out at the edge of the Dogona, while a golden figure of fortune swings freely above them to tell Venice which wind prevails. The mystery of Venice is the coexistence of exquisite beauty with a folk memory of horror and tragedy. A Iago might have taught the lions' mouths to open to treachery, an Othello set slaves to hammer out the time.

What do the words exactly mean? *Calle, Rio, Fondamente, Sotoportego, Riva*. Each one seems to offer the same medley of bridge, path, pier or blank wall, only mixed in more generous or more niggardly proportions. What mad Venetian civil engineer designed alleys that with one twist discard the crowds and become passageways of disturbing narrowness and isolation, corridors that derange the compass with their sudden gyrations? Stone, water, uproar, silence, piercing light and chilling shadow.

Half an hour before midnight, in St Mark's Square, two gangs of teenagers, liberated from the tedium of galleries and churches, are kicking

A feral cat claims a ledge between green shutters with a proprietary flick of its scent glands: the Dorsoduro.

The Lion of St Mark, symbol of the cruelty and beauty of ancient Venice, presides over the Piazza San Marco.

Opposite: Two of the mosaics which decorate the west façade of the Basilica di San Marco.

And another commands the Torri dell'Arsenale, behind whose gates Venice armed to confront and dominate the Mediterranean.

Opposite: The Basilica itself, about to be invaded by tourist hordes.

A nervous awakening near San Zaccaria.

At the Rio Tera Drio La Chiesa, two cats are already on early morning patrol in case one of the 'mothers' turns up with free food.

Santa Lucia on the Grand Canal: 'peace and light to Italy, and the world'.

a football beneath the impassive basilica. In darker corners other tournaments, of adolescent lust, are being played. But—observing an etching in the window of an antique shop—I'm not sure that bear baiting in the same arena would be any more edifying or any less noisy. Anyway, the time to see the piazza is at daybreak, when you share it with the pigeons, the cats, a few sleepy cleaners and a couple of policemen. You walk away from St Mark's at night, maybe past the Fenice Theatre, watching the lamps turn

The infamous Bridge of Sighs. 'The State is all,' said the constitution of the Republic. 'It is for the individual unconditionally to serve the State. No one person may rise above the others, no cult of personality will be tolerated.' Those with other ideas enjoyed their last glimpse of the free world through those latticed windows.

to torches in the solemn, black undulations of the canals, over the Academy Bridge and across to the Dogona or the Zattere, where you can watch boats and buildings send festivals of light dancing across the lagoon. Vague or strident sounds pulse in the night. The blizzard noise the *vaporetti* seem to make before they pull away from their jetties. The shouted conversations of boatmen, who always turn their engines on before they talk. Cries from youngsters leaving a dance or a discotheque. Bells: muffled, light, or ominous. Each one rises to the margin of consciousness, only to be thinned and swallowed as the city tries to fall asleep. And Venice has much to dream about, for in her archives there are a quarter of a million books and documents, the largest civic collection in the world, recording conquests, treaties, trading agreements, reports from spies in every foreign court, rumours of domestic treasons, sumptuary laws that forbade ostentation in dress and deed, regulations governing the colour of gondolas (black only), tax returns and customs tariffs, and the names in the *Libro d'Oro*, the book of gold, described by one author as 'a perpetual studbook of Venice's aristocracy', proving the ancestry of the mighty and limiting to them alone the right to join the courts and councils which dictated the destiny of the ancient republic.

Silence. Only the wash of water against marble. A half-dream, perhaps, induced by a mix of red wine and the local dish of liver and onions (sounds dull, is delicious) of pauper women diving to the mud at the bottom of the lagoon to search for a golden ring. Silence; except, like the bugle calls of a scattered infantry, the noise of a few members of the legions of cats sating their grosser appetites. 'Unpaid municipal ratcatchers', Helena calls them. Sifters of garbage, porters of fleas, emerging from their lairs for the night patrol.

* * *

The lion (beauty and cruelty) is the emblem of the city's patron saint, Mark the Evangelist, and sculpted lions, from small to monumental, adorn every part of Venice. But if the lion is the custodian of the city's spiritual welfare, for centuries the cat has been her physical guardian. Those early settlers on a wilderness of marsh were prey to all the diseases that ferment

One of the earliest cats to come to Venice: an ancient wooden sculpture of the Lion of St Mark, now stored in the Basilica museum.

when mosquitos and a damp, warm atmosphere are in concert against men and women. Numbers of islands were tried and then deserted in a search for the most salubrious environment. Then came the undetected and unwanted stowaways who follow every merchant navy: rats, shipping plagues between the farthest ends of the world.

It was a doge in the Middle Ages who made the mental connection between rats and cats, and sent to Syria for a consignment. The mass of Venetian strays do have a Levantine look to them: lithe, large-eyed with attenuated jaws, tabby or ginger. You sometimes bump into a likeness of one of their ancestors if you happen to be browsing among the classical artefacts in the British Museum. But there are also strays of other shapes and colours, because over the years unwanted domestic litters have been dumped on the streets to join the descendants of the original workforce.

Venice's debt to the cat is acknowledged in a number of unobtrusive places. You'll find a Campo delle Gatte, a Salizada delle Gatte, and a Ramo delle Gatte as you walk along the canals and across the squares. After all, cats were the only creatures which could protect the city's granaries and save her from desperate famine and incurable sickness, and still they continue—you see them all around the complex of open-air food markets near the Rialto—to keep the rodent population under control. And yet there is a curious ambivalence in Venetian attitudes to the animals. Or perhaps, and more fairly, there is a curious ambivalence in humanity's attitude to any functionary, be he or she a cat or a roadsweeper or a labourer on a sewage farm—the execution of whose daily tasks involves activities which the rest of us find it distasteful or disgusting to contemplate. Gratitude succumbs to a rising revulsion when we imagine the actual performance of the job. So it may be that a generalised ambivalence was simply brought into sharp focus by the continuing relationship of Venice and her cats, and the opportunity to study it that was afforded by the intervention of Helena and her friends and colleagues.

The fascinating, if disturbing feature of the episode was the revelation not just of neglect, but of limited and local outbreaks of real cruelty. Of course, there will always be in any society (perhaps until Helena's pursuit of the beatific vision is universal) sadists who take pleasure in tormenting their fellow creatures. But leafing through hundreds of pages of reports prepared over the years by Dingo, the Anglo-Venetian Group for the Protection of Stray Animals, one encounters time and again a more systematic, a more organised expression of cruelty, as if the cats were somehow to be punished ferociously for reminding the city of that diseased and decaying underside beneath the glistening palaces, for being the emissaries whose presence advertised during the hours of daylight the rats that infest the dark corners while the sun shines, and then enjoy the freedom of the night.

This report came sixteen years after Helena had begun her medical, surgical, and propaganda war on behalf of the cats:

> All over Venice, the Cat Mothers, women, often in the face of opposition and even violence, feed the cats. The Cat Mothers make use of our veterinary forms to put down newborn kittens, and to spay an increasing number of cats. As well as the feral rat catchers, there are many much loved pets. What the visitor does not see are the numerous acts of brutality, by individual vandals and now, it seems, by bureaucracy.
>
> The Cat Committee . . . had been asked to report on a situation

Before dawn near the Rialto marketplace. Shop and restaurant shutters have provided night-time shelter and protection.

involving a neighbours' row. Allegedly there were forty or fifty cats in a house. In fact there were twenty-nine. Signora Salvalaggio, chairman of the Cat Committee, visited the house in question and found that the owner was trying to move to the mainland to a place where she could keep her cats. She telephoned the environment department and spoke to a surveyor, who replied that if that was the case, he would cancel a court order for the cats' destruction. He also asked for written confirmation.

As she was leaving to take the confirmation to the municipality, Signora Salvalaggio received a telephone call that the cats were being taken away. She went to the house and found pandemonium. Firemen were hammering on the door. Women were screaming hysterically, swearing and hurling invective. She asked the surveyor and the police sergeant there to read her note. They refused. The surveyor denied that he had promised to cancel the court order. Finally, the police sergeant lost his temper and told his men to take Signora Salvalaggio away. They threw her down some stone steps, and she was cut and bruised. Another welfare worker arrived, and they both returned to the house. After a while the cats were brought out, stuffed into sacks and hen battery cages. The men turned these on their sides, like suitcases, for easier carrying, so that the cats fell on top of each other. They were poured like potatoes into baskets, and taken away to the slaughterhouse where they were gassed.

When the owner and her daughter returned they were unable to lock the broken door behind them. They had to barricade themselves at night into a house that was covered in disinfectant, cat urine and fur. Similar incidents have been reported, and Signora Salvalaggio suspects that this behaviour is more common than is often realised.

Helena then translated a comment on the affair which appeared on July 16, 1983, in a Venetian daily newspaper called the *Gazzetino*:

July 14 is an historic day, from henceforth not only for the French, who celebrate the fall of the Bastille, but also for the Venetians. A house in the Cannaregio district was invaded, in the absence of the owner, by five firemen and their officer, a sergeant of police and two policemen, and seven local government employees. The cox'ns of four launches brought this gang to 20 people in all . . . All this to catch and destroy eighteen cats and eleven kittens . . .

With rubbish floating on the canals, and lying about attracting rats, the litter-scattering Venetians had paid for a military operation, in the name of hygiene. Unfortunately no vet or animal inspector was present.

And Helena's own footnote:

I hope no one will be shocked, or misunderstand me, if I say that this incident looks to me like a little simulacrum of the Calvary. Women looking on helplessly while men do unspeakable things. There were no women in the raiding party, or men among the watchers. Cause for reflection on the roles of men and women?

A miscellany of other paragraphs and snapshots from Dingo documents:

A woman was given the keys of a Venetian boatyard by the owner so that she could feed eleven cats. A neighbour objected and told her rudely to go away. She persisted, and one day this man and his wife attacked her. They shook her, pulled her hair, used foul language and finally punched her face. A man was watching, silently, noting down as they occurred their breaches of the Italian penal code. He was a cat lover—and a judge. He drew up the *denuncia*, the formal legal complaint, and there is a possibility of a prison sentence. Meanwhile the cats are now being fed by the owner of the boatyard . . .

* * *

A good deal of anxiety is being caused by the disappearance of cats. No one seems to know who is responsible. An elderly woman, now in hospital, who feeds about a hundred cats, is very worried that they are vanishing one by one. Ten are already missing. Who takes them, and why? Naturally one thinks of the fur trade, or the laboratories at Padua. We spent a miserable two days searching for a little, shy, affectionate grey and white cat which Signora Scarpabolla had fished out of the canal. She had found a home for it because her flat is already filling up with cats, including two kittens which she had rescued from two horrible brutes. Luckily it turned out that the person to whom she'd promised the grey and white had collected it without telling her . . .

* * *

I stood between two children and a cat they were chasing in a *campo*. They went away, and then one came back. I resisted the temptation to slap the little horror's face. By the time we'd finished glaring at each other the cat had gone. I made sure it wasn't in the canal. Incidents of this kind, and much grosser acts of cruelty, are only too common. There have been wanton acts of sadism: petrol being poured over cats which are then set alight . . .

A colony of cats at a hospital were removed with considerable brutality by local dog catchers and crammed into hen battery cages. This is also the subject of a prosecution . . .

* * *

Killing cats by the local authority leaves much to be desired. They are still lassoed and gassed, and if they raise their heads to escape the gas, they are beaten down . . .

* * *

Many cats are astonishingly tame. In view of the amount of vandalism, it terrifies me to see cats sitting beside the canals where they could easily be kicked in. In almost every area there are women who feed the cats. As you know, they used to be called the Cat Mothers, but this has now become a derogatory expression in Venice, and they

Before the Sanders crusade, Venetian strays shunned humans for fear of cruelty. Now many are astonishingly tame.

> now prefer just to be called the Cat Women. Even so, they are liable to abuse, ridicule, and sometimes even violence. They not only feed the cats, they take sick and injured cats to the vets, collect newborn kittens to be put down where necessary, and, where possible, take cats to be spayed . . .

* * *

What does Chekhov have Yelena say to Uncle Vanya, woman to man? 'In all of you there lurks a demon of destruction.' And Vanya replies, 'I don't care for all this philosophising.' Well, perhaps I don't care for it either, when it takes this particular turn, but it is imperative, I think, to acknowledge the plain sexual dichotomy which appears when the issues of cruelty and charity are investigated. Helena herself, after years of watching the sexes at work and at welfare, wrote: 'The more I see of men, the more I love my doctored cat. Men are unwise and curiously planned. I find them incomprehensible.'

Of course there are dozens of men in Venice who help to provide food and medical treatment—and, where necessary, euthanasia—but very seldom when a story of vandalism is told is there a female in the castlist. Once, when I saw an old woman crossing a square with a little tray of food and a swarm of cats and kittens writhing round her legs, I called her to stop, wanting to take a photograph. And she turned her back and rushed away, fearing, I suppose, that I was going to attack her verbally or physically, or that if I took her picture it might be used to prove that she was committing a nuisance or contributing to a public health hazard. It was her instinctive expectation that as a man my intention must have been to cause her grief. An Englishwoman recognised that there was an indefensible malaise in the transactions between Venice and her thousands of stray animals. Her husband, although by no means an unkind man, was barely conscious of the depth of the problem or in what way it might be susceptible to any solution, and twenty years into the work, talked to me in terms of amused irritation about 'this cat business', and how he occupied his time while his wife was about it. When that woman was first mobilising her campaign to sort the situation out, her most enthusiastic and pragmatic supporters were Venetian women, led by the painter Gina Scarpabolla, stoic in the face of all the vilification that the menfolk chucked at them, optimistic despite widespread insistence that nothing they did could possibly make an impact on a set of circumstances, however undesirable, which were the result of centuries of neglect.

In fact, those circumstances were poised to change disastrously when fate introduced Helena Sanders into the equation. The human population of Venice had declined significantly; the cat population continued to rise, and some estimates polled it as high as 30,000. Vermin were under feline control, but these were the 'sixties, when public authorities throughout the developed world keenly sought artificial remedies for natural ills. Potent rat poisons had been invented and were used throughout the city. Cats fed on the carcasses of rodents and suffered agonising deaths themselves. Poison seeped into the canals and began to disrupt the already fragile ecology of the lagoon. Dingo was able to raise a public debate, pointing out that if the money spent on lethal chemicals was diverted to the business of keeping cat colonies down to an optimum number, and up to an optimum state of health, rats and mice would automatically be brought under control, and the city would have a clearer conscience and be a safer place in which to live. By and large, the poisoning has stopped.

Effecting psychological repairs continues to prove a subtle and elusive goal. At least half the citizens of Venice keep a pet, but often the same people who pamper a domestic cat will spurn a stray. As a local writer and animal lover, Antonella Barina, has written, Dingo members and their allies are addressing a complex of educational deficiencies:

> Love for the cat himself is decreasing. He is often abandoned by those who move to the mainland, or by fools who suddenly decide that 'cats are dirty', or those who stupidly imagine that 'cats can look after themselves'. That this is far from the case is evidenced by the flood of urgent calls made to cat-rescuers. A lot of efforts have to be made to discourage cruelty, and one effective means is the summons, but these are only possible when there is detailed proof of violence. But Dingo issues warnings, such as the one to a pair of quiet gentlemen who were catching cats with fish hooks. People have to be taught that cats are not a health risk, and careless workmen have to be taught to think before they wall up some derelict building and imprison a colony of cats inside to starve to death.

It is still true that in many cases all Dingo can offer is a swift and painless death to an animal which has been barbarously maltreated (a vet told me of a kitten he had put down which had had its claws torn out). But public and corporate attitudes are changing. Notices warn of the penalties for cruelty. The Town Council has voted to allow the Island of San Clemente—ironically, it was once an asylum for insane women—to be converted into a sanctuary and hospital for sick cats, and in the city itself the Council has supplied a number of wooden boxes, big enough to admit a fleeing cat, too small for a human. The battle against fur-traders, vivisectionists and sadists is beginning to attract official support. Antonella Barina again:

In Santa Croce: some cats disdain involvement in a cliché . . .

Some know their station . . .

And you, Venice cat, what do you think about it all? What does being a Venetian cat mean? It means waking up behind a window overlooking the Grand Canal, with sunlight on thick fur; it means being savagely beaten during the night by someone who cannot face himself; it means having a bed, a brush, and some food, or a litter of thin kittens with runny eyes; a poisoned titbit or a bowl of milk; a cruel boy or a family that looks after you; an active cat rescuer, who decides to deliver you from a life of hardship; the wheel of a car or a drowning in a canal; a song of love, the wing of a struggling pigeon, or the tail of an escaping mouse.

There is no unique or even exceptional problem of cruelty or negligence in Venice—it is simply that the city's isolation enables a flaw in human nature both to be examined and attacked. Broadly speaking, the citizens no longer believe that contact with animals is unnatural, that they are insensible and disposable items in the divine scheme. But in parts of mainland Italy that view continues to prevail, and authority often winks or connives at brutal treatment. The life-expectancy of a stray cat in Venice is now three years. Not long? On the Italian mainland it is one. And add this, from Dingo's first annual report, in the uncompromising words of its founder, Helena Sanders:

> Before any English get ready to throw the first stone, give a thought to the abandoned animals in England, sometimes thrown from moving cars, like a boxer puppy in Truro last summer. They are numbered in hundreds of thousands. Give a thought to our factory farms, our badger baiting, unknown on the continent, our farmers who persist in sending hundreds of thousands of cattle, sheep, and pigs abroad (yes, and horses too, in spite of the law) when they know the appalling conditions of travel that exist on the continent—*inferni di piombo,* leaden infernos, is how they were described by an Italian journalist.
>
> Shooting live captive pigeons, whose wing and tail feathers have been cut to make them easy targets, is revolting. Some of the injured birds land near our dog sanctuary at Lazzaretto Vecchio, off the Lido, and there is a proposal to establish a pigeon shoot on the island. But I could take you to an estate where pheasants are 'preserved', and where there are often shots heard at dusk, or in thick fog, when conditions make clean shooting impossible: where all wildlife other than feral mink has been virtually exterminated, and where fen traps, said to kill small animals humanely, are used. We are not told what happens if a large animal, like a fox or a badger, gets caught.
>
> As for the well-known quarrelsomeness of Venetian animal lovers, after experiencing the behaviour of individuals and societies in

England (although not Dingo, let me hasten to add) I sometimes feel inclined to take refuge in the calm and peaceful atmosphere of Venice.

Put down those stones.

From philosophy to facts. In the last year we provided veterinary treatment for 233 cats, 69 treated, 29 spayed, 30 castrated, and 115 put to sleep . . .

CHAPTER FIVE

THE SOCIAL WORKER

The Mastery of Sex, Helena's unofficial syllabus for instruction in human relationships during her first days at Oxford, captures both the innocence and the severity of moral attitudes which were swept aside in the secular revolution following the Second World War. If its author is occasionally adroit at finding a wrong tree up which to bark ('one hopes that the youth of today will develop the "Youth Movement" on similar lines to the movement in Germany, with its opportunities for fresh air and healthy companionship'), he is at the same time surprisingly liberal in his advocacy of candid sex education, explicit in his descriptive examples of the kind of education he proposes, and vivid in his illustration of the psychological and physical horrors which ignorance can cause. But Christian law circumscribes every aspect of experiment and performance. Sex is a delightful function of matrimony and matrimonial procreation, and outside marriage there seems to exist only a sinful range of solitary or mutual perversions, all prefiguring misery, disease, and disaster.

Helena graduated from university, with third class honours, in 1933, emotionally preoccupied with her still unstated and unsated love for Bernard, her ears still hot with her father's anger after he found out about a mild flirtation she had enjoyed with an Asian student ('It isn't that they're worse than us. They're different. And we just don't have any contact with them'). The weeks that followed were despondent and desultory, vaguely looking for work where nothing serious or challenging seemed to be available. She travelled backwards and forwards by train between Camberley and London, attending interviews—among them, one for the job of manageress in a Lyons Coffee House—and rightly rejecting her successes as unworthy of her mental abilities.

She had almost abandoned the quest for work, deciding that 'the only possible thing to do is to get married', when she encountered an advertising campaign that held her in check, revived her intellectual enthusiasm and, within a very short time, turned her once more from potential victim to energetic helper. Bodies like the Industrial Christian Fellowship, the

London Council of Churches Care Committee, and the Charities Organisation Society were campaigning to recruit social workers whom they could deploy in the distressed East End of London. Helena's membership of her various university crusades had already alerted her to the scale of deprivation. She had tried to persuade her father to adopt a slum child, and although he had demurred at that proposal, he did agree to set aside his ambition for his daughter to take up the refined if precarious career of a book reviewer, and supported her while she trained at Bedford College in Regent's Park, his one stipulation being that she shared rooms with Gerard in Finchley.

The recruitment meeting Helena attended had been a chaotic enough affair, with a speaker who muddled his way through his notes, and only three in the audience. But enough was said to persuade Helena that she had found a vocation, and her conviction did not diminish when, after her graduation from the college, a posting to the Princess Club in Jamaica Road, Bermondsey, began a period of sustained exposure to the poverty, unchastity and despair of life in the East End.

Princess Christian, a granddaughter of Queen Victoria, had founded the settlement in Bermondsey after the German princeling to whom she had been married divorced her for failing to bear him a male heir. She was an altruistic, autocratic woman, and maybe her humiliation by her former husband was one reason why her original plans envisaged a club for women and girls only. But one of her first directors, Nellie Hooker, was an aggressive and a progressive thinker, and she declared that it was ludicrous to suppose that anything could be achieved for the poor by separating the sexes. Under her guidance, and despite some pretty stiff opposition, Jamaica Road became the first mixed settlement. Helena Charles reported to Nellie Hooker.

Her style was to develop the critical and debating faculties of her protegées by consistently adopting contrary positions. 'She was always pushing Christian Science down my throat, and Anglicanism down the throat of a Christian Scientist. In fact her own position would be described today as ecumenical,' Helena remembers. 'She warned me I would soon find that the unemployment ground me down, and insisted that everyone should rest for at least twenty-four hours in every week.'

Five nights in every seven Helena worked in the settlement's various clubs: for the over-25s, the over 17s, and the youngsters. During the day her job attached her to a Schools Care Committee. She might be trying to find second-hand clothes for children, or taking them for treatment to get rid of lice, or simply hammering away at their parents to make sure that doctors' recommendations were implemented. 'It was extremely hard and exacting work. None of us ever seemed to get enough to eat.'

Bermondsey, as Helena recalls it, was 'a sink into which people fell, and out of which they never rose.' The daily scramble for piece-work at the docks seemed to be designed by a conspiracy of employers and bureaucrats to keep families permanently on the trailing edge of subsistence. If a labourer managed to find three days' work in a week at the equivalent of about 53 pence a day, he qualified for one day's unemployment benefit. If he worked for four days, no benefit was paid. Means testing prevented whole families from receiving support if one member happened to be earning, even if the wage was totally insufficient for their collective needs. In one case that recurs in Helena's recollections and her books, an unemployed grocer whose two teenage sons were working and lived at home had to beg his children for a penny if he wanted to buy a newspaper and scan the meagre advertisements of situations vacant. The toll on human dignity was immense. 'His wife gave him hell. She had a real problem with her attitudes, and after a year I managed to get her to attend the psychology department of Guy's Hospital. The psychologist first asked her whether she was physically attracted by her husband. At which she got up and left.'

But the most hideous feature in the hell of Bermondsey was the Wolseley Building, a complex of 200 two-room flats, with two lavatories serving four flats, and as many as a dozen people in each. The building housed more people than the entire Mayfair postal district.

'It was the Wolseley that made a vicar cry out for the shedding of the blood of the bourgeoisie. I remember photographing its horrors for the Royal Institute of British Architects, and we endlessly tried to get the local council to do something about it. I used to think that if the building could be evacuated, the Kingdom of God would have come. Well, during the war it was evacuated, and after the war it stayed empty. I went down to the East End to see it, but there were no particular signs of the coming of the Kingdom of God. It's very depressing, fifty years later, to find that people are still fighting appalling housing in London and other cities.'

Helena's duties included collecting statements from families who were applying for help. It was around this time that Baldwin made his dole cuts in spite of a budget surplus. The three shilling (15 pence) weekly allowance for dependent children was cut by a third, and while the British Medical Association calculated that the cost of a minimum subsistence diet was about 6s 7d (33 pence) a week, the sum available for most families to spend on food was five shillings (25 pence). Helena and her fellow social workers organised a lunch to try to demonstrate how very little food even the BMA diet could buy. Everyone left the table hungry, except the wife of an unemployed man, who declared that the meal had been an extraordinary luxury. Most people in Bermondsey were living on bread and margarine, using strong tea with condensed milk to anaesthetise their hunger pangs. For hundreds of thousands, the normal condition of life was starvation.

Helena travelled England during the depression, and discovered the same distress in the North, the coalfields, and the Midlands. The Ministry of Health stated publicly that it had found no evidence of malnutrition in areas of mass unemployment. It must, she says, have been unique in reaching that conclusion.

Not surprisingly, she never forgot the physical and moral degradation she witnessed in Bermondsey. Here she is, writing in her book *The Christian in the Modern State*, in the straitened and rationed world of the early 'fifties, with the memory of that jobless grocer still vibrant after twenty years. She begins by clearing aside the peculiar notion of the post-war generation that somehow it confronted instabilities and uncertainties more acute than any of its predecessors':

> Life today is not more precarious than it ever was. We who live our lives under the shadow of atomic warfare are apt to think that to live in constant fear of death is a terror new to our age. We forget that for the majority of people, for most of the period of human existence, life has been a dangerous and unhappy business. The austerity of the 1950s is nothing compared to the starvation of the 1840s and the misery of the unemployment of the 1930s.
>
> When unemployment numbered anything between one and three million, the fear of unemployment darkened the lives of many millions more. Even when the horrible threat did not materialise it produced nervous strain and friction, often resulting in quarrels between husband and wife. But the worst attack on family life came from the administration of the means test, the law providing that unemployment benefit should be cut in proportion to the earnings of other members of a family. Only those who were in close contact with its effects can realise the havoc and human suffering for which this iniquitous measure was responsible. It resulted in unemployed parents being dependent on their adolescent children who were working for the bare necessities of life. There were such cases as an unemployed father having to ask a sixteen-year-old boy for a penny to buy a paper. The result was that the father was despised by his own children who took his place as breadwinner. Young people who wished to get married were prevented from doing so as long as they lived at home, as they were compelled to give up their earnings to support their parents . . .

Helena, who had begun her work at Bermondsey determined 'to do something about terrible poverty and bad housing', found after a while that she, too, became 'case-hardened', unable to evoke her original indignation as suffering family after suffering family appeared for ministration. But her passion gave way not to resignation, but to a certainty that she and her fellow undergraduates were right when they diagnosed the ills of society and prescribed not the repair and maintenance of the status quo, but radical change. The young girl who had prayed each night for a Conservative Government began to entertain a rather more left-wing position.

Meanwhile, as her political ideas continued their long gestation, she exhausted herself at the Princess Club, often heckled and harassed by the very people she was trying to help. She admired them, nevertheless, praising their courage and good humour, although she was disturbed by their unswerving assumption of their own impotence. One unemployed man actually admitted to her that 'the difference between us and you is that when we hear a sad story we cry, and when you hear a sad story, you do something about it.' Helena shed what sweetness and light she could among the sadness, organising dances and talks, taking parties to exhibitions at the National Gallery, arranging and accompanying groups on holidays at home and abroad. Some of the girls saw these excursions as opportunities for romantic rather than cultural adventures.

'Haven't you noticed,' said one of the organisers of a trip, hoping to lead by example, 'that we don't pick up strange men and go off with them?'

'Yes,' replied a girl, 'we have noticed that. We feel rather sorry for you.'

Occasionally, a case was fraught with such misfortune that it pierced the shell Helena had built around herself. 'I remember sitting on Bernard's lap one night in complete silence for a very long time. He asked me what I was thinking about, and what I was thinking was that one of my families was going to be evicted on Christmas Eve for non payment of rent.'

Bernard, the former theological student from Brasenose College, looms through the Bermondsey period of Helena's life. The son of a naval chaplain, he was 'a great big hulking man, with very blond hair and blue eyes, a rugby player, gentle in spite of his enormous physical toughness and strength, which enabled him once to pick up me and my sister at the same time.' Was it strength or gentleness or the mixture that attracted Helena? 'I suppose the best adjective to describe him was "nice".' And you really have to hear Helena pronounce the word, at a distance of fifty years from the relationship, to learn how barbed it can be.

As we have seen, for two years Helena's upbringing and inhibitions forced her to disguise her love, while Bernard, she presumed, refrained from any declaration because he was frightened of being snubbed by a girl who had adopted the completely phoney pose of a hardbitten woman of the world. Twice the charade nearly collapsed. On both occasions it was October 16 ('there was no significance in the date') and on both occasions Bernard asked Helena to join him for an evening's dancing at Prince's Golden Brasserie at the bottom of Regent Street, while protecting his emotional flanks by couching the invitations in a somewhat disdainful formula—'Will you come out with a rather bored young man?'

Now dancing, for anyone schooled in the Leslie Weatherhead doctrine of interpersonal behaviour, is an activity of huge portent: 'There can be no reasonable doubt,' the scholar and psychologist averred, 'that originally dancing was a preliminary to the short courtships of primitive days, and was looked upon as a preparation for marriage . . . I would personally encourage dancing in these days since I regard it as a way in which the sex instinct may be sublimated.'

Sublimate they certainly did, the young couple at Prince's Golden Brasserie. 'All our frustration seemed to go into the dancing,' Helena recalls. But if the wraith of Weatherhead was there, hoping that frustration would evaporate as perspiration chilled when the dancers turned out into Regent Street, he would have been disappointed. 'I think if I crossed my legs and stood on my head you would follow me,' said Bernard to Helena, in a strangely ambiguous compliment. The genie of love the couple had stoppered up grew and grew until he escaped in the early hours of that New Year's Day of 1934, when an obtuse or obdurate younger brother was finally despatched to bed with words which composed themselves into an unintended declaration. Bernard and Helena became unofficially engaged.

'We had a very happy time for a couple of years,' she says. 'We spent a great deal of it walking together, perhaps for fifteen or twenty miles at a go, discussing heaven only knows what. I still don't understand why it had to come to an end. Bernard had a curious streak of insensitivity, and I was extremely aggressive and much too possessive.'

He was a curate in Southampton, she a social worker in the East End, but whenever her duties allowed she would travel by train to see him, staying at St Luke's vicarage. 'One day early in 1936 I went down there, and I could sense immediately that something was very wrong. I asked what it was and he just said brutally: "I don't love you any more and it's off." I spent a long time in the lavatory on the train home crying, until the ticket collector banged on the door and I had to come out. And that was that, and I had a sort of nervous breakdown. It was so totally unexpected.'

Eleven years later, when the war was over and Helena had been buffeted by other relationships, Bernard came home from Lusaka in Africa, where he was rural dean, and sought out his ex-fiancée. 'It was during the great freeze-up of 1947, and it was wonderful having him back.

The couple slithered around in overcoats, mufflers, gloves and galoshes, laughing together, warming themselves over cups of tea, Bernard visiting Helena in her lodgings and explaining the problems of the Third World while she sat on his lap and matched his concerns with her new anxieties and opinions about the need for a Jewish state. She was too glad and grateful to hold an inquest into his earlier treachery, and he, perhaps, too diffident to volunteer an explanation. And then he was gone, just as swiftly as he had appeared, and the next news Helena received was that he had married. Helena Charles, it seemed, had been a useful machine to keep out the chill during his vacation. It was 1977 before Helena heard of him again, when he arrived to preach at the parish church where her second half-sister worshipped. Elizabeth introduced herself to Bernard after the service, explaining who she was. 'It's no use delving into the past,' he said, without a single question about Helena's health and circumstances. A year later he died, and the reason for his sudden defection at Southampton is now a mystery that will never be solved.

* * *

Sorting through the notes that I had folded together for this period of Helena's life, I found the remnants of a curious little song, familiar only at its edges. Although most of the names sound Cornish, the experiences seem to pin themselves to the Bermondsey years:

The Nightmayor

Housing, water, and public health
Go round and round in my brain
As I lie in my third class sleeper
And try to sleep in the train.

A mean little man in a mean little room
Sat at a desk in Whitehall
And wrote a Government paper
That didn't make sense at all . . .
Mrs Tremeer has a single room
For her man and her kids and she,
And nobody ever stops to think
Of the things those children see.

Mr Polmeer is out of work,
They cannot pay the rent.
They'll have to get tick at the grocer's
When all the money's spent.

Mrs Penrose is the worst of all,
The councillor said, 'Who knows?
But it's all so sad
And my memory's bad,
But what's wrong with Mrs Penrose?'
Mrs Penrose has a leaky roof,
She's got no kitchen sink . . .
Water, water, everywhere,
Nor any drop to drink.

Envoi

Awaiting the council dust cart,
The sanitary buckets stink.
Water, water, everywhere,
Nor any drop to drink.

Helena's commitment to Bernard had been fierce, and the security their love gave had sustained her through the social atrocities she witnessed in Bermondsey. But the breakdown that followed their separation left her physically and mentally disarmed. How could she contemplate the renewal of her work in the East End?

The extent of the damage can be gauged by the extent of the preceding love. When Helena and Bernard proposed to join a college friend and her fiancé for an innocent holiday, Frank Charles protested. Not that he suspected the Southampton curate and his daughter of plotting immoralities. It simply 'wasn't done' to go away unchaperoned. And Helena's response was to write him a note saying that she was going ahead: she would rather defy him than deceive him. At the time her father was very ill, so perhaps she was lucky that Barbara Davidson, her stepmother's companion, who often acted as a buffer between Helena and her parents, intercepted the letter.

Delve back even further, and look at the chances, the hesitations, the hours or weeks of diffidence that redirect a life. One casual meeting may blossom into a relationship which precludes another casual meeting from finding a space in which desire can plant its roots. Bernard was not Helena's first love. He was a man called Harold Redman.

'Harold was a young officer, a Captain at the Staff College in Camberley. I did not know or like any of the young men in Camberley, nor they me. The Sandhurst cadets always seemed immature, and superficial, and I think they thought me a blue stocking. So my Aunt Ethel was often called on to produce a man for dances and meals and so forth. Harold Redman, who had been my Uncle Ronald's ADC in Afghanistan, came to a dance at our house near the end of my time in school. He made no impression on me then, although a friend asked, "Who was that nice young man?"

'In the spring of 1930 I came home from school for a weekend after the various college entrance exams for Oxford, and went to a 21st birthday dance. I was nearly 19, and Aunt Ethel asked Harold to escort me to this party. Apart from his physical attraction, although he was not what you might call handsome, he was charming, a good deal older than I was, and much the most intelligent young man I had ever met. Instead of saying, "Oh, my God," when I told him I was hoping to get into Oxford, he said he envied me. He also expressed a liking for the French, whom I liked, and explained that he had been teaching French soldiers to play hockey. Perhaps most importantly, he treated me like an adult. Later, he apologised for not calling at our house after the dance, and asked how he stood. It had never occurred to me that he should call. There was a point-to-point the next day, and I said I would like to go, because he was riding in some of the events. He said: "If I'd known you wanted to go, I would have taken you, but I've fixed up with somebody else." It's just as well he didn't take me—he had a bad fall and was ill for some time afterwards.

'During the summer vacation of 1931 he came to lunch. My stepmother was at one of her cures, so I presided. My father monopolised him completely, and we had almost no conversation. I sat miserable and silent at the head of the table. After lunch they played golf. Harold, I still remember, wore green golf-stockings. I trailed along behind. I loved him for considerably more than a year. I do not think he ever had any feelings for me, or any idea of how I felt, but I still think of him as one of the most attractive and admirable men I have ever met.

'In 1940 or thereabouts my stepmother told me that a Colonel Redman had called to see me when I was out. He'd been posted to Minley Manor, a branch of the staff college. This was post-Bernard, and I was much involved with the French who were with us, and I did nothing in reply to his call. I have never ceased to regret that. Decades passed. I read in the newspaper that Princess Margaret had been entertained by the Governor of Gibraltar, General Sir Harold Redman. I asked my Uncle Ronald who the Governor of Gibraltar was, and he said: "that's my old ADC."'

Looking back after more than fifty years, Helena comments on the break-up with Bernard: 'I did not become, nor am I a misanthrope, or anti-clerical. Bernard could not do anything to control his feelings. As we were not married, or engaged in an official sense, he was under no obligation. I do not deny that he was lacking in sensitivity in the way he did what he did.

'An Israeli, who once said to me, "Among the many, you were one of the very few," also said, "You Christian women torture yourselves with abstinence.'' I hope you will make it clear that I was a virgin when I married. I do think that, in spite of ''*la donna e mobile*'', and ''*souvent femme varie*'', and ''go and catch a falling star'', women are more constant than men. Several times I have had a lovely evening with some young man or another at a party, laughing, dancing, and mildly flirting, and then next day I have met him and said hello, and have been cut dead. I could never understand this. It happened quite often. But I had my revenge. Once at a party I danced the whole evening with someone else's partner. Next year, I met him again at the same house, and mindful of what had happened on other occasions, I turned my back on him.'

* * *

By the summer of 1936 Helena was largely over the mental trauma of Bernard's defection. She allowed herself to be drawn into her stepmother's social activities. 'My stepmother was terribly keen on all that sort of thing. She made my father attend a levee one year so that she could go to Ascot. In 1936 she'd arranged to present my half-sister Anne at court, and she asked me if I'd like to be ''done'' as well. If I remember rightly it was the first court of King George VI and Queen Elizabeth. We went in a hired car, and queued for hours in the Mall. All the debs were there, and so were two or three people from the Princess Club who'd turned up to watch, and I think ours was the only car waiting which had two dirty urchins standing on the running boards. When we finally got into the Palace we were ushered into a corridor, and finally we were presented. A footman whisked my train from my arm, someone called out, ''Mrs F. R. S. Charles,'' and we were in front of the King and Queen. My stepmother said, ''May I present Miss Helena Charles?'' and I curtseyed, and that was it, really.'

She also remembers a Buckingham Palace garden party, which she attended with her stepmother, her sister Anne and Uncle Ronald—General Sir Ronald Charles, KCB, DSO. Helena was his goddaughter, and because he did not marry until he was in his sixties, she often presided at his table. That summer, when the Lord Mayor of London gave a dance for the Territorial Army, Sir Ronald asked Helena to accompany him. 'We walked in procession behind the Duff Coopers. Lady Diana (*née* Manners) was wearing a backless dress, and I remember that her back was covered in scratches, as if she'd been attacked by a cat.

'Uncle Ronald became Chief Royal Engineer, and President of the Old Contemptibles. When he died in 1955, several of them came to his funeral, and I obtained permission from his widow to write to the Mayor of Landrecies. He turned out to be the son of one of my uncle's close friends,

Helena, aged 25, dressed for her presentation at Court. 'My stepmother was terribly keen on all that sort of thing.'

On the way to a Buckingham Palace garden party. Helena, on the right, walks with her Uncle Ronald Charles. Beside him, Helena's stepmother Nancy, and her sister Anne.

and told me that he was still remembered there.' His name is still to be seen, inscribed on the bridge at Landrecies, in tribute to his gallantry in wresting the village from the Germans in 1918, leading 600 men.

* * *

The Bermondsey experiment was over, though Helena's concern for the welfare of the disadvantaged never abated. She began to cast about for new work that would sever her from past associations. In the meantime, she bought 'an enormous dog, a cross between a bull mastiff and a St Bernard, which was a lovely puppy, but which, when fully grown, would attack any other dog on sight.' She also acquired a very old and slightly decrepit small car. In a short time she had studied for and obtained the Archbishop of Canterbury's certificate entitling her to become a parish worker. She passed, it should go without saying, with distinction in doctrine. The jangled nerves and emotions were now soothing themselves, and she recorded with some satisfaction a colleague's observation that 'people who've travelled the world and have been kissed' make better social workers than the single-minded and ascetic sort who simply want to dominate a battalion or two of their fellow human beings. She and the dog set off in the car for Mitcham in Surrey—'a lot of small, lower middle-class houses. Nice little houses, with nice little gardens.'

The wasp was back in her tongue . . .

CHAPTER SIX

REFUGEES

Helena was installed in reasonable comfort in two rooms she furnished belonging to the postmistress, Dot Dawes: a minute bedroom and a sitting room, space enough, perhaps, for a bachelor girl, although the enormous dog would have made a detached villa seem congested. Miss Dawes would regularly protest about the dog, which in turn would regularly draw on the bull-mastiff in its soul to menace Miss Dawes. Four days a week Helena worked in the parish of the Church of the Ascension, a new building which had been thrown up to serve the residents of new housing estates, and which doubled as a hall. Two rather more demanding days were spent in London at the offices of the Industrial Christian Fellowship, on the staff of the Youth Committee.

After Bermondsey, Helena no doubt welcomed the order and hygiene of Mitcham, but her duties were comparatively unexciting. She enjoyed helping confirmation candidates and working with the girls' club and the communicants' guild, but her round of parochial visits was tedious, and occasionally she must have wanted to spirit a family off to Bermondsey to show them real distress. By and large, the bill of fare was tea and gossip, although a marital difficulty sometimes offered itself for dissection and solution. In the prim but lethargic Surrey environment, Helena rediscovered a predilection for morning slumber, and it got her into trouble.

'I have a very peculiar clock inside in my body. Always, all my life, I've been frightfully heavy and sleepy in the mornings. I tend to wake up quite late at night, and I can be very active well into the small hours of the morning. But in Mitcham I found that I just could not get up, and I was forever late for the daily Mass at the church. The vicar was a very good priest, but to use a modern expression, our chemistries didn't really mix very well, and I couldn't get on with him, and he didn't like me. We just had to do the best we could.'

Their disagreements sharpened when Germany annexed Austria in 1938, moving towards the creation of a 'Greater Germany'. The vicar declared that by allowing Hitler to satisfy his territorial hunger the rest of

Europe was taking out an insurance that underwrote a continuing peace. Helena was among the minority who were convinced that the man's hunger was insatiable. Where were the boundaries of this putative Teutonic empire? And if you accepted an immemorial right to erase frontiers allegedly imposed by succeeding dynasties of 'treacherous' monarchs and politicians, weren't you also compelled to swallow a detestable potion of racial theories? 'I'd been extremely worried for a very long time by the news from Germany and Hitler's rise,' Helena recalls. 'I'd read about and heard about the long anti-semitic campaign. When they marched into Austria and were just allowed to take the country over I knew that a terrible thing had happened, and that it implied even more terrible things to come.'

The difficulty was how to tackle and convert the vicar, and all the others whose obstinate yearning for the quiet life distorted their vision of the facts and, indeed, led them to interpret those facts as a model of world affairs which promised peace. As ever, Helena Charles decided to proceed by practical demonstration. Freda Troup, one of her college friends, had been working as secretary to Mrs Phyllis Forbes Dennis, who had been in Vienna with her husband during the *Anschluss*. They had seen gangs of agitators silencing opponents with sticks and boots, and witnessed the almost immediate and horrifying consequence of annexation for the Jewish population. Helena persuaded Freda to persuade Mr and Mrs Forbes Dennis to address a local society. The picture they drew was vivid enough to unsettle, at least, the quiet-lifers and raise the blinds with which they were so anxious to obscure the more ominous details of events across the Channel. But before she left, Mrs Forbes Dennis made a request that secured Helena's enlistment to the campaign for Jewish refugees, and set in motion a process that was to lead to the disruption of an orderly life only recently achieved.

Could Miss Charles possibly help some orphaned Jewish children from Vienna?

Well, yes, of course she would do what she could. What were the circumstances?

They were looking for a school to take two girls. One was fifteen and the other seventeen. A tragic case. Both parents had committed suicide. The girls were stranded in Austria, and desperately needed somewhere to recuperate, and a place where they could pick up the pieces of their education.

Unsurprisingly, Helena was not just moved, but moved to action. She made contact with the woman who was directly involved with the girls' case, an Austrian Jewess called Lily Wright, who became a lifelong friend, and whose husband was an Englishman. The facts, it transpired, were rather different from those related by Mrs Forbes Dennis. Neither parent had committed suicide, the girls were eleven and fifteen, and they had already arrived in England in a family group of such exceptional complexity that it was difficult to establish who was married to whom, and when, and above all why. However, the unravelled circumstances may help to explain the chaos that the Fischer family wrought wherever they moved, and how they very nearly undermined that pillar of fortitude, Helena Charles, to the point where the pillar collapsed.

Alone at the start had been 'the old father who was very quiet and depressed'. He was joined—and the silence was exploded—by his volatile second wife and the two daughters, 'who were in a very bad state of discipline'. For three months, as the Nazis consolidated their Vienna power-base and until the family could secure a passage out of Austria, the girls' mother had been too frightened to allow them to leave the house. They had become all but unmanageable, and whatever excursions Helena proposed by way of compensation for their recent traumas had a habit of ending in a sort of anarchy, both sides jabbering with mutual unintelligibility in their native languages.

Helena decided that a dose of the medicine that had served her so well as a child might get the girls back on the rails. She contacted her old headmistress at St Stephen's College in Folkestone, who said she would be delighted to take in two young Austrian pupils, promising to supply uniforms free of charge if £20 a term could be raised to cover the cost of meals. With very little money to spare from her own meagre income, Helena made a vigorous and successful nuisance of herself among relatives and friends until an annual subscription of £60 had been guaranteed.

Their mother treated the childrens' departure for school as a family catastrophe, a cause for lamentations that were loud enough to engulf her entire household, but within a single term, two intractable young Jewesses had been transformed into demure English schoolgirls, talking, albeit with a middle-European accent, the sort of slang that was celebrated in the novels of Angela Brazil. They might have stayed at St Stephen's throughout the years of war, but their very race and religion entailed a difficulty which Helena, as an Anglican ex-pupil, had failed to foresee. 'Sister Jean Marion, the headmistress, said that if they were to stay on they would have to be baptised, and of course, that was an absolute anathema to their mother who was an ardent, if not particularly practising Jewess. The girls first of all wrote home and asked if it would be all right if they knelt down during morning assembly, and their mother very sensibly said they mustn't be different from anybody else—they must do what the rest of the school did. But that was really just the beginning of a campaign which became almost a battle to have the children baptised.'

For the first time in her life, Helena profoundly disagreed with her old headmistress. 'I didn't think it was right to take advantage of the sorry situation in which any refugees were placed by trying to insist that they should be converted.' Two terms passed with the family and the school establishment in a state of *impasse*. Meanwhile, attracted like moths to the candle of Helena's practical compassion, more Fischers began to arrive from Austria, bringing cousins and friends in their train. All of them betrayed the shocked disorientation that is typical among refugees, waiting helplessly and numbly to be helped. One, it transpired, had an interest in rearing trout. Frank Charles obligingly opened communications with a business associate who owned a trout farm, to see if a job might be made available.

Suddenly and without any warning—although negotiations and fund-raising manoeuvres must have been continuing secretly for some time—almost the entire clan decanted to join relatives in the West Indies. The two daughters were left behind, but their mother instantly inaugurated a long and hysterical correspondence intended to extract them from St Stephen's and get them across the Atlantic. Helena was disappointed, depressed, and furious. 'The children were in great security, and I couldn't see why she wanted to break it up. But she was howling and whining and saying she must have the children with her, and her sick and elderly husband wrote as well to say that his wife was having a nervous breakdown because she was parted from the girls.'

It had all begun relatively simply: a clear-cut series of altruistic acts which should have freed Helena within a month or two to concentrate on her job in Mitcham. Instead it began to worry at and devour all her energies. The school holidays arrived. She arranged for the girls to stay with some friends. Orders came from the West Indies countermanding the arrangements and sending both daughters to a different location. The next term brought some weeks of respite—although not from the cycle of wailing letters. When school broke up again, Helena was suffering from 'flu during the critical days when dispositions needed to be made, and she surfaced to discover that there was apparently nowhere for the girls to go. She applied to the friends who had offered to help before, but they argued that since they had been stood up once, this time they were not inclined to volunteer.

'So there I was, living now in a three-roomed flat with two other adults, and suddenly faced with the prospect of squeezing two girls into the place as well.' She managed to billet them instead at Clarewood for one night, and then they were transferred, after a remarkable piece of persuasion, to a camp in Sussex which was accommodating Basque children who were refugees from the Spanish civil war.

Helena had earned herself another uneasy intermission, but her own relations with the school had been prejudiced because the girls had contrived, on their earlier and unscheduled visit to their mother's English connexions, to take away a huge trunk of clothes, and had returned to St Stephen's with a small suitcase. Whatever inquests were held produced no satisfactory information, and staff at the school could only assume that uniforms which had been charitably supplied were now clothing unknown children.

In the summer of 1939 their mother's demands for a reunion reached a new stridency. 'Sister Jean Marion said, since pupils who were paying full fees for the school couldn't afford to go to the West Indies for their holidays, she saw absolutely no reason why special provision should be made for these two girls.' But the cries of anguish, the bellows of despair, and the threats of imminent mental and familial disintegration were now so loud that eventually the English faction was bludgeoned into surrender, the money was found, and the girls were sent. They never returned to the school—an outcome, perhaps, which Helena must have been covertly willing.

* * *

But who were the 'two other adults' who had settled themselves in Helena's flat? In the job-lot of volatile mother, sick and elderly father, capricious daughters, friends, relations and aspiring trout farmers, there were two individuals who had been clearly labelled 'not wanted on voyage'. A first wife, and the 38-year-old son of a first marriage. No vociferous appeals were made for their transfer across the ocean. No unexpected contacts were excavated to find them an amiable place of residence. They had been beached at Mitcham, and at Mitcham, it appeared, at whatever cost of embarrassment and inconvenience to their busy and distracted host, they intended to stay.

Gerhard Fischer had been a journalist on a popular Viennese newspaper before the Nazis expelled the Jews from any place where opinions were formed and disseminated. He, too, had arrived in England poleaxed by his sudden translation from social pilgrim and man of influence to nonentity and non-person. He and his mother were not in the first wave of the Fischer family who had come to England. Once again, it was Helena's indefatigable resource which had extricated them from impending horrors and arranged their passage to freedom.

'They'd managed to get out of Austria on false passports and were living in Czechoslovakia, and the Czech police were in a desperate situation. They knew it wouldn't be very long before the Nazis invaded, and they were trying their very hardest to get rid of all the refugees who were pouring in from Austria, before the calamity happened. I got in touch with my father, who was as generous as ever, and promised to help me get this woman and her son out. I moved heaven and earth. The Home Office was being incredibly slow, as government departments always seem to be, and at the same time the Fischers were given an ultimatum to get out by the Czech police; it was being said that the Nazis were waiting on the borders to arrest refugees as they were expelled.

'I had some misleading information at this point from the Home Office, who said that the entry permits had been granted, when this wasn't actually the case. But I telegrammed that the permits were ready, in all innocence, and actually that saved the day, because when the Czech police arrived to turn them over to almost certain incarceration and probable death in a concentration camp, they were able to show the telegram, and they were given a reprieve. With my father's money to back me, I managed to get them a place on a 'plane. The initial plan had been that they'd go to Bolivia. But you know the usual story with the Civil Service: there were delays and delays and more delays. After what seemed like months of waiting they arrived at Croydon, and I went to meet them.'

While she strove to help the Fischers escape, and sorted out the difficulties of her other refugees, Helena understandably began to neglect her parish duties. The day the 'plane touched down at Croydon had been appointed for the confirmation of a group of candidates she had been tutoring at Mitcham. It was not that Helena made a judgement that she would rather witness the promotion of a mother and son to freedom than the promotion of a party of youngsters to full membership of the Church; it was just that she was so obsessed with one event that she completely forgot the other, and failed to turn up at the Church of the Ascension to arrange veils, flowers, and prayer books.

'Of course, the vicar was extremely annoyed, and actually I don't blame him, because I was falling down in my responsibilities as a licensed parish worker. But the one thing that this distressing and trying episode did teach me was that in this human condition as it is now, very often it is only possible to help one set of people at the cost of causing pain to others. I don't know what the answer is. One of the people whom I caused most pain to, and I remember it with sorrow, was Dot Dawes, my landlady. She was furious at having her house invaded by foreigners. Not just the normal irritation that anyone would feel at having strangers imposed upon them without a by-your-leave, but a pathological resentment which made her really ill.'

Until the arrival of the Fischers, Dot Dawes and Helena had been close friends. Curiously, that 'pathological resentment' might be a clue to their

The view towards San Agnese on the Dorsoduro.

Opposite: Crossing the Grand Canal by gondola between *traghetti*. Guy Sanders, in his years as 'honorary gondolier', used to ferry the empty boats back to their landing stages.

Mad dogs and holidaymakers may prefer the sunlit side of the Rio di San Vio. Wise cats seek out the shade.

Opposite: The Dogona di Mare – the seventeenth-century Venetian customs house. The figure of Fortune on top of the gilded globe is a weathervane.

And in the heat of noonday the shadows of nearby trees bring a welcome relief.

Slumbering near the marketplace.

affinity, because the landlady always said that her hatred of intruders originated in her childhood, when a new baby arrived and a rather uncongenial nurse was introduced into the household to look after the first child, usurping, in Dot's eyes, the place of her mother. The experience, she claimed, had left her permanently wounded, and irrationally anxious to dictate who should enter or leave her home. Whatever sympathies she tried to conjure up for the refugees whose arrival was none of her contriving, she nevertheless saw them as new usurpers. 'She was extremely jealous, because I stopped going downstairs to chat to her after meals over a cup of coffee, and she accused me of staying in my rooms to play the lady bountiful with my foreigners. For all of us it really was a terribly trying period.'

The plan to post the Fischers on to South America collapsed when Bolivia imposed a ban on immigration, and mother and son remained suspended, as it were, in mid flight, two unhappy cuckoos stuck in the nest which Helena herself had only borrowed, while a landlady and a priest—whose views on the nature of politics and the prospects for appeasement made him less than sensitive to the plight of refugees—became increasingly belligerent. The vicar seemed oblivious to the greater tragedies that were seeding themselves beyond comfortable Mitcham and across the Channel. Helena's eyes were not turned inward to respond to the demands of her parishioners, but outward, if not to the ends of the earth, then certainly far enough to contemplate the forces that threatened European civilisation; for the vicar, however, Helena's were the eyes of an impertinent fool, and an increasingly turbulent one as well. Quietly, he schemed to replace her with a deaconess. 'And then he just said brutally, "I think you'd better pack up and go".'

Helena was marooned, for a while, in Mitcham, with a hostess who had become hostile and two stateless, helpless lodgers. 'It was a terrible strain on my financial resource. The small private means which I had from my father were ample to keep me in the simple life that I'd been leading, but once they had to be stretched to cover two other people I found myself in a major crisis, and I was terribly hard up. I found a room for Gerhard in an old lady's house. His mother slept in my room while I slept on the sofa. I had to pay his rent, our rent, and feed both of them, and give them a little money of their own. I know it was much easier for me than it was for millions and millions of people on the continent, but it really was a very stressful time. Not least because the old mother and I took a violent dislike to each other at the airport.

'She always told me she wasn't a Jewess. I didn't know whether to believe that or not, because I never knew if I could believe anything she said to me. I have to say that even when I was most angry with her, I still felt sorry for her. We just came from different worlds. It was like trying to strike up a relationship with someone from a different planet. Like all refugees she was very difficult to deal with because of the state she was in—the state they were both in—when they arrived in this country.

'I suppose if they'd been in some sort of hostel, some impersonal place, they might have found it easier, but living with me must have been trying for them, because I was such an arrogant young woman. I remember her telling me that she wasn't at all a democrat by nature, and I replied that she was jolly well going to be democratic while she was with me. I believed that anybody who shared my home had to think along the same lines as I did.

'Meanwhile poor Gerhard had never managed to break free from his mother's influence. She was twined round him like a snake. She used to sit in the room with him while he was getting dressed in the morning, in case he needed anything—a button sown on his clothes, for example. And I asked her rather cruelly once what she thought he was going to do when she died, to which her answer was that he wouldn't want to go on living if she was dead. I naïvely thought that I could break this bond. It was far too late, because the damage had been done many years before. He was a very good man, high minded and conscientious. But quite apart from this mother syndrome he was a weak character. I found him terribly lacking in any ability to stand up to me or his mother, or anyone else.'

* * *

Even now I am unsure how any of the details or impressions in Helena's recollections of her attempts to disentangle a man from his predatory mother could have rung the bell that prompted me to check the later career of Gerhard Fischer. My mind somersaulted forward some thirty years, to a time which marked my own journey from studenthood to work.

The building which houses *The Western Morning News* in Plymouth is a grand, if rather bourgeois edifice of red brick that partially defies the otherwise uniform alignment of New George Street. That defiance is a token of survival, for Leicester Harmsworth House escaped the blitz through luck, and through influence and a certain intrinsic grandeur also escaped the frenzied zeal for redevelopment which later beset the local council. The first floor of the offset wing once housed the Reporter's Room.

I joined the staff in October 1968. There was a large and clerical desk where the Chief Reporter sat, a smaller bench for his deputy, and four huge tables around which the rest of the staff were grouped. Along the northern wall were a few telephones under hoods, against a partition, and behind that, someone later that day tersely explained, was 'the morgue'. It was a stuffy space crammed with filing cabinets and shelves which housed *The Western Morning News* library of cuttings and reference books. It smelt of old newsprint, paste, and tobacco smoke, and the man who snipped the first, splashed the second, and dispensed the third unceasingly was Gerhard Fischer.

Buildings like Leicester Harmsworth House may resist demolition by asserting their differences, but the average man or woman, equipped with no excess of courage, will better endure in a new society by finding the shadows and practising their imitations of native traits until it is safe to emerge, and to attempt to merge. And yet, unconsciously, the project can sometimes drive itself to caricature. Gerhard Fischer seemed to me, when I finally went into the morgue and began to consult his dusty envelopes, like the figure of a kindly male uncle, drawn by a novelist who was over-eager to pin down a notion of Englishness. Silver hair, clipped moustache, kindly eyes; polished shoes that seemed to contradict a pair of slightly baggy trousers and a venerable tweed jacket patched with leather at the elbows; the pipe commuting regularly between fist and face; a wool-gathering and absent air with which he solved the mysteries of what I now suspect was a darkly creative and deliberately perverse filing system. One might, for example, find 'sewerage' under 'rivers', 'traffic accidents' under 'motor cars', and the entire Royal Family reposing behind some tattered cuttings that chronicled the jubilee or funeral of Queen Victoria. Only a quest for material explaining some detail of the Second World War, and in particular the Plymouth Blitz, was certain to produce, from Gerhard's store, a literary trump.

No matter how soft his voice, and how excellent his vocabulary, they could not disguise the vestiges of a middle-European accent. None of this mattered a damn to an 18-year-old apprentice, born a few years after the end of the war. The mystery lay in the attitudes of a couple of senior colleagues, who saw me chattering to the librarian and made discouraging sounds and gestures. It was nothing to do with the national obsession with rank: there was something more arcane at work in the desire to keep Gerhard at a proper distance from the men and women with whom, if you were to remove a few telephones and demolish a partition, he shared a room.

At first, when I was digesting what Helena remembered of her early relationship with Gerhard, I wondered if the weaknesses she diagnosed were the reason for his apparent isolation in the newspaper office. Now, although I reckon they were probably contributors, I do not think they can have been the entire or even the major cause. It seems that somewhere in the psyche of those war veterans (even those whose only active service was to juggle with a fire pail or a barrage balloon) there was, even after more than two decades, a vague contempt for the refugee. It was a victor's determination to remind the first victims of the vanquished that they were pensioners, allowed, on sufferance, to sit at the table, but not to join all the laughter and the songs.

* * *

There were certainly few occasions to provoke either a smile or a fleeting whistle within the uneasy troupe which left Mitcham after Helena's peremptory dismissal, and took up new lodgings in London, in a two-bedroomed flat within a building that belonged to the Duchy of Cornwall. The landlords were more inclined to fear immorality than assist altruism, and only under pressure accepted that Helena was not trying to instal on the premises a lover and his complacent mother as well as one fractious and gargantuan dog. Almost the first letter to arrive on the new doormat was an angry demand from the Vicar of Mitcham for full settlement of outstanding debts for board and lodging. Once again, the intercession of Frank Charles just prevented a financial disaster. 'I can't manage without another four pounds a week,' Helena pleaded, and her allowance was increased by that much while what she called 'this extraordinary regime' lasted.

Mr Charles urged his daughter to try to find the Fischers some fresh means of support and new accommodation, but she had the measure of the couple's helplessness, and could not see how they could possibly survive on their own. By now so many refugees had arrived in England that almost all those who combined kind hearts with a sense of international duty had filled their vacant rooms and committed their surplus income. The government might be willing—after much cajoling—to issue entry visas, but it preferred to leave private charitable organisations and individuals to cope with the fugitives' needs. From the moment she had first heard of the plight of Austria's Jews, Helena Charles had been playing a bizarre and thankless game of pass the parcel, involving relatives, friends, her old school and any amenable-sounding soul whose presence was reported in the neighbourhood. Now the music seemed to have stopped, and she was left with the task of stifling Mrs Fischer's moans, and endeavouring to help Gerhard to clamber onto his own two feet.

'In my stupid inexperience and pride I thought I could do something to make him more of a man. It would never have worked. And so we just suffered. I tried to give them a good time. I used to take them out in my little car, but there were an awful lot of rows, some of them quite terrible, mostly between her and me.'

Helena managed to escape during the day after she re-enlisted as a full time worker with the Youth Committee of the Industrial Christian Fellowship. She was instructed to write a pamphlet from the point of view of a young unemployed Marxist. The text was called 'God and Suffering'. There no longer seem to be any copies in existence, although some of the flavour of her thoughts about communism can be gathered from fragments in her other writings: a quotation, for example, from a Russian refugee called Berdyaer, who believed that 'communism is the result of the failure of Christianity to produce an order of society based on charity'; and her observation that while in Russia the Church had ruthlessly sided with reactionary and aristocratic forces, in England branches of the faith had separated from the mainstream when it began to behave like 'the Conservative party at prayer', and had expressed themselves in various nonconformist groupings which were, through their chapels, the allies of the deprived and suffering classes, and the inspiration for many trades union movements.

The pamphlet enjoyed a wide circulation among the youngsters who were the ICF's target audience, and Helena was sent out to carry the torch of 'the beatific vision' to youth groups and women's societies, to argue again and again that society needed a theological overhaul because 'British democracy is the result of the emancipation of the commercial middle classes through the industrial revolution, and is constructed on a false basis . . . and in so far as this is true, democracy is merely another aspect of the struggle for power which is the basis of all political systems . . .' adding as a palliative, and perhaps with a sideways glance towards Berlin and Moscow, that British democracy, despite its moral imperfections, represented 'a great advance on other systems'.

One of the 'other systems' then advanced into Poland. Chamberlain made a speech for which, if royalties had been charged, film, television and radio producers would by now have paid some hundreds of thousands of pounds in reproduction fees. An air raid warning promptly sounded, and Helena Charles, bowling along in her little car, shot up the high street in Streatham, and charged through a red light before she regained her composure and reasoned that this first lament by the sirens was probably a false alarm. 'It was one of several occasions in my life when I deserved to have an accident and didn't.'

Given the circumstances, it seemed more appropriate to embark on the defence of that flawed British democracy rather than continue to expose its deficiencies. Helena resigned, for a while, from the Industrial Christian Fellowship and enrolled with the London Ambulance Volunteer Service, whose staff delighted in using its acronym: LAVS. LPVS would have been a less diverting but more appropriate set of initials, for LAVS lacked even a single ambulance, and its organisers had commandeered instead a number of large and small pantechnicons, furniture and laundry vans, augmented by a few private cars for the sitting wounded. At least, that's the vehicle muster Helena recalls. And she also says that the period she spent with the Volunteer Service ranked among 'the most inglorious few months of my life'.

This was the celebrated phoney war. The members of the London Ambulance Volunteer Service waited in the headquarters they had borrowed from a garage, and pasted paper over the windows which would undoubtedly have shattered anyway if a bomb had fallen nearby, and worked their shifts, and became increasingly moody and quarrelsome. You could be on duty from 3.30 in the afternoon until 11, or from 11 until 7.30 in the morning, or from 7.30 until 3.30. And when you were not in training you were waiting, all keyed up, as Helena says, to a pitch of enthusiasm, with nothing at all to do. The volunteers included a squash champion, a chiropodist, a taxi driver, and a society hostess who was anxious to lend her support to the national effort on behalf of an apparently non-existent war. There was also a former prison officer, who once said to Helena, when they were being trained to reverse lorries in pitch darkness without any lights: 'You're right, the night was made for love,' and although Helena tended to agree, she had no recollection of making any remark to that effect herself.

'We were a motley bunch with absolutely nothing in common, and we seemed to spend the whole time arguing. On no point of principle at all we found we fell into two camps which were always at loggerheads. If you went into a room where members of the other camp were sitting they all shut up immediately. The tension came out of sheer boredom. Morale was rotten. All alcohol was forbidden, but on Christmas Day, when we were on duty, somebody brought in some gin, and we disguised it by putting it into a water jug. All I can say is that it was extremely fortunate that nobody inspected the station on that day, and even more fortunate that no bombs fell.'

It was not a very inspiring piece of service for a woman of vision and energy, and her standing among the volunteers and organisers deteriorated when she decided to use the Fischers' presence at her digs to quench a thirst for a new language. Given the aptitude she had already demonstrated with French, it is hardly surprising that in a very little time all the conversations at home were being carried on in German; but sometimes she began to respond instinctively to questions at work with one of her newly learned words, phrases or sentences. Although the Second World War brought little of the dachshund-kicking which had distinguished the first, it was hardly a propitious time to be acquiring and showing off one's prowess with the enemy tongue. Nobody went so far as to accuse her of disloyalty, but there was a certain sniffiness to add to the other discomforts and the profound tedium of life in a garage, waiting by a laundry van for a bomb which never fell.

When the Industrial Christian Fellowship invited Helena back to run the Youth Committee, she resigned from the LAVS without hesitation, and returned to a sphere of work which seemed to her to have more consequence in the real world. She also wanted the ICF to find some sort of pigeonhole for Gerhard to occupy, and busied herself trying to obtain a work permit for him.

But in May and June of 1940, whatever mask of phoneyness the hostilities had worn was pulled aside. Belgium, Holland and France fell to the invading Germans, and the nightmare and the valour of the Dunkirk evacuations finally disillusioned those who had thought the war would never arrive on their threshold. Another tidal wave of refugees crossed the Channel to England. With them, the authorities suspected, were large numbers of German agents, and complacency gave way to panic and a groundswell of xenophobia. For months, with little other subject matter available with which to excite the jingoism of their taproom audience, sections of the popular Press had been stirring up a John Bullish 'intern 'em all' vendetta against refugees from enemy territories. So far, the government had found their soap box oratory easy to resist, but now those shrill editorials acquired a plausibility that recruited more and more MPs to their cause, and eventually the Cabinet succumbed. In the national mythology, a sinister knock on the door and arrest without charge had largely been a feature of novels and films that dramatised the insecurities of alien and totalitarian states. But when the goats were allegedly dressing up as sheep, then both sheep and goats, it seemed, had to be closely penned. All adult male refugees from German and Italian dominated countries were rounded up.

'One morning, very early, the police came and took poor Gerhard away. Perhaps it was necessary. The nation was suddenly in an absolutely shocking situation, perhaps the lowest time of the whole year. As my father pointed out to me when I went off the deep end, this sort of injustice always happens to innocent people in wartime. But I set about trying to get not only Gerhard released, but everyone else who was innocent. I wrote suitcases full of letters to MPs and to anybody I thought might have some influence and be able to help. I eventually discovered that Gerhard had been sent to Huyton, near Liverpool. The camp was in a shocking state, unprepared and dirty. He and the others were being guarded by soldiers who had just come back from Dunkirk and assumed they had custody of Nazis. I can see now that it was inevitable in the circumstances, but at the time I was outraged. The BBC, for example, had been employing a number of Italian anti-fascist refugees to make broadcasts on the overseas services, and they were all put into a camp with fascists. Nobody seemed to know the difference, and it was an absolutely horrifying situation. I joined up with some like-minded people and we conducted an extremely vigorous campaign to try to get each individual's case history re-examined so that the genuine refugees could be released and only the Nazis kept in prison.'

Reviewing the case histories that Helena and her associates assembled and distributed to sympathetic members of Parliament and prominent liberal-thinkers, it does seem that the measures ordered by a Cabinet Committee hint at careless haste. It was left, for example, to individual police officers—the rank was never apparently specified—to judge whether a refugee was too old or too sick or in too important a job to be taken away and locked up in camps where, according to one observer, the public were able to gaze at the inmates through the barbed wire as if they were animals in a zoo. In many cases the policemen concerned seemed to be adherents of the 'intern 'em all' philosophy.

There was a man who had been a professor of chemistry at a German university for 23 years, one of the world's leading authorities on dyestuffs, whose seminal book was translated and printed at Harvard. To deny any other country the benefit of his knowledge and research, the Nazis at first refused to let him leave Germany, then they threw him into a concentration camp and brutally tortured him for 17 days. When he was released, he escaped to England where he was awarded a research grant to continue his work with a leading company. On the announcement of internment his employers applied to the Home Office for an exemption, and when the police arrived at his flat he showed them the letter of application and asked them to postpone their decision until a reply had been received. They refused, told him to prepare for immediate internment, and left, saying they would return shortly to collect him. How was he to envisage any difference between the consequences of arbitrary imprisonment in two separate societies, both of which clearly regarded him as an alien? When the police came back, they found that he had swallowed poison and was dead. There was a significant exchange at the inquest. When the man's widow was asked if he had been a Jew, she said that although he was born Jewish, he had later been baptised. That piece of information might have counted for nothing in Germany, where prejudice was racial rather than religious, but the policeman who had visited the flat admitted he might have agreed to defer internment had he known the scientist was a Christian. He told the coroner he had assumed there were no grounds for granting exemption to a Jew.

Other histories from the dossier:

Age, 53; refugee from Nazi oppression; arrested in the streets of Leipzig during November pogrom; three months in Nazi concentration camp where he contracted diabetes. Now living on daily insulin. His only child in English sanatorium with chest disease; offer to serve Britain three times refused. Has this morning been detained by the CID for immediate internment as enemy alien. Fainted; carried away semi-conscious . . .

Several scores of factories, workshops, and agricultural settlements have been stripped of directors and key workers . . .

The managing director of a company carrying out contracts for Government ministries, totalling £500,000 in value, has been interned . . .

Between 600 and 700 nurses have been turned out of hospitals all over England because they are considered to be 'of alien nationality' . . .

Among the men interned are sufferers from heart disease, diabetes and glaucoma . . .

Huyton Camp has been inundated with refugees. It is almost completely devoid of chairs, tables and beds. Elderly internees are forced to sleep on the floor on mattresses or straw. They are forbidden access to newspapers or wirelesses, and were forbidden to take with them their own books or such comforts as, for example, their own violins . . .

* * *

A knock at the door, behind which lodge, now, only Helena Charles and the increasingly distraught Mrs Fischer.

'Miss Charles?'

'Yes?'

'May I come in?'

'You are?'

'A police officer.'

Hope, perhaps, as they walked back towards the tiny living room, that there was good news, not bad, from the miseries of Huyton; that the policeman was not doubling as the padre whose duty was to announce that Gerhard in his squalid solitude had committed some folly or been trapped and killed by Nazi prisoners.

'Well?'

'Miss Charles, are you aware of the Defence Regulations?'

'Vaguely.'

'I have been sent to ascertain whether or not you should be arrested for contravening them.'

'I beg your pardon? What am I supposed to have done?'

' "Subject as hereinafter provided, any person who publishes any report or statement relating to matters concerned with the war which is likely to cause alarm or despondency shall be liable to imprisonment for a term not exceeding one month, or to a fine not exceeding £50 or to both such imprisonment or fine." '

'So?'

'You've been circulating reports regarding conditions in Huyton and other internment camps?'

'Yes.'

'I have to tell you that these reports are considered gross exaggerations by the authorities . . .'

'Rot . . .'

'They've been described to me as false statements amounting to anti-British propaganda.'

'Anti-British? You can be against injustice without being anti-British . . .'

'But what you've been saying simply isn't true.'

'Not true? Not true? Have you been to the camps?'

'Well no, but I . . .'

'Just look at these.' And Helena handed over two letters from MPs who had been provoked to examine the facts by the information Helena and her group had supplied. The police officer read them.

'Well?'

'I shan't be recommending an arrest, Miss Charles.'

'I should think not.'

'Actually, I wish you luck with all this. It's a shame I can't do something about it myself.'

* * *

The evidence that Helena's team supplied was used at least twice by Parliamentarians in debates which eventually persuaded the government to review its policy and adopt a more discerning approach to refugees who had crossed the enemy's frontiers because they shared our hatred of his ideology and were in turn, by race or conviction, his enemy. Only one man was unshakeably dismayed by Helena's involvement in the campaign: Frank Charles. 'I thought that as he'd always taught me to stand up for the weak he would have been pleased at what I'd been doing. But he was absolutely furious. The idea that I might have gone to prison was a disgrace that he just couldn't stomach.'

No matter how loud his wrath, Mr Charles was powerless to prevent Helena from pursuing her crusade. Indeed, one doubts whether she could have stopped herself, even if she had agreed to withdraw from the spotlight to protect the sensitive plant of the family's honour. The Mitcham pattern was repeated in the offices of the Industrial Christian Fellowship, whose Youth Committee Leader, instead of deploying her time on behalf of the immortal souls of London's juveniles, found herself inundated with requests for information and assistance from the relatives of interned refugees, and from the relatives of Jews and dissidents still trapped—now, most likely, inextricably—behind the lines of the thousand year Reich. More readily than the parochial authorities at Mitcham, the ICF recognised an overriding spiritual and moral importance in the work which was now preoccupying Helena. Of all the tragic histories that passed before her, one in particular stayed in her mind, perhaps because it demonstrated a level at which even she was impotent. A woman called Trudi Friedman came into the ICF building and said she had just heard that her brother had been put into a concentration camp. All Helena could do was commiserate with her; there was no message she could give, no action she could take, to deflect their minds from the awful outcome the news portended. Only lame words.

Gerhard and most of the other internees were sent to Canada, where Nazis and non-Nazis were, at last, segregated. He spent a year there, while Mrs Fischer continued to live with Helena—'we pursued our miserable existence'—until the start of the blitz. Helena's introduction to those night fires and night fears came one evening towards the end of 1940. She had doubled back on her way home to collect a fur coat inadvertently left behind at the ICF offices. A siren sounded as she resumed her journey home, and this time the bombs began to fall. 'I went into a pub, just opposite St Thomas's Hospital, and spent the night sitting on three slats of wood in the cellar. It was full of people sheltering from the raid. When I came out in the morning I could see that bits of the hospital wall were down, and bedding and blankets and mattresses were hanging out into the street.' It was Helena's first encounter with the savagery of modern warfare, and she had no idea how widely the devastation was spread. 'I went back to our lodgings in Walcott Gardens, and the house next door to mine was flat. There had been a very nice old woman who'd lived there with a daughter who was married to a merchant seaman, and there was a beautiful baby we were all very fond of, called Ivan. The merchant seaman had wanted his family to go to Canada where they would have been safe, but his wife always said, "No, it'll never happen to us,'' and the very first night of the blitz Ivan was killed. The grandmother survived. I'm not sure now what happened to the baby's mother.'

The charming infant who had won the street's devotion was a first and terrible casualty of war in Helena's neighbourhood. Surely it was understandable that her greeting to Mrs Fischer appeared to lack warmth? Shock tends to leave people more numb than effusive. But a terrible row ensued. Mrs Fischer had spent an anxious and solitary night, fearful that the source of her support had also been destroyed in the night's attack. Reason broke down on both sides. Helena was exhausted, and needed to sleep. Mrs Fischer was agitated, and wanted affectionate chatter and comfort.

For the next couple of nights, the couple shared the stresses of the blitz. 'We spent one terrible evening in the air-raid shelter, with bombs whizzing down all round us. There wasn't very much damage done in our vicinity, but the East End was flattened, and we were both very frightened. She couldn't see any point in the silly jokes that the rest of us were making. There's that very powerful English defence mechanism—the more frightened you are, the more you try to find something to laugh about, to release the tension. But Mrs Fischer just sat there miserably, with her mouth down at the corners, and her head sunk on her chest, and of course, her fear was very infectious, and made all the rest of us that much more frightened.'

Then Frank Charles arrived, and strode into the typical chaos that tended to make Helena's lodgings look, even in peacetime, as if a smallish bomb had passed by. He wanted his daughter to return to the comparative safety of Clarewood. But there was a difficulty. Camberley was surrounded, now, by military training camps, and had been declared a prohibited area, off limits to alien refugees. 'I just can't leave Mrs Fischer,' Helena pleaded. 'I can't just walk off and abandon her here.' Obligingly, Mr Charles trailed round police stations until a sympathetic officer granted the old lady a permit to make her querulous invasion of Surrey.

'Actually she lived there for quite a long time. You can just imagine what it was like having her and my stepmother in the house together.' At first, Mrs Fischer was almost unctuous in her gratitude. After all, she had been translated from some fairly frugal and claustral lodgings to a grand house, a situation more in keeping with her anti-democratic inclinations, reminiscent, perhaps, of a halcyon and imperial Austria. But the distant shuddering of bombs and guns, and the visible if inscrutable manoeuvres of the adjacent soldiery, reminded her of the catastrophe that had fragmented her world. Mrs Fischer's native pessimism prevailed, and she adopted a favoured perch in front of a radiator. 'What are you doing?' members of the Charles family would ask. And she would draw in a breath and explain, in ominously accented tones: 'I am waiting for something dreadful to happen.' Perversely, in an exercise of that very humour which Mrs Fischer found so inimical, Clarewood's household found the catch-phrase as amusing and serviceable as any on the radio.

Dislodged from the radiator to join what she was certain, each time, was a last supper, the old lady sat in anguished silence. 'On one occasion my Aunt Ethel came to lunch. She was a dear thing, but one of the most tactless people I ever met. And she suddenly looked across at Mrs Fischer and asked her to say something funny. Of course, it had the reverse effect.' The mouth turned down even further at its corners, and the melancholy deepened.

In other circumstances, Helena might have brooded over the unpredictable emotional chemistries at Clarewood, and over a more secret grief: she had decided to have her boisterous dog put down, both because her training at the Ambulance Volunteer Service had convinced her there would be gas attacks, and because she feared the animal might run ferociously wild in an air-raid. But there was much to distract her. She had been promoted to the executive of the Industrial Christian Fellowship, and had begun an enervating curriculum of writing and lecturing—more than two meetings a week for over a year, travelling in constant difficulty and danger. The pamphlets she produced looked away from the war to problems that had preceded it and would endure, without legislation, after any armistice. 'The Fact of Malnutrition' drew on her Bermondsey experiences to propose some national consideration, if not supervision, of diet. 'From School to—?' reminded its audience that while England had covered some moral distance since the Victorian age, the protection of young people employed in factories and shops was still not entirely adequate.

New friends and associates provided new stimuli. The Reverend Gilbert Shaw was a lawyer turned vicar whose mission had a strong tendency to mysticism (his friends claimed that light-bulbs flickered when he entered their rooms). Her namesake Alice Charles was, she says, one of the few thoroughly good people she met during her life. Alice's father, before his elevation to the Bench, was a barrister who specialised in the defence of priests who had been accused, under a statute introduced by Disraeli, of deviating from the established liturgy. In an unlawyerlike piece of research, Charles discovered a loophole in the law—the need for episcopal approval, which was seldom forthcoming, before any prosecution. His colleagues accused Charles of killing a goose which had laid golden eggs for decades.

Alice and Helena diverted themselves for a while by trying to find a common ancestry. They discovered no relationship, although both families had originated in Scotland. Alice's forebears were farmers,

Helena's fleshers. 'So we supplied the raw materials for your trade,' Alice joked, and in a sense that sort of relationship continued, for Alice, a generation older, provided from her knowledge and experience facts and ideas for Helena's talks and booklets. They played on their interchangeable names by interchanging engagements, so that different audiences, comparing notes, would argue furiously whether Miss Charles was a young woman or middle aged. And when it was reported that the Reverend Gilbert Shaw had expressed a deep admiration for 'Miss Charles' work' they were unable ever to establish which Miss Charles he had in mind, and he, presumably, was too much of a gentleman to settle the dispute.

'One of the things which this extraordinary company of people did for me was to make me very dissatisfied with anybody else,' Helena admits. 'Almost any other group of people I found slightly boring, and slightly sub-standard, so perhaps it wasn't completely good for me.' But almost in the same breath she qualifies her confession of acquired arrogance with a familiar phrase of self-effacement. 'The meetings I addressed during those years have very largely been merged into a sort of blob in my memory. I can't remember very much about them.' Perhaps that's unsurprising given the congestion of her appointments calendar. Once, turning up to give a lecture, she knew *en route* from railway station to hall that she had been to the place before, but no matter how hard she tried, could not recall the date or subject. It was flattering that her audience remembered, and brought up those previous themes in the open session following her talk.

Perhaps the abiding memory for her listeners was that this 'slip of a girl', as some of them called her, had a habit of leaving chastened and bedraggled hecklers in her wake. Both ardent communists and cynical capitalists might suppose they could glibly demonstrate that the Christian socialism of Helena's message had woven itself into romanticism or stamped itself into anachronism on the looms and letterpresses of the William Morris movement. Instead, they confronted an austere, dogmatic, and thoroughly modern thinker, whose texts might be timeless, but whose images and arguments were collected from the contemporary world.

'It was a very happy and very satisfying job, apart from its weariness, and all the awkward situations of travelling. I thought I was really getting somewhere, although now I'm not so sure.'

CHAPTER SEVEN

WARTIME

The war's metal and explosive horrors spread to Camberley. Already, as the blitz reached its height, fires burning in London shed enough light in Surrey to allow the residents of suburbia to read or eat without the use of their own electricity. Beneath Clarewood lay a series of cellars: a corridor flanked by a dairy, a laundry, a wine-cellar, a boiler room and a larder. 'It was like a flat with subterranean windows underneath the house.' Frank Charles converted it into a spacious air-raid shelter, which the children nicknamed 'Dr Goebbels' coffin'. The family's use of it was at first diligent, and then rather more casual, until a German aeroplane in flight jettisoned its bombs, demolishing one nearby house and damaging another. Fortunately the only casualty was a canary.

'One day we were sitting in the shelter when Anne came in from a party she'd been to and said she had a very important announcement to make. She'd just been introduced to some Free French officers. That was the beginning of an extraordinary relationship. A stream of young men had just poured into England from France in response to De Gaulle's plea for a fighting force. They had practically nothing with them, no arms, no uniforms, but our Government had accepted them as the basis of an army, and had put them into a rather hastily prepared camp on a common near our house. I think we all felt the same. It was great fun having them to the house, and dancing with them, or going out with them, but there was also a deeper aspect to it. They were far from home, they had lost their country, they were living in very rough conditions, and many of them were not military minded at all—they were volunteers who'd decided to do what they could to defeat Hitler and regain their country. All this seemed to us to be reason enough to entertain them, and incidentally to have a very good time with them. Of course my stepmother didn't like them coming to the house, and my father was petrified that they'd seduce one of us, which never happened. They used to come to tea, or to dance—and we took up the carpets and rugs in the billiard room and played the gramophone. All in all it was rather a happy time, despite the war.'

When Helena was at home, she and her sisters would scavenge the woods for logs and branches to build fires—there was scarcely any coal to be had—and browse the orchards for apples and chestnuts to augment their meagre food supply. One night they organised a party at a nearby restaurant—Mr Charles, whatever his misgivings, was once again his daughters' financial backer—and combed local society for girls who had a working French vocabulary. The transport to and from the house was described on postcard invitations as a 'convoy', and rumour of it caused at first some alarm among the local military. After dinner, the party returned to Clarewood to dance, and a young French officer to whom sister Anne had taken a shine (his Christian name, of course, was Charles) decided he rather preferred Helena.

'After a while we were dancing only with each other. As the evening drew to a close Anne came into the room and found us kissing, and she was not unreasonably upset, and I was rather upset that she'd seen. But Charles Boyer and I had five marvellous weeks, striding about together on the Common. I was rather possessive and jealous, and insisted on going to a farewell dinner that he was giving. But after five weeks he went. He was the world's worst correspondent—I think I had one letter from him. I did hear news from time to time. He ended his career in Paris. I could have asked to meet him again but I didn't, because we were both of us married by that time and I thought one of two things would happen: either we would both be disappointed in each other or the whole thing would start again.

'But that was one of the brighter moments of life at that time. One by one all our friends went away, because, after all, it was a training camp. We had one wonderful outing at the end when Charles, who was an army doctor, and the beautiful Eduoard and Anne and I went off to a dance in the officers' club at Aldershot. Anne had been forbidden to dance because she had a poisoned thumb and her arm was in a sling, but the doctor said it would be all right for her to take the sling off for just one evening.

'I remember that Charles was driving the military ambulance. We came out, indulged in a short necking party, and drove off. When we got home we looked in the back and there was nobody there. It was a November night, it was dark and foggy, and there was an air-raid. I left a note on the table saying that we'd gone back to Aldershot to look for them. We only had dimmed sidelights with bits of tissue over them, and when we'd travelled the six miles back to Aldershot we found Anne and Eduoard sitting back to back on a bench. Apparently Eduoard had tried to kiss my sister and she'd taken great exception to his behaviour.'

Eduoard and Dr Boyer moved away, at last, and in their place arrived a

'Fortuna' swings on his golden globe – and beneath him, two metal slaves memorialise the source of the Republic's power and empire.

ALLE
RMESINI

SALVIATI
SALVIATI

Opposite: Backstreet Venice, and the wild cats disdain a tethered dog.

Inside the Campo di Ghetta Nuovo, the main Jewish quarter since 1516. On the left, a Jewish bank. On the right, a scrawled slogan – *'Juve Merda'* – recalls Helena's campaign against anti-semitism in the heart of the city where she later campaigned against cruelty to animals.

Opposite: A palace sparkling with mosaics on the Grand Canal.

Graffiti on a wellhead in the Santa Croce. Tourists mingle with shoppers and commuters away from the holiday honeypots.

Dignified and alone, a Venetian cat 'mother' strolls towards the main landing stages near the Piazza San Marco.

large group of Frenchmen who had escaped from German prison camps into Russia, only to be the victims of even harsher treatment from the Bolsheviks. Helena and her sisters heard horrifying stories of gold fillings being extracted from teeth, and prisoners being confined in rooms which had been adapted to exacerbate whatever illnesses they might be suffering—someone with a chest infection, for example, might find himself trapped in a continuous current of chilly air.

The Charles sisters prescribed a tried and immediate remedy for the ills of their new arrivals: a dance. The rugs and carpets in rolls against the skirting like apt draught excluders; more apples and more chestnuts, more brushwood, more logs, the fire blazing cordially, the handle of the gramophone warm from the warmth of the atmosphere and from constant cranking. *Un petit Français qui s'appelle Jean-Louis*, nine years younger than Helena, fell instantly and violently in love with her. 'I didn't know what to do about it. There was no question of anything between us except that I felt desperately sorry for him. But I did find that if I let him cuddle and kiss on the sofa for quite a long time it would calm him down. He was in quite a

'The beginning of an extraordinary relationship . . .' One of the Free French soldiers who joined Helena (right), Anne (centre) and Elizabeth at Camberley in 1941. 'You have given me life and sweetness,' he wrote on the back of this snapshot.

bad state of nerves after more than a year in prisons of various kinds. If I resisted him he got more and more excited and upset and went home completely unfulfilled. He left when his time came, and suddenly changed his attitude and wrote me a very abusive letter, followed up by one saying he was very sorry for this reaction, because he knew I'd been very kind to him, and could I write to his mother through the Red Cross and let her know that he was getting married. So I wrote—she was in the Vichy—and she was terribly upset, because he already had a girl at home.' It must have been difficult gently to break the news of the latest twist in the young Frenchman's sentimental weathervane: Red Cross regulations demanded that whatever the matter of a letter, it should be conveyed in a maximum of twenty-five words.

Naturally it was a diversion for Helena to allay the neuroses of war, and leaven a local society which she had always found somewhat uncongenial, by mixing with the Free French troops and refugees. But in a sense, she was paying a tax for her pleasure—the extension into a new field of the pastoral care for which she had trained since Oxford. For Jean-Louis, she was an *ersatz* sweetheart, and perhaps every attractive Englishwoman was going to play that role until one appeared who was convertible and would supplant his real love. For another Jean, Helena was confessor.

'He had been married for several years, and had a little girl of four, and he was missing his wife and child most terribly, and would tell me all about them. He had been taken prisoner after the fall of France, and had trekked through the countryside with a gang of orphans they'd met. They had no food, and one day they found a van laden with liqueurs, and desperate for some sort of sustenance, they'd all become terribly drunk. Then he was arrested and sent to Russia, and finally managed to get himself transferred to England. He was so unhappy and we would talk for hours.'

Finally, as he became more sure of Helena's willing and confidential ear, Jean disclosed that his sorrow was underpinned with guilt. 'It was a very sad story. He'd met another refugee, a girl, who'd been machine-gunned from the air and had scars all over her arms. They'd had an affair and he was feeling awful about it because she'd written to say she was pregnant.' Helena got in touch with the French priest who was trying to salvage something from the triangle, and through their persistent efforts they discovered that the 'pregnancy' was a trick. The girl eventually married, and Jean was a guest at the wedding. Through the economical manipulation of her twenty-five word Red Cross missives, Helena also managed to re-establish contact between Jean and his wife, and to maintain a line of communication between them when he was posted to North Africa.

Her task was not always to turn herself into a clue to lead a young foreigner from his emotional labyrinth. Sometimes, relations were refreshingly simple and platonic. Frenchmen encountered during that unique year at Camberley still exchange cards and letters with Helena, and occasionally pay visits to her cottage in Ely when they come to England. How many more friendships might have been forged, and how many more riddles of male behaviour solved, if the period of contact had been extended, remains a hypothesis, for a new figure was preparing to disrupt the unlikely idyll.

'For just over a year we were really very happy, but it all came to an end in a flaming row with my stepmother. One night my sister Elizabeth and I were entertaining three Frenchmen. To see them thawing out in front of a roaring fire on a bitter night as we roasted chestnuts was an absolute delight. It really was the most respectable party you could imagine; I suppose it went on until eleven o'clock, or perhaps midnight. Anyway, some time later, after they'd gone, my mother went along the corridor to the bathroom and saw the light beneath the door. Elizabeth and I were alone, reading Lewis Carroll's *Sylvie and Bruno*, and laughing aloud at it. The next morning my stepmother gave us a terrible row, and I stormed out of the door and went up to London, and didn't go back for a very long time. I continued to work for the ICF from London, living in a very uncomfortable bedsit.'

The problem of what should be done with Mrs Fischer was averted when the Government succumbed to a campaign—to which Helena had continued to contribute—to bring deported refugees back from Canada, and, after re-examination, to liberate non-Nazis. Gerhard by this time had learned a system of shorthand, and was able to find himself a secretarial post with sufficient income to set himself up in lodgings with his mother. By now there was a kind of rhythm to the war, which is to say that its participants expected no quick resolution. Sister Anne joined the WAAF; sister Elizabeth, the WRNS. Sister Helena continued to lecture and to write, and to enjoy the companionship of Alice Charles and Gilbert Shaw.

Archbishop William Temple organised a series of major meetings, reports of which were broadcast throughout Europe. One was on the subject of 'Youth', and Helena was invited to take part. The Malvern Conference followed, charting a Christian course through the post-war years in anticipation of victory. Once again, Helena was among the participants, trudging through thick snow and the blackout and remembering, as she arrived, that she had forgotten to bring her hat, despite the cold and even though the event was being held in a consecrated building. Had not St Paul suggested that a woman who appeared in church or chapel without a covering on her head should have the said head shaved? As Archbishop Temple passed she called over:

'Your Grace, would you mind if I come in without a hat?'

Helena in 1941: the year of the Free French 'invasion' of Camberley, and of her decision to leave the family home and take lodgings in London.

'Of course not, of course not. By all means. The angels will never see you through the blackout.'

The angels made sure, though, that a million copies of the conference report were circulated. Flying bombs, however, managed to disrupt the deliberations of a later working party whose manifesto was entitled 'Towards the Conversion of England'. On one occasion nobody turned up to preach the cause at all.

From bedsit to bedsit, Helena moved, during these hectic years. From time to time she would return to Clarewood, initially wooed by Frank Charles, who had been saddened and ill after her departure. She would go back for Christmas, perhaps, but her links were substantially severed, and for the rest of her life home would be a place of her own determining. And, for a while, a place to which Free French soldiers, the grapevine flourishing, felt they could resort without notice for a chaste and convivial evening. 'On one occasion, with no warning at all, two of them turned up. They seemed decades younger than me. I asked what they wanted to do, and they said they'd like to go to the Hammersmith Palais de Dance. So off we went. There was a band at either end, and we danced for so long that there was no chance for them to get back to Camberley. All the hostels were full up, and the only alternative would have been for them to sleep on benches in the underground. So since I thought that was rather hard I asked them to come back with me. We none of us undressed, I gave them each a pillow and a blanket, and they lay down with their boots on. We all got the giggles shortly after I'd turned the lights out. In the morning I woke up and all I could see was a row of upturned boots poking out of the blankets. It looked just like the pictures one had seen of casualties.'

Lingering souvenirs of the pleasant year at Camberley. Which perhaps explains why Helena was drawn to Victoria Station to watch an anarchic parade of Free Frenchmen passing the statue of Marshal Foch, and joined the crowd from which emerged, with an invitation to a cup of coffee, a Latvian refugee called Leo.

* * *

Leo was a refugee from a different terror: a Russian Jew, the grandson of a rabbi. He told Helena there was a parchment in his family which described a pogrom in his village, a murderous procession led by a monk brandishing a cross. The parchment record stopped abruptly, and the family could only deduce that those collateral ancestors had been annihilated.

Leo and his mother had fetched up in London after their escape from the Russian revolutionaries who were invading Latvia, and destiny was to bring him face to face with Helena that day at Victoria Station. She must have recognised that he was a foreigner, because although he spoke to her in English, the approach was very direct, and very untypical of the manners of her countrymen.

'Do you want a cup of coffee?' he asked, and she looked round in surprise at the stranger and saw a dark and saturnine youth, about her own age. She agreed, and over coffee began to sort out his story: the escape from Russia with his mother, with whom he lived (his father was in Canada). How he had gone up to Oxford—they must have been contemporaries, but they had never met, and she did not think she would have forgotten those very distinctive Russian features—but left without passing his degree. His command of the language was extraordinary. 'Almost perfect', Helena recalls, although he betrayed himself with one of the English expressions he affected, 'hang it all', which tended to emerge from his lips as 'hang-gitall'.

Now he was trying desperately to make ends meet. National sympathy for refugees was focused sharply on fugitives from Nazism, and the plight of those who fled from the Russian Revolution was a matter of indifference, or even of embarrassment, as Russia's own sufferings in the war and her defection to the Allied cause began to evoke a sense both of pity and fraternity. Leo wrote odd pieces for the *Evening Standard*, and did a little jobbing work as a translator. But he was, he told Helena, constantly short of money. She paid for the coffee.

And then, for six months, silence. It was prophetic of the nature of their relationship, and perhaps Helena should have been warned. But so far it had only been the most casual encounter, perhaps invested with a slight depth by the coincidence of their Oxford years. Besides, Helena was busy with her ICF work, and assisting in a multiplicity of other causes. She found somewhere more permanent to live, a flat at number seven, Philbeach Gardens. A friend agreed to share with her: Sybil Richardson, a music graduate from Oxford, the devoted daughter of a doting father, born by caesarean section as her mother died. Perhaps one could chain together from that traumatic birth the reasons for Sybil's claustrophobia; anyway, her territory consisted of the dining room and a small bedroom, while Helena encamped in the big sitting room, and the couple made a pact to avoid chaos in communal areas.

After the half year had elapsed, Leo suddenly telephoned and invited himself round to the flat. 'It was quite a pleasant evening,' Helena recalls. And it was the start of a relationship that was to last for three years. 'He was very clever and full of charm, but utterly selfish. He wouldn't bother, for example, to turn up for a date if he decided there was someone else he'd rather see.' Sybil was uneasy about the egotism of this suave newcomer, and time and again tried to persuade or force him to demonstrate his affection by some practical gesture. On one occasion Helena's duties took her out of London, making it impossible for her to present her coupons and claim her tiny meat ration for the week. Sybil made Leo promise to collect it on her friend's behalf. It was a costly effort to instil some sense of consideration—he forgot, and Helena's wrath on her return made him ill for two days.

Gradually, Helena was drawn into Leo's home. His mother was a nervous, suspicious sort of creature, and at first she detested the cat that

Helena introduced into the ménage. Later she would be discovered cradling it in her arms and crooning Latvian lullabies. She spoke no English, so conversations were conducted in German. The young linguist had hoped to add Russian to her vocabulary, but Leo could not be bothered to teach her. There was, however, one subject which excited him passionately—the sufferings and destiny of the Jewish race. Perhaps the Gentile Helena should have guessed from this obsession that the friendship which was becoming increasingly serious to her could never be more than a detour along Leo's forward path. But given her own passionate and instinctive empathy with the victims of oppression, she was, she says, fertile ground for Leo's polemic.

'He made me into what I have been ever since, a very convinced Zionist. I came to see that the betrayal of the Balfour declaration which had promised the Jews a homeland had denied them a refuge and delivered them to the Nazi holocaust. The first refugees who'd attempted to settle in Palestine suffered poverty and malaria, and the onslaughts of the Turks, and the nations who'd promised them support just ignored them and went back on their word. But more than that, Leo opened my eyes to the terrible things the Christians had done to the Jews throughout history —particularly the pogroms in Russia, and the repression which excluded Jews from various avenues of work and sections of society. The very idea of Christianity was repugnant to them for those reasons, and for the first time in my life I was ashamed of my faith, or at least of the way some people had practised it, repudiating the command to love one another and preach the gospel to all people.'

While Helena was having history lessons in anti-semitism's past cruelties, flying bombs were swarming nightly over London, engines growling before suddenly cutting out into silence some seconds before a crash and a fearful explosion. Helena remembers the model prayer that A. P. Herbert composed for the time: 'Let that noise stop now, O Lord, that I and not some other chap may die.' It was an ideal which stretched even Helena Charles' capacity for virtuous intentions. 'We used to look at the railway and all around us and say, "Look at all the places where a flying bomb could fall and not fall on us . . ."'

At the same time, Sybil was being agitated by a different lapse from virtue: the top floor of 7 Philbeach Gardens appeared to have become a brothel. As always, the resilient Helena was expected to find some sort of remedy. 'Sybil begged me to do something about it, and told me the noise was deplorable, but I pointed out that unless I caught them at it there was very little action I could take.'

Sybil was doubly disturbed because Helena had started moving out of the flat at nights—hence her inability to catch the whores performing their professional duties—and was minding Leo's mother while he worked shifts translating Russian broadcasts for the BBC external services. The old woman was distraught every time the bombs began to fly. 'One night there were seventy-six of them,' says Helena, 'and I was completely unable to sleep—not because of the noise they made, but because the sound of Leo's mother in a continuous panic kept me awake all the time.'

The next night seemed mercifully calm. A widow whose home had been destroyed brought her small son to Philbeach Gardens and begged accommodation. There was room to spare because Helena decided to continue her duties with Leo's mother. Only one bomb materialised, but it was still enough to provoke hysteria. 'I said, "Oh, do be quiet, it's a long way away and I really must try to get some sleep."' Eventually the old woman was persuaded to rest, and when morning came Helena went straight to her office at the Industrial Christian Fellowship.

One can picture the interior of the ICF building, and Helena approaching her office door, hearing an excited jabber from inside. As she enters, inexplicably silencing her colleagues, one of them says—more a bewildered inquiry than a greeting—'Miss Charles?' And then the scene at Earls Court: a monstrous cairn of bricks, smouldering timbers, and eviscerated furniture. Limbs are threaded in and out of the heap, some naked, some partly covered with strips of uniform, others in bloodstained bits of night attire. These were the customers of the brothel and its staff. The houses either side of 7 Philbeach Gardens had collapsed, and another seven were badly damaged.

'Just that one flying bomb had come over, and it dropped through my bedroom window. The whole house had collapsed into the bedroom. As well as the naked bodies and the uniforms, Sybil was found in the rubble. Dr Richardson had identified her. The thing that worried us was her claustrophobia. We were terribly depressed at the thought that she might have been buried alive. But I found a pillow in the road with her name on it, and there was very little blood, so we suspected that she'd died from the blast, and hadn't suffered too much.'

Unsurprisingly, the shock of discovering Death's visiting card on her doorstep was enough to reconcile the differences—temporarily—between Helena and her stepmother. She returned to the family home, but continued to commute to the ICF in London and to travel the country lecturing and distributing her pamphlets. The tally shows a total of 497 talks, urging support for the Fellowship's dogma and strategy. The first world order of capitalism, they believed, was being consumed by the second totalitarian order of fascism and communism, because the capitalists had long since abandoned the moral heights to quarry depths of materialism, and by that selfish act had alienated the mass of the working people, making them fodder for despots with promiscuous tongues and evil intentions. When the bombs stopped falling and the senseless destruction of friend and foe ceased in a truce of mutual despair and horror, one hope would be left for mankind: a third order reaching back beyond the mercantile treachery of the Renaissance to find in a purer medieval theology the basis for a Christian order in which work served man, and labourer and master were united in pursuit of the beatific vision.

As Helena wrote in *The Malvern Way*, a book she published in 1949:

'Economic gain must be subordinated to the real business of life, which is living the fullest possible life for the glory of God . . . Trade must be carried on and goods produced not in order that merchants and producers can enrich themselves, but in order that people's needs may be satisfied . . . Those who engage in it must ensure it is carried on for the good of the whole. They must not make profits, except such as may be regarded as wages of labour. Moreover, they must be ready to share such wealth as they acquire among the largest possible number of people.'

And all the time the bombs continued to fall. One night, a vicar and his wife with whom Helena was staying woke to find their window shattered and a rock on their pillow. They bailed out to an air-raid shelter, leaving their guest asleep in the house. Once again, unscathed, she discovered next morning that the war had whispered near her ears. And yet, like many of her fellows, Helena experienced the paradox of those whispers of mortality. They fuelled a sense of urgent creativity; demanded, instead of an unswerving patriotism, the revaluation of every social value; they forged unlikely and fruitful alliances. There was Leo, of course, appearing and disappearing in the shattered landscape, the negligent suitor who by turns astonished her with his eloquence and depressed her with his indolence. But on the greater scene she was, in her own words, 'ruthlessly exposed to excellence' between 1940 and 1946. In the midst of bombed buildings in Soho, St Anne's Church had created a 'Mission to Intellectuals', and Helena began to attend its lectures. 'Absolutely no concessions were made by the speakers,' she says. 'The lectures were designed quite deliberately to appeal to the most intellectual levels of society.'

Once she took Leo to a session on Marxism. He was enthralled. 'It was like being in a mental bath—I feel so refreshed,' he told Helena afterwards. She wondered diffidently whether she should confess that somewhere in the shuttling of prothesis and antithesis her mind had hit the net, but was relieved when another member of the audience, the writer Dorothy Sayers, confided that the arguments were too subtle for her as well. If the translator of Dante (and therefore student of Saint Thomas Aquinas) had foundered on this particular retail version of Marx, maybe the text was abstruse, and not the listener obtuse.

'I never found anything but kindness in Dorothy Sayers—no arrogance at all. Often we had discussions about the strict Christian laws of marriage, the canon law. I discovered later that she was married to a divorced man and had an illegitimate child. She must have been hurt very badly indeed by what was said, but she never showed any sign.

'Looking back, I realise that I quite took for granted the incredibly privileged position I was in.' More than that, although she was still a comparatively young woman, and hardly a celebrity in the company to which she was now being introduced, Helena was quite unabashed in her appraisal of the brighter lights in her new circle.

'At a lunch given by the committee of St Anne's Church House, I sat opposite T. S. Eliot. I must say I didn't really take to him. He was cold and aloof, and he didn't make a fuss of me. He just sat there, and I suppose we had a little conversation. I cannot understand his poetry and I have never been able to understand it, and even at the time I was shocked by his anti-semitism. I've since been told by my nephew that the reason for the extreme pessimism of poems like *The Wasteland* is his guilt over his first wife's illness. At the time Leo belonged to a club at Student Movement House, which was run by the Student Christian Movement, and was open to people of all ages and religions; the rather aggressive, positive warden was called Mary Trevelyan, and our gossip was that she and T. S. Eliot were very friendly indeed.'

Helena allowed in mitigation of Eliot's literary anti-semitism his personal friendship with a number of Jews, and in particular with a poet and archaeologist called Steiner, who was to play an indirect role in an imminent but unexpected period of grief. As the war ended, Helena decided to live in London again, moving via rooms in St Stephens Gardens, North Kensington, to a flat in Longridge Road, Earls Court. Leo, meanwhile, travelled to Canada to visit his father, and despite the austerity of the times, sent his sweetheart no letters, and more importantly, no food parcels. His mother had decided to go to Paris, and Helena found herself additionally burdened with the job of pacifying a landlady who was already aggravated by Leo's constant shortage of funds and the uncertainty of ever receiving her rent on time.

Back from his absence in Canada, far from showing a redoubled fondness or any gratitude for Helena's protection of his tenancy, Leo was offhand and evasive. He was broke, of course, and through contacts at St Anne's, Helena managed to get him freelance work re-researching and rewriting the notes for a thesis on anthropology and slavery which Steiner had managed to leave on a train. Leo fell ill, and since the income was essential, Helena volunteered to deputise. 'All I can remember now is that in some African languages the words for son and slave are the same.'

Perhaps in the *patois* of some East European states, the words for girlfriend and slave are equally interchangeable.

As she divided day and night between her work for the Industrial Christian Fellowship and Leo's work for Steiner, Helena developed conjunctivitis in one eye. 'Stupidly I struggled on, and as a result the eye had to be bandaged. I went back to the bedsit, and while I was trying to light the fire a piece of wood jumped out and struck me in my good eye, which then became infected. I was virtually blind, and in hospital for a week before my sight was restored. And while I was in hospital I got a letter from Leo saying he was married "to the daughter of a well known MP"—I never found out who, and the next I heard he had gone to Israel.

'Leo,' says Helena, 'had the typical refugee mentality of insecurity which makes people selfish. The family had, after all, escaped once from the Russian Revolution into Latvia, and then again from Latvia before the Russians invaded. He always wanted to go to Israel, or Palestine as it was when I first knew him, but there was no chance at the time. I used to get furious with him for his selfishness, but I knew that if I threw him over, he would go to Stalin's Russia, and the people who did that got murdered. What angered me more than anything was his refusal to tell me whom he had married. It was so pointless. He wrote to me once in London, and once from Israel, saying how bad he felt about me.'

* * *

Is there a pattern? Perhaps we can see, at least, a compelling force-field at one pole of which is the word 'mother', at the other the ghost of a 'stepmother', Leo and his mother, Guy and his mother, a story still to come; Gerhard and his mother, a grey episode for which Guy supplies the lighter, Leo the darker counterpoint. So many times in her encounters with men, Helena resorts to a particular metaphor. The mothers are twisted like serpents round their sons. Their power of suffocation is supplemented by a very venomous approach to prospective suitors.

* * *

And what of Gerard, the younger brother whom we last glimpsed sharing his Finchley flat with his sister in 1933?

The infant whom Helena had wanted to clout over the head on the voyage home from India—and long after—grew, like many sickly children, into a prodigious athlete, sticking at his games until all the other competitors were begging him to let them leave the pitch. If his sister's childhood and adolescent memory was of an obstinate and tiresome boy who teased her whenever the opportunity was presented, the adult recognised a man of high principle and devoted faith whose teasing, perhaps, was the remedy he proposed for her own moodiness and sense of isolation. Helena's declarations of independence and determination to escape from the family straitjacket we have already seen. Gerard, eventually, flew the heritage of all his Anglican antecedents, and was received into the Roman Catholic Church, becoming, along the way, a tertiary of the Franciscan order—that is, a lay member with obligations to the order, who works and lives in the secular world. According to Helena, his defection from the family faith caused enormous grief.

He was destined to work in the jute business with his father, and was therefore, as a young man, subjected to a commercial monasticism which matched his Franciscan self-regulation. George Henderson and Son, you may remember, would not allow a member of their white collar staff to marry until he had earned a partnership. Were employees who consistently failed in their attempts to join this inner circle obliged, one wonders, to remain celibate until they received their inscribed gold watches?

Gerard was in India when the Second World War broke out and, for him, Germany's progressive occupation of continental Europe was the means of liberation from a job at which he chafed. He enlisted, soldiered first in the Middle East, and then joined the Eighth and Ninth Armies in North Africa, taking part in the campaign that led to Rommel's defeat. Crossing into Italy, he was involved in a series of bloody battles. In one engagement, he was the only officer left alive, successfully led both artillery and infantry divisions, and was awarded the DSO for his courage and resourcefulness. Later, talking to his family about the medal, he revealed that he had previously faced far more dangerous situations, but was prevented from discussing them—a hint, perhaps, that he had also been involved in undercover operations of some kind.

After the war, Gerard decided to spend some time in Surrey with his family. He privately confessed that the prospect of returning to a desk in India and superintending the progress of jute between the various merchant centres of the world filled him with horror. Perhaps a calm family conference was on the schedule, to debate his reluctance to resume a sedentary and unglamorous profession, but if it was, the appearance at Clarewood of a woman by the name of Dorothy—'that bitch', in Helena's cast list—disrupted their domestic harmonies.

Gerard was now 31, and had met Dorothy first at the age of 22, when he was just embarking on his career. Obviously he must have fallen heavily in love, but she was not the sort of woman who dutifully waits until obstacles are overcome and promised partnerships materialise, particularly since her would-be lover could set no term on the delay. So she had married someone else. Clearly Gerard mourned her loss deeply, for according to Helena, he was only just getting her out of his system when, ten years later, she arrived without warning in Camberley. Whatever the real cause of her disaffection with her husband, it was unlikely to have been the one she gave Gerard as the reason why she was renewing their friendship and seeking to revive their love. But she knew it was the only reason that would work. She told him her marriage had never been consummated. As a loyal Catholic, Gerard would never contemplate wedding a divorced woman. But an unconsummated marriage was void in the eyes of the Church, and that cleared an orthodox route to the altar. Excitedly, he began to investigate the processes that must be followed to secure an official annulment. Helena watched glumly from the touchline. I have only once heard her use the word 'cat' as a part of her rich store of derogatory epithets. When she described Dorothy's antics with Gerard as 'cat and mouse', no compliment was intended to the predator.

The mouse, meanwhile, was devising a new future. George Henderson (and Son) agreed to transfer him from India to the Gold Coast. From there he planned to move swiftly to Kenya and establish himself as a farmer. Maps were bought, passages booked, authorities consulted on the likely timetable towards the dissolution of Dorothy's marriage. He left the country first, and within a day or two of his embarkation, the bored cat announced that she was returning to her previous mouse. There was going to be 'a reconciliation'.

The Charles family were never able to fathom or forgive Dorothy's motives. Gerard, grieving even more deeply than before, lost himself in his work in Africa, and became so beloved of the local population that after his death they erected a monument in tribute to his labours as a town planner, a vocation he discovered in West Africa. He returned home just once, in 1951, and the family joined together to dance the Flora Dance in Helston for the first time since the First World War. Then Helena and Gerard drove to Dover to meet Anne, and Rebecca West and her husband, and the quintet went on a touring holiday in Europe, examining Romanesque churches in France, and travelling into Italy by way of the highest Alps, on each of which Gerard's van pretended it was about to expire. Anne was now Rebecca West's secretary, and in the conversations on the road and in wayside *auberges* (assuming that the subject was not still too delicate), the novelist and critic may have been able to shed some light on the Dorothy episode. After all, she had been attending the Nuremberg trials, and was to write a book called *The Meaning of Treason* about the strange transformation of William Joyce into the traitor 'Lord Haw-Haw'.

Helena had been horrified when Gerard decided to go to the Gold Coast.

The climate was notoriously evil, and it was with some sense of premonition that she sat with him in deep depression as they waited for the boat train that would take him to Africa. 'After he'd gone I thought, well, never mind, he'll be back in a couple of years. They took account of the climate, after all, and never allowed Europeans to stay there for very long at a spell. But in 1952, just when we were looking forward to having him back, we heard that he was sick. At first we couldn't work out what it was. I sent a telegram asking for news, and all I got by way of reply were two words, "very ill". It turned out to be a form of pneumonia, a virus in his lungs, and for three months he was more or less at death's door. He would improve, his temperature would go down, and then he would relapse. They tried antibiotic after antibiotic, until at last they found something which apparently suited him, and he began to make what looked at first like a remarkable recovery.

'Anne was always closer to him than I was, even though they were half-brother and sister. She flew out and stayed at the hospital with him, and reported back to us that his condition was greatly improved; but the doctors told her that he was still very weak, and that unless he was moved to a better climate his health might be permanently impaired. I'd wired that I would meet him anywhere in Europe, but it was decided that he ought to spend his convalescence at Tenderah. And then on Easter Saturday, shortly after Anne had left him to sleep, he suddenly became breathless, and he died. They said it was pulmonary embolism, brought on by the massive doses of antibiotics he'd been receiving. The doctors had always realised it was a risk, but if they hadn't given him the medication, the virus would have killed him anyway.

'He was buried on Easter Sunday, in Accra cemetery. We later sent out a granite tombstone from Cornwall, which we felt was appropriate. For a long time Aunt Kit refused to have his name mentioned, almost as if he had done something shameful. She simply couldn't bear any reference to him, which made it all the worse for the rest of us, because we wanted to talk about him very badly. Then one day a man—a total stranger—sent us a selection of photographs of the garden which had been laid out as his memorial. It was in a triangle of land where two roads met, and among the flowers was the stone with his name written on it. Apparently when it was dedicated there'd been a great ceremony with all the local dignitaries and representatives of the British colonial power. Clearly he'd loved the people of the Gold Coast, and they'd returned his love. And it was because of his fondness for the place and for its citizens that he stayed there too long, and contracted a terrible virus.

'For some reason, once she saw the photographs and had heard about the tributes, Aunt Kit thawed and felt able to talk about Gerard, and the ban on the mention of his name was lifted. He was thirty-six when he died, and I've always thought it was a tragedy that a person with his gifts should be taken from us when the world has such an urgent need of people like him: charming, high-principled, and a devoted Christian.'

CHAPTER EIGHT

THE ZIONIST

The Second World War was over, but although she might be relieved at the defeat of Nazism and her own and her family's survival after so many skirmishes with disaster, Helena had very little to celebrate. Leo, for all his aggravating behaviour, had been a constant point in a weary and itinerant life. Now that he had vanished, the burden of five years of almost incessant travelling and lecturing seemed to redouble its weight. Maybe, now, capitalism was being shaken at its foundations, but were its assailants crusading under the right banner? The nation might have decided that it wanted its reconstructions supervised by a Labour government, yet the reforms proposed, although they attacked many of the social ills the ICF had sought to cure, were hardly pinned into that luminous vision of a Christian society which the Federation propounded.

Gradually, Helena identified the reason for her own malaise. It was rootlessness. In particular, she was sick of making her devotions every Sunday in a different church. A parish, after all, was the model of the family, and someone who drifted like a stranger from one parish to another, a welcome guest, no doubt, but not an intimate of the congregation, could hardly derive the nurture she needed from her weekly communion. The solution was to sever her ties with an organisation which kept her travelling constantly by road or rail; to dig herself in at her flat in Longridge Road, Earls Court, and to find a job that confined her wayfaring to a daily dash to an office and back by underground or bus.

The British Social Hygiene Council no longer exists, or if it does, it has either moved out of London or changed its name. It was one of those euphemistically named national organisations whose function, when its title is examined, seems to be a bit of an enigma. What exactly is, or was, 'social hygiene'? In fact, it had begun its life as the 'British Society for the Prevention of Prostitution', but at some stage its organisers had realised that this ambitious manifesto erred towards naïve optimism, and coined the phrase 'social hygiene' from which it could be concluded, even if the prostitutes were never swept from the streets, that the Council had done its work as long as it could demonstrate that some sort of damage-limitation had been achieved.

Her mind still enervated after five taxing years with the ICF, and her thoughts still lively with the ideals of Zionism, a legacy of her relationship with Leo, Helena went to work for the BSHC in 1946. It was, she says, 'a hell-born institution'. Appointed as the Secretary's assistant, she felt her stomach knot when she was informed that one of her tasks would be to make sense of the petty cash. In all her various schools and colleges, nobody had managed to instil the most rudimentary principles of financial literacy. As well as the key to the black tin box, she was given a coloured pen and told to chart the progress of the Council's appeals for funds. 'I can't do it,' she protested. 'We'll all end up in a fearful mess.' But they were adamant that they had always intended, when recruiting her, that she was to assume the duties of an amateur accountant. So she picked up her coloured pen and worried at the appeal returns, and tried to draw a clear and vigorous graph. Then there was a discrepancy in the petty cash, and Helena's determination to blame herself brought another cloud across her desk until the professional accountant checked his own figures and found that he was to blame.

His confession did little to staunch the growing void in Helena's self-confidence. She was becoming an unpopular figure—and a useful scapegoat—in the office, and seemed, as one does in those circumstances, to attract misfortune and opprobrium. Invited to be the principal speaker at a meeting in Liverpool organised by the Reverend Ambrose Reeves, who had found a Christian solution to a dockers' strike, her absence coincided with the day the BSHC Secretary decided to succumb to an illness, and a cluster of administrative problems came together and erupted into a crisis. Rather like Cinderella, Helena returned from the north to be blamed by everybody for whatever disasters had occurred while she was away. She even got into trouble for voicing her own opinions at a public meeting and expressing her view that some form of population control was necessary, at a time when the official BSHC policy was to urge the nation to breed without restraint to prevent a decline in British power and influence.

'Then I made the most frightful hash of a meeting of their Venereal Disease Committee. I was told to ring up the members, who were all doctors, to find out if they were coming along. Of course, being a totally inefficient secretary, I forgot to have a pencil with me when I made the telephone calls, never made a note, and gave an absolutely incorrect account of who was going to be there and who wasn't. And after the meeting I tendered a completely hopeless set of minutes, an entirely inaccurate account of what had taken place, and I got the sack. Looking back I can't say I blame them. I was a square peg in a round hole. It was a totally unsuitable post for me, and it was their jolly bad luck that they'd given me the job.'

It must have been around this time that Helena wandered past the Wolseley Building in Bermondsey, and noted that despite her pre-war belief that if the building were evacuated the Kingdom of God would have come, there were no signs of the Kingdom materialising. But it was in Bermondsey that she had mapped her way from a vocational crossroads, defied her father, who intended her for a mooring in the calmer waters of literary criticism, and begun a career by finding a job that united an income with the satisfaction of that ardent concern for social welfare that had been imbued by Archbishop Temple's mission to her university. Now she resolved to find a practical outlet for her espousal of Jewish rights. She joined the staff of the British Association for the Jewish National Home in Palestine, based at Palestine House in London.

'During the last period of my work with the ICF I'd rather naughtily brought the needs of the Jews and the sufferings of refugees into the discussions at our meetings. The horrors of the holocaust had just been discovered, and it was very easy to introduce them into our question and answer sessions, though I think I brought them up more often than I ought to have done.' Inadvertently, Helena had groomed herself for the post she was about to assume, and rehearsed with groups who had assembled to hear a Christian message the Zionist arguments which were to impress her prospective employers at her interview. It did not seem to matter that the essential tools of her new trade included a familiar and occasionally depressing chattel—one she already possessed and had frayed in previous service: a suitcase.

'For more than a year I travelled the country, talking to Rotary Clubs, Church of England Men's Societies, anybody who would give me a hearing, about the need for a Jewish homeland. There'd been a White Paper intended to cut down on immigration into Palestine, and in effect it trapped the Jews in Europe. Although Hitler had been overthrown, and Germany was completely defeated, there was still a great deal of anti-semitism. All those people who had been fortunate enough to escape from concentration camps were now displaced and had nowhere to go. The obvious place was Palestine, and the British government was breaking its word by inhibiting immigration.

'One of our great enemies in the Arab Office was Kim Philby. We didn't know at the time that he was a Russian spy, and in fact he was believed to be extremely right wing and pro-Arab, blocking every move we made on behalf of the Jews.'

Palestine House was a weave of exhibition and propaganda centre,

Helena with friends at her sister Elizabeth's wedding. Beside her is Rebecca West, with whom she later travelled in Europe, and between them, Rebecca's husband Henry Andrews.

funded, although the staff were instructed never to reveal the details, from an intricate variety of Jewish sources. Its displays celebrated the skills of immigrants who had managed to settle in Palestine, and commemorated the disasters of European persecution. Dignitaries visited, of course, but so did individuals with more shadowy credentials—members of Irgun, the group which had sworn to use bomb and bullet, if necessary, to secure an independent homeland.

During the intervals in her lecture tours, Helena conducted uninitiated visitors round the displays, working to elicit pity for the Jews' catastrophic sufferings, and admiration for attainments in the Middle East that were traced back to the time of Solomon. 'I achieved as little there, I think, as I achieved for Christianity when I was working for the ICF, but at least we had an illusion that we were accomplishing something.'

On the basis of a partition that attempted to reconcile the conflicting goals of Zionism and Arab nationalism, the State of Israel was created on May 14, 1948. The arrangement was pregnant with a violence that still continues, but at the time a divisive compromise seemed the only way forward. Jerusalem was supposed to remain an 'international' city. 'There'd been a United Nations resolution, carried with a clear majority, for the creation of Israel,' Helena recalls. 'The British abstained, and the Arabs, understandably, voted against the proposal.'

There was, equally understandably, a huge party at Palestine House when the new State was founded. The staff danced late into the night, until they were begged to switch to a less muscular form of celebration by staff who pointed out that the delicate tracery on the Adam ceilings below was in danger of falling apart under the percussion of their stamping. Helena arranged a treasure hunt, with clues in English and Hebrew, making sure of her accuracy by extracting the phrases she needed from scripture. 'It was a complete failure, as it turned out, because neither the English nor the Jews knew anything about the Bible.' Came the dawn, and the staff were congratulated for their tireless work on behalf of the Jewish nation, and told, since the nation now had its homeland, that their mission was done, and they were all being sacked. And could they clear out as quickly as possible, because the builders were moving in to convert Palestine House into an Israeli Embassy.

Helena had exhausted herself on behalf of a cause which devoured her goodwill and her leisure. The stress of that sudden and 'very ungracious' dismissal provoked a new bout of nervous prostration which took her, for a while, back to hospital. And her instability was exacerbated by the blind alleys and bleak prospects of a new romantic attachment which in some ways had become an emotional mirror image of her commitment to the Jewish national campaign. No amount of coaxing, cajoling or bribery will ever force her to reveal the man's identity. He remains tantalisingly anonymous, described only as 'an exceedingly prominent Israeli citizen', who visited Palestine House on a number of occasions. Clearly he was engaged at the highest level in the strategies which were evolved and deployed on behalf of the State of Israel.

It seems that their relationship developed swiftly, but was the kind of clandestine affair of which Helena had no experience. He would ring her office. She would agree to meet him, or murmur in Hebrew, 'I am not alone,' if anyone else was in the room. The man was not only married, but a grandfather. No hint of their liaison could be allowed to escape among the rest of the staff. If their paths happened to intersect during the day, more likely than not they brushed past each other without a glance. A senior Jewish diplomat would hardly chatter casually to one of the Gentile assistants, however fervently she was writing and lecturing on behalf of their shared ideal. The 'exceedingly prominent Israeli citizen' was, however, love-stricken.

'The first time he asked me to visit him during the evening at his hotel I thought that his wife would be there, and she wasn't. But I thought no harm would come of my seeing him if he was as anxious as all that for my company—and after a while I was completely hooked as well. He was very much a married man. What we were doing was against all my principles, and yet, it was one of the most wonderful things that ever happened to me. I knew that he would be going away in a month or so anyway, and so we continued to meet. In one of the pictures I carried away in my mind, and which I still treasure, we sat up in his room until about two o'clock in the morning, drinking Israeli whisky, which I didn't very much like and wasn't accustomed to, and argued about the meaning of adultery in Mosaic and canon law. I was at times reduced to praying out loud. I have no doubt that many of the things I did and thought were wrong—but I didn't let him seduce me.'

Someone once said that the perfect affair lasts twenty-four hours, beginning and ending with a luncheon. Knowing that the enchantment has a fixed duration, that its term will expire before their appetites are sated, quickens the actors' pleasure and absolves them from the inevitable remorse of a future of subterfuge. Helena had a month, and at the beginning of it she gathered reassurance against the affront to her morality from the very limits promised in her lover's timetable. At the end of it, as he left England, she was 'shattered and broken-hearted'.

There was another man to complicate the frame, whom I shall call the Reverend Alec Marshall. He was a senior priest in a provincial city, who had become a close friend and something of an unofficial confessor. Clearly the couple must have met during the war, because Helena remembers that he found her once when she was lost during a blackout. Marshall's wife was completely deaf, and Helena obviously supplied some of the companionship that he lacked. 'We would sit talking for hours about everything under the sun. I looked upon him as a sort of guru. I never knew anybody like him before or since; I trusted his judgement absolutely.' A few years later, however, when Guy Sanders, after his engagement to Helena, arranged to see Marshall, the priest was out when he called. 'I wrote to him later,' says Helena, 'and received a brief note in reply saying his wife had died and he had remarried. Many years later I read his obituary and discovered that he'd been living just a few miles from us in Cornwall, but had never tried to make contact. I found that absolutely incomprehensible. I was sad and upset at an extremely puzzling end to our friendship. Looking back on it now, I think that he probably was in love with me. He certainly began to get fonder of me than I was of him, but I saw ours simply as a spiritual relationship.'

It was to Marshall she turned for comfort when Leo abandoned her, and she sought solace from him again when the eminent Israeli was leaving for Palestine. What straw was she clutching at when she told him she had discovered that the Israeli's wife, according to Mosaic and Christian law, was among the categories of women whom a man is forbidden to marry? What should she do about it? 'Nothing,' Marshall replied.

London, the landscape of so many aspirations, joys, reverses and tragedies now tired her. She wanted to be rid of the associations that clogged every part of her orbit, of the memory of lovers whose replies to each last invitation to join the dance of her youth and then maturity had been to plead, in one more sense than Oscar Wilde intended by the phrase, 'a subsequent engagement'. Some years previously she had invested a little capital in a small cottage at St Day in Cornwall, unsure at the time whether it was to be a holiday home or a place to rent out as a source of income. She had not lived in Cornwall for twenty-nine years, since her father's remarriage at the end of the First World War had divorced her from the magic garden at Tenderah. Now she decided to pack up books and clothes and settle in the West Country, taking with her the only two survivors of her romance with Leo—Tiger and Panther, the pets they had once shared. If her own feelings about a fugitive move were equivocal, because deep sadness had provoked it, the cats at least would enjoy their migration from Earls Court to the open spaces of the Duchy.

CHAPTER NINE

RETURN TO CORNWALL

There is a dream of Cornwall that sustains some people through 50 weeks of non-negotiable drudgery each year, and helps their spirits to transcend the brutal or banal experience of living in urban settings. It begins with the crossing of the Tamar, where the yachts and frigates are sprinkled in the estuary below; continues along the river valley towards Liskeard; passes through Launceston and Lostwithiel and on to the fishing ports of Fowey and Polruan, and the earthworks of Castle Dore (was this where Tristram brought Isolde to meet King Mark?). It lingers over Bodmin and the solemn moors, then makes for the sea and a last swoop westward, out past Mousehole and the heathland of Penwith, to the monumental granite cliffs where Cape Cornwall braces itself to meet whatever seas and winds the Americas have sent.

But there is another Cornwall, a drizzling, foggy sort of place, where the mud plucks your shoes off and a blind man with a keen ear and sense of smell has the best notion of the line between the end of the precipice and the start of the void that falls to a butcher's shop of rocks and waves. Every year there are new retirement guests who get a chilly shock as the season ends, the tourists depart, and Cornwall wraps itself in a damp blanket to brood until spring over a barrel or two of bitter, or pot upon pot of stewed tea. The people who have been nurtured for centuries in a climate that alternates between balm and rheum, honey and gall, are by and large a welcoming sort; the visitor is greeted cordially, accommodated and entertained, and admired if he or she can discriminate between authentic and *ersatz* culture. But there is another frontier as sharp and perilous as the cliff edge, soon discovered by the 'incomer' who tries to become a native. The Cornish admit to obstinacy, and to an ineradicable conservatism which seems to cut across the Duchy's liberal and nonconformist traditions. And they will confide that if there is one thing they can't stand, it is 'being interfered with'.

Helena Charles surely had enough Cornish blood in her veins at least to qualify her for honorary membership of the nation. On the other hand, she had been away for nearly three decades, and spent most of them around London, a version of Babylon for folk who hardly ever ventured further than Truro, and viewed Plymouth, the western bulwark of Devon, as a foreign part. True, there was the value of her years of work among the underprivileged, a community which was well represented in Cornwall; but she'd as like as not filled her head with upcountry notions and gotten the airs of a charity lady. Bit of a busybody, by all accounts.

In the first place, Helena had to contend with the underside of Cornish meteorology. Certainly, there was running water in her cottage: running down the walls and dripping from the ceilings, leaving dingy arabesques and blooms on paint and paper. Water trickled under doors and searched the roof for promising crevices. It decided that chimneys were meant to convey liquid down, not smoke up. All that the building lacked to give its aqueous concert a helpful outlet was a tap. Instead, when Helena wanted to boil a kettle, take a bath, or brush her teeth, she was obliged to tramp to a spring about a quarter of a mile away. Tiger and Panther picked their way among the interior and exterior marshes and did what they could, as animals always do, to comfort their mistress during 'a most dreary, lonely, and terrible time'.

Helena, however, had come to Cornwall for the change that amounted to rest, but not to rusticate, or even to rust. Hers was not a temperament that lets grass grow under feet, moss on carpets, or fungus on walls. With cement, bricks, plaster, pitch and paint she sealed out the damp and sealed in the warmth. She built another room onto the property and turned it into a tiny and genial fortress, whose new ramparts a Cornish winter might rage against but never penetrate. Once the fire was alight, and the lid of the kettle was chuntering gently, Tiger and Panther could forget the amenities of Longridge Road, while Helena held the Duchy she was now discovering at arm's length, as it seemed to want to hold her, and turned it round and round to see where it might fit into the jigsaw of her experiences.

St Day was more than 200 miles from Palestine House, and Cornwall itself, in the late 1940s, was several decades from London, and quite a few generations from discovering any affinity at all between its own condition and the Jewish suffering and struggle which had been answered by the creation of a nation state in Palestine. Even today, there are English people who think that the concept of Cornish nationalism belongs in the realm of quaintness and mummery. But as Helena contemplated the Duchy and its people she perceived the Cornish as a race, and her diagnosis of their relative poverty disclosed the canker of a colonial relationship with the rest of England. Her contact with Zionism had led her to believe that a separable group of people needed not only to sense that theirs was a

'A poor thing, but mine own . . .' Helena in the doorway of her Cornish cottage, Prasigow, in 1948. In her arms, Tiger, one of the pair of cats who joined her on her journey west from London.

unique community, free from enforced adulterations, but also to have the government of their resources and dispose of them in a way that was mutually acceptable and profitable. Helena became a pioneer of the Cornish national cause. If her mother's forebears had streaked her with Celtic obstinacy, a dynamism derived from the soldiers of the Charles family quite neutralised that local conservatism which very often tended to inertia, a quality she now began to encounter in glutinous abundance.

'I was very distressed by the fact that the majority of people in Cornwall who were active in any way came from outside the county. The Cornish language was to all intents and purposes dead. I set myself the task of making the local folk themselves conscious of their own culture, and that occupied a great many years of my time. I had also thought that when I'd set myself up I would be able to go on with my work for the Industrial Christian Fellowship, but I was rather quickly disabused of that idea. During my five years of travelling I had never been to Cornwall once on ICF business, and I began to understand why. I absolutely failed to persuade anyone in the Church or anywhere else to allow me to promote the Fellowship's aims and ideals.'

Fancy London notions? Entirely rubbing the wrong way against networks of individuals in webs of influence that were as abstruse and almost as shadowy as Chinese triads. How was Helena to know, when she mounted a loud and successful crusade, drawing on the lessons learned in Bermondsey, against a plan to put Falmouth's dock workers in tied accommodation, that a leading local councillor, whose support she tried to enlist, stood to gain from the deal through his private interests? 'He never forgave me. He wouldn't even join the Old Cornwall Society, a quite innocuous historical group, because I was a member, and when a mission based along ICF lines was organised in Falmouth, he threatened to boycott that as well if I was a part of it. So I was pushed out of the one event where my training would really have been useful.'

It wasn't simply a matter of resident hostility to a newcomer whose ideological seven-league boots had hobnails on them. There were also philosophic differences at work. The Industrial Christian Fellowship, directly and indirectly, was a force directed against the Church of England's drift towards rural dotage. Its arguments fell on stony ground in Cornwall where, although there was a substantial proletariat, it was not gathered in a city, but fragmented between moderately sized towns and tiny villages; and its Methodist schooling fostered a degree of quietism and insularity which, fortified by the local dislike of any outside interference, presented an insuperable barrier to any stranger or strange organisation hoping to evangelise in the spheres of politics and religion. No matter how cogent the message, no matter how aptly tuned to local needs, it was usually received with suspicion and hostility.

As for the Church of England in Cornwall, Helena found to her dismay that Archbishop Temple was almost hated. She tried to organise a mission to the china clay workers, established valuable contacts among managers, trades unionists, and scientific researchers, and explained at an inaugural meeting that her intention was, by disseminating a spiritual message throughout the workforce, to effect a transformation which would naturally lead to a happier, healthier and more creative and rewarding industry for all concerned. 'But those are Temple's ideas,' exclaimed the senior clergyman who was with her, evidently horrified. He made sure that the mission was aborted.

Every time she tried to hitch herself to some engine of reform she was frustrated. 'I went to Cornwall County Council and explained about my experience as a social worker in London. I told them I would work for their children committee full or part time, voluntary or paid. The answer came back from the children secretary that she would very much like to have me on the staff, but the County Council wouldn't support her because they were unwilling to pay my travelling expenses. So then I went to the Workers' Educational Association and asked if I could work for them—I was very used to conducting meetings and study groups, of course. I got no joy from them either. I then went to the Cornwall Council for Social Service and persuaded the then secretary that theirs was work I was very much interested in and qualified to perform. And they gave me a job which any clerk could have done. And then one day out of the blue they said to me that they were sure I was very busy with other commitments elsewhere, and I shouldn't bother to come in any more.

'In other words, all of the occupations for which I had experience were closed to me. I didn't ask for pay, I just asked if I could help, and without exception the door was slammed in my face. So I threw myself with enthusiasm into the Celtic movement. I started to learn the language, and got in touch with other enthusiasts, and in the end four of us went off to a meeting in Truro and founded *Mebyon Kernow*, the sons of Cornwall, to work for recognition that the Cornish were a people.'

There was then, as there is now, a feeling in Cornwall that a lot of the most important posts—and particularly those of formative authority—were being taken by outsiders who really wanted to retire prematurely to an agreeable environment and maintain their incomes by working in positions that carried lots of prestige and few onerous duties. 'Cornish Jobs for Cornish People' was the battle-cry of *Mebyon Kernow*, and Helena did not stop to think whether the realisation of the slogan's aim would entitle her only to a half share in a job. She began to assemble and restore the evidence that would prove to Cornish ears and eyes that theirs was indeed a tribe apart, distinguished by its rich artistic traditions. She spoke at meetings whenever she could, and helped to revive a section of an ancient Cornish saints' play, which was performed in the original language by a cast of sixty actors, singers, dancers and wrestlers at the Piran Round, an Iron Age fort which had last been used as a theatre in Elizabeth times. 'It was really an extremely successful project, and I produced it again for the Celtic Congress the following year, at the Falmouth Methodist Hall.'

* * *

Cornish nationalism and Cornish culture would continue to occupy Helena, intermittently, for twelve years. 'I wouldn't have been nearly so committed to it if all other doors hadn't kept so firmly shut—I couldn't persuade the Church to let me do anything at all.' Her zeal and vigour were rewarded when she was chosen to represent Cornwall at the convention of an organisation she nicknamed 'The Cong of Min', short for 'Congress of Minorities', whose other and rather endearing name was 'The Council of the Small Peoples of Europe'. It was a forum where the continent's largely forgotten subject races could pool their discontents and

Helena at Prasigow with her first family of goats.

celebrate their cultures and their differences. Altogether more than forty races gathered together—including Scots, Irish, Welsh, Cornish, Bretons, Manx, Catalans, Basques, Walloons and Flemings.

Helena attended successive congresses in Friesland, Denmark, Baden-Baden and Cardiff. 'Everywhere I went I was given VIP treatment, and my linguistic abilities were a tremendous advantage. I could translate extempore from either French or German into English or vice versa, while the university people who had volunteered to come and help were laboriously trying to get the speeches down on paper before rendering them across.'

She was quickly promoted from the audience to the platform, the organisers recognising that she possessed quite a parcel of useful qualities. Not only could she understand what most of the delegates were saying as soon as they had spoken, and instantly offer an intelligible version in two other languages—but as a woman she could also defuse some of the more politically fraught moments. When, as sometimes happened, a delegate tried to storm the podium and annexe another's speaking time ('I represent a million people. I demand the opportunity to give a longer speech . . .'), Helena's appeal to gallantry and common sense usually disarmed the besieger ('and don't forget, you have to allow five of your fifteen minutes for translations . . .').

'I thoroughly enjoyed myself, taking the chair in English, French, and

German. And I remember in Baden-Baden there was a party, and I had a French person on one side and a German on the other, and I carried on two simultaneous conversations.' In Denmark, the Congress included a top-level reception and dinner given by the Foreign Ministry, where the question of lost minorities was high on the agenda. Helena, who had discreetly tried to hide herself among the lower tables, was called to the top to sit between the Danish Foreign Secretary and the former leader of the Danish Resistance. 'The dinner was in the most sumptuous room, with waiters in perukes: a really stately occasion. The Danes have a quite delightful habit of catching each other's eye and raising a glass, so I toasted quite a few people in the same way. And there was a Welsh priest among the people there, who by the end of the evening was saying, "I'm a deacon from Wales and I've never had alcohol before—and I feel good."' He so delighted Helena that at a subsequent Congress in Britanny she described his antics to amuse her neighbours at the supper table. 'Oh yes, him,' said another of the guests. 'He's sitting right behind you.' Helena did not dare turn round to see if he was continuing his behavioural experiments with grain and grape.

Helena propagated the Cornish and Celtic gospel with her feet as well as her mouth. She formed a team of dancers who specialised in dances from Britanny, Ireland and Cornwall, and found an eager supporter in the bakery of the Tregenna Castle Hotel at St Ives. Mr Courtney was an Irishman and a Roman Catholic whose saffron kilt and crimson plaid became a familiar spectacle at fêtes and fairs. Once, Helena got him to dance at a church party in St Day. Poor Mr Courtney was reported to his priest for performing in 'an heretical place of worship', and earned a stiff penance. His was the sort of Celtic exuberance which bred optimism for the Cornish cause.

But another Irishman, whom Helena met at a 'Cong of Min' in Paris, betrayed the more chilling side of nationalist politics, and recalled her encounter with Irgun terrorists at Palestine House. 'As I was so much taken up at the time with Breton dancing, I was staying with a woman who'd written a book on the subject. We used to practise our steps while we travelled underground on the Metro. Anyway, while I was there my host had a visitor who belonged to the IRA. It was quite impossible to talk to him, or make contact. We told him about our interest in dancing and he snapped back that he disapproved of it because it took people's minds off politics.'

Undeterred, Helena continued to blaze a trail for Cornwall and Cornishness in Europe. But her reception each time she returned home reminded her of the days when she was alternating the roles of celebrity speaker on the ICF circuit, and drudge at the British Council for Social Hygiene. Only her band of sixty-odd fellow enthusiasts (and they were odd, as far as the rest of the Duchy were concerned) welcomed her with applause. 'We'd had all these immensely interesting discussions and debates, but I just could not provoke any general interest, and I became more and more disillusioned by the narrowness of the outlook of most of the Cornish, and their indifference to new ideas. A few of us had learned to have a conversation in Cornish, but most of the people who'd said they were going to learn, if you addressed them with the simplest sentence, would stare at you and say, "I'm afraid that's rather beyond me."'

In one of Helena's favourite quotations, G. K. Chesterton remarked that Europe was a unity born of its diversity. Cornwall, perhaps, was not in his mind when he devised the equation. Ahead of her era, Helena crusaded for the Cornish to forge alliances over the Channel, to use Europe as a forum within which the Duchy could, for the first time, articulate its concerns and ambitions with a separate voice. But the people she addressed were as impervious as the native granite rock from which they quarried the stone to build their houses. 'And it wasn't just apathy and silence. Dissension and opposition seemed to greet every plan we put

Austerity Britain forgotten for a couple of weeks, Helena enjoys a French picnic in 1949.

forward. There was one old boy who was a prominent journalist and a very bad archaeologist. He was an intelligent man and he ought to have been a great help to us. Instead he did nothing but try to sabotage not only what I was doing, but everything that all the other forward-looking people were trying to do.'

* * *

It was during this period that Helena came across the Cornish poet Jack Clemo. She had read his novel *Wilding Graft*, and wrote to complain that while she was excited by the story, the implication of his arguments seemed to be (with a certain element of the 'old hyper-Calvinism') that 'if you believe in God you get your girl, and if you don't, you don't.' She met him and became compassionately involved in the battle to save his failing sight and hearing. His Calvinist background and that of the Anglo-Catholic social worker and journalist were not entirely devoid of parallels. Her senses were lamed by no physical disability, but instead there was the memory of the less than kindly stepmother whose appearance on the stage of Helena's infancy might have induced slavish obedience in a child of weaker temperament, willing to trade independence of mind for affection and a quiet life. Instead, Helena had learned to despise unquestioning conformity, to challenge ambiguous loyalties, and to eschew the comforts with which her social position might have environed her, in order to work for the more visibly deprived.

Clemo had also been a rebel all his life—against school, against organised religion, against convention, and latterly against nature, which seemed to him to mock his disability. Helena paid for him and his mother to visit Godfrey Mowatt, a blind man, who had been commissioned by Archbishop Temple to conduct healing services in London. Only a brief remission resulted, but Mowatt's statement that God can sometimes abolish painful circumstances without effecting a physical cure, was to have a profound influence on Clemo. It was a revelation which would help him make a happy marriage with Ruth and approach an inner calm.

At some point during the 'fifties Helena resumed a number of her duties with the ICF, and for two or three years edited its magazine, *Man Today*. She attended a conference in the Midlands on the purpose of industry and the principles which ought to govern relationships between management and workers. The conclusions reached were written into a document which the ICF circulated to every newspaper. Not a single line was printed, a measure of the ICF's gradual dissociation from the centres of national politics. By the middle of the decade, Helena was dividing her months equally between St Day and London.

St Day itself was hardly the most idyllic place to settle in Cornwall. Maybe that typical Helena Charles scruple drove her to make her home in one of the more desolate parts of the Duchy. In the Middle Ages, it was prominent as a centre for pilgrimage, the last overnight stop for priests wayfaring on the ancient route that led through Glastonbury and Tavistock to St Michael's Mount. St Day declined after the Reformation, but then suffered a brutal sort of renaissance during the mining boom of the eighteenth and nineteenth centuries, when the town was said to contain the richest half mile in the whole of England. Eviscerated by prospectors and speculators, it was soon disfigured by spoil heaps that rose higher than Truro Cathedral, and when the metal and mineral tide turned, it left a mini-mountain range of barren ground, the constant threat of subsidence, and a community which became known as 'the waste-paper basket of Cornwall'. When Helena arrived it was distinguished by a series of those statistical 'highests' that delight demographers and destroy local morale: highest illegitimacy, highest unemployment, highest rate of mental deficiency . . . in effect, a bucolic Bermondsey. The church was falling to pieces around a congregation that was weary and disillusioned after years of neglect, and Helena noted that 'a parish priest would very seldom spend more than two years before he left, his heart broken by the despair of the place.'

She bustled in from the start, of course, taking over the organisation of the Girls' Club and Girls' Friendly Society, arguing with the Parochial Church Council until it waived a rule that tried to limit membership to those who regularly attended church, and set aside a prejudice which worked to keep the youngsters out of parochial and civic buildings, on the grounds that terrible poverty and terrible housing had conditioned them only to cause as much damage to as much public property as often as they could. For a busy and productive couple of years, Helena was at the hub of evangelistic societies ('I don't think we ever evangelised anybody, but we used to meet to discuss what could be done'), nativity plays, and her various groups of 'little rapscallions' who would occasionally get out of hand, but by and large calmed down after a firm and friendly word.

Then a new priest arrived and decided to freeze her out. Maybe he was simply irritated to find affairs so efficiently disposed and packaged before his installation. Loud arguments ensued, sometimes conducted in the streets—it was at this point in Helena's life that a sympathetic archdeacon warned her that 'a priest's temper is worse than a priest's lust'—and she was on the sidelines once again. Nevertheless, this petty and domestic example of her exclusion from any of the movements that might be working in the Duchy for reform encouraged her to pick up her pen again, and was the wellspring of some of her most powerful writing. She composed a series of articles for *The Church Times* which one by one examined and despatched the more eccentric sects which were proliferating on the margins of religion—spiritualism, theosophy, astrology and British Israelism—and others which were swimming nearer the mainstream—Christian Science and Jehovah's Witness. 'One week I got my copy of *The Church Times* and opened it, and there on one side of the page was my article, and on the other was a review of a pamphlet which I had written on Christian Stewardship. The reviewer said that "good pamphlets are rare, and excellent ones are pearls of great price." Actually in retrospect it seemed to me a very ordinary piece of work.'

The pamphlet had been a tradition in Britain for centuries, a compact polemic, widely read and distributed, often published at the risk of fine or imprisonment. And yet within thirty years, how much of a curiosity and an anachronism it has become. The very word 'pamphlet' is avoided by modern political studies units, who distribute 'policy documents', and 'discussion papers'. The man or woman who approaches you in the street and says, 'I have a pamphlet here . . .' is instantly committing a kind of social hari-kari. Who turned the pamphlet into a hive for bees out of bonnets? During the mid 'fifties, radio was in its maturity, television in its adolescence: the next stage for Helena Charles might have been the broadcast essay, assuming that her orthodoxies were in harmony with those that emanated from Portland Place.

By now her philosophy had reached a crossroads. In the 'thirties she had preached greater government intervention; by the middle of the 'fifties she was beginning to feel her way towards the idea of 'voluntarism' that has become very much a contemporary vogue. Why was she pushed outside the circles of social endeavour in Cornwall? Because, like the pamphlet, her sort of effort was being made redundant by modern trend and technology. Now the functions that she and her fellows had discharged from their privately-funded and theologically motivated bases were being folded into the apparatus of national and local authorities. However adequate their training and experience, there was increasingly no place in the system for people who were regarded as 'amateurs'.

* * *

Helena had chosen exile from London after a series of abrupt endings, romantic and vocational. Now, as winter followed Cornish winter, and there was little sign that the frosts which kept her outside the various establishments would ever thaw, she began to warm herself with the idea that she might abandon her West Country retreat and make herself a neighbour, once more, of metropolitan vitality by taking a house in the

Home Counties. There had been exciting times—the reception of her Cornish play, the Cong of Min, the creation of a linguistic society which met once a fortnight in Falmouth to chatter in French, Italian and Spanish, and only disbanded when the Suez crisis and petrol rationing made the journey impossible for most of its members.

When she drew up the balance sheet, however, it was not satisfactory. It was not so much failure, as frustration. It was a time for a change. But would she be simply moving her isolation a couple of hundred miles from one county to another? She was now in her mid-forties and one wonders, when she advertised in carefully chosen journals for a woman companion, whether she was implicitly resigning herself to spinsterhood.

'Professional woman seeks another to share house, possibly in the Home Counties.' There were fifty replies, which Helena, with her habitual caution, divided into two piles: hopeless and just possible. The latter were invited to join her at St Day for a brief trial, and in almost every case relegated back to hopelessness. Two applications, however, were intriguing. One came from a venerable geologist whose discoveries about the nature of certain Cornish rock formations had been nationally recognised. In deference to the lady's status, Helena went to visit her.

'I decided pretty quickly that although she was extremely interesting from the point of view of geology, she was totally deficient in any sort of domestic economy. I'm bad enough, but she was hopeless. To give you an example—because although we didn't become companions we remained friends—one Christmas Guy and I took her over some lunch, and when we arrived there wasn't a single clean saucepan, plate, knife or fork in the place. And to tell you the truth, there wasn't much besides geology that she could talk about, which was a bit of a bore.'

As a postscript, Helena adds that shortly after the geologist's death, the ungrateful rocks pitched her house from the cliff edge at Mullion into the sea.

'The other woman who sounded interesting was partly Polish, and I'll call her Margo. She was very intelligent, a linguist, and widely travelled, and we got on fine at first, and I thought that this was, perhaps, the right person, and we began to see more of each other. But then I discovered that she was what some people call a manipulator, and I call a cannibal. She expected to be waited on all the time. She was cross because during petrol rationing my old cat had to go to the vet every six weeks to have an injection to keep him going, and I took him in the car. She begrudged me using the petrol for the cat instead of taking her on trips. I had to cancel any engagement which I might have made when she announced that she was coming to stay, and after she had stayed with me for a few days it took me a month to recover. When she wasn't talking about the peculiar cult she belonged to, whose name I'd better not mention, she was very interesting and we had a lot in common. But her devotion to the cult was fanatical, and she used to read me screeds and screeds about it, and I found it more and more tiresome, while in between it was "get me a sweetie", "drive me here", "take me there", "no, don't go and do whatever you've arranged to do, I want to do something else". There was obviously no question of us sharing a home, but I realised I would have to do something to be rid of her.'

Margo rang up in the spring of 1958 and asked if she could come to stay for nine days. Helena reluctantly agreed. But then she received another invitation with far more appealing implications. She wrote to Margo and tried to reduce the nine days to four. In reply she received a cross letter full of self-pity and complaint. Helena then proposed that they should forget the Easter visit and allow themselves three months during which tempers might cool and both could reflect on the nature and obligations of their relationship. When the three months had elapsed Helena received a postcard inquiring after her health, but the conclusions of her own reflection prevented her from replying. 'I quite obviously couldn't have a cannibal in my house.'

To soften Helena's occasionally harsh character assessments, the following quotation from a letter she wrote quite recently may help to redress the balance:

> I know two men who were at the Pencalleneck School for the educationally sub-normal in Cornwall. Both have IQs of less than ninety, and neither reads easily. One of them can pick up tunes by ear, and either sings them beautifully, or plays them on a penny whistle, and is also a crack shot. For a number of years he was an assistant cellarer at a bar, and presumably ordered the drinks and kept the accounts. The other man can draw the most amusing caricatures, and for some time managed a rabbit processing factory. I couldn't do any of these things. And at the other end of the scale, I must remember that although I had to do two days' worth of washing up before I could give my geologist her Christmas lunch, she was absolutely brilliant in her field. Rocks were named after her, and if she went to a conference the proceedings never started until she'd arrived . . . St Paul had the right idea when he said that we all have different abilities and vocations.

The text from St Paul, in the seventh chapter of the first epistle to the Corinthians, is revealing:

> For I would that all men were even as I myself. But every man hath his proper gift of God, one after this manner, and another after that. I say

> therefore to the unmarried and widows, it is good for them if they abide even as I. But if they cannot contain, let them marry, for it is better to marry than to burn.

The invitation which encouraged Helena to send Margo the cannibal on the spoor of a fresh victim came from Guy Sanders. He had been asked to design the church exhibition stand for the Royal Cornwall Show, and had been told that Helena was an authority on the Church and industry. Would she help? It was like a longed for change in the weather. An unsought opportunity to get the sleeves rolled up again and work on a new project which drew on years of solid study and expertise. She happily accepted. 'Watch your step,' his vicar added, when she did a little research into her new associate's background. Guy was 45, Helena 48.

* * *

Guy Sanders was a thought-provoking man: brusquely charming, knowledgeable, a largely self-taught but accomplished sculptor and craftsman with not one perceptible trace of the artist-bohemian in his appearance or demeanour. He was six feet six inches tall, and had the physique and bearing one associates with the Royal Marines, in whose reserve he remained after his marriage. At 47, he earned his commando's green beret, taking assault and obstacle courses with ease, and concluding a 25-mile march by carrying a nineteen-year-old companion's rifle as well as his own. The youngster had weakened, so Guy also gave him his sugar ration—and fainted himself as a result at the end of the course.

He was almost obsessively meticulous, and sceptical about anybody else's ability to pay attention to detail, convinced until the last touchdown, for example, that travel plans made by anyone else would collapse disastrously ('and when they do, I have a number of plans myself which will get us home'). 'I always think it was the baggage that ruined our holidays,' Helena ruminates. 'He always took much too much, and since we couldn't afford taxis and I found it all too great a burden, he'd end up carrying the lot, and we both got thoroughly tired and bad tempered.' All of which must not be taken to mean that he was not delightful company, for he had a lively sense of humour.

Guy and Helena had disrupted childhoods in common, although in his case the nature of the convulsion was different, and the result, because of his isolation, perhaps even sadder. He was an unwanted baby, born when his mother was forty and in the middle of an acting career which she had no desire to suspend or abandon. Because his cries kept his parents awake, he was sent away to a home. After a year they brought him back, and subjected him, in Helena's phrase, 'to a most severe and limited upbringing'. When he was about to leave school he applied on his own initiative for a job as a commercial artist. His parents tore up the reply before he had had a chance to read it, because they had not been consulted. 'He was always completely suppressed by them, and developed a real need to feel wanted.' That, Helena understood, was why he relished his participation in the drills and manoeuvres of the Royal Marine Volunteer Reserve, and why he applied himself with such panache to the administration of the performances and clarification of the politics of Cornwall's multitude of brass and silver bands. Essentially, and identifiably, when one met him, he was a loner, and so he revelled in his membership of formal societies whose rules of behaviour and association were exact and beyond equivocation.

By the time he met Helena, Guy was working for the ambulance service at Cornwall County Council's headquarters in Truro, and his relationship with his mother had developed into something rather morbid. In the phrase she first used when she met Gerhard and Mrs Fischer, Helena describes how Mrs Sanders was 'twined around her son like a snake'. But she qualifies the comparison. 'In Gerhard's case it was an excess of mother love. It was different with Guy. His terrible mother, who nearly kyboshed our marriage, was frightfully repressive. He hadn't been allowed to bring any of his friends to their house, and she still demanded the right to make all the major decisions in his life, even though he was now 45, and he couldn't seem to stand up to her. Because her husband had been crippled in the Great War she'd had to take another job, and became a gardening consultant. She had a warped view of sex which had affected his attitude to girls, making him very shy and wary. He'd been through the Second World War, lived at home for a while, moved to Bristol, returned to Cornwall to live on a yacht, and finally bought his own tiny cottage near Truro. But he still couldn't seem to get free, and openly told me that if his mother disapproved he wouldn't be able to go ahead with our marriage.'

There was already a girlfriend of a sort in Guy's life, of whom his mother more or less approved, because theirs was a very clinical, precise, and occasional alliance, with a vague and rather abstract prospect of marriage at a date which was never discussed. But both the lofty Marjory (who had affronted Guy's punctiliousness, anyway, by once leaving her handbag somewhere) and the supercilious Mrs Sanders were unprepared for the tenacity of the campaign Helena launched when she decided that Guy was her man. It was game, set, and match in a little over a year. Mrs Sanders refused to visit the couple for several months after their marriage, but was eventually reconciled. One of Guy's aunts cut him out of her will and never spoke to him again for the supposed disloyalty of abandoning his old mother. In fact, as Helena wryly points out, the ageing parent had a far better time with a daughter-in-law who was happy to take her on motoring trips, run errands, and, finally, to nurse her through her last illness until her death in 1962—the same year, coincidentally, that Helena's stepmother died.

The legacy of more than 40 years in thrall to a cold and stifling woman was a secret melancholy that fed on solitude and sometimes overthrew the strenuous attempts Guy made to control it by setting himself exhausting programmes of work and study. 'He was not a manic depressive, but a sufferer from depression, like at least half of the world's artistic people. Sometimes, for months at a stretch he would absolutely fail to take any interest in life at all. I remember one Christmas he went through a completely silent phase. I cooked the lunch and put a bottle of wine on the table, and he never bothered to open it. We sat and ate the meal without saying a word, and then he went to lie on his bed and stayed there for the rest of the day. In the evening he came downstairs and apologised, and suddenly the depression lifted, as it always did. I think he was too inhibited to say what the matter was even if he knew. I was puzzled, but didn't want to intrude.'

Helena admits that as far as many of their friends were concerned, she and Guy seemed totally unsuited, and she will even go so far as to concede that, in one sense, each was the other's 'last hope', as their two lonely and rather bruised souls were blown towards the far thresholds of middle age. But then again, both had separately schooled themselves to disguise their emotional depths, and perhaps it was at those profound and obscured levels of their beings that harmonies sounded which it might, by then, have been hard to raise to the surface and articulate. 'I've frequently been asked what it was that attracted us to each other, and in some ways I'm not sure. I was attracted to him because I saw that he was a good man, and terribly conscientious, and I felt something for him which I had never felt before. I don't know what attracted him to me. He used to get very cross with me sometimes.'

The place where their courtship began was a black iron bridge—so obvious a symbol of the moods to which both were prey that their recollections of its gaunt and lugubrious structure were always rich with amusement. The bridge led over a road to the site near Truro where, for six weeks, they prepared the Royal Cornwall Show stand—a massive exhibit depicting in various tableaux with cycloramas and costumed wooden mannequins the involvement of the Church with youth, the sea, and healing. Helena laboured to paint 'acres and acres and acres' of wood, colouring it green, or red, or grey, or blue, to barked instructions from Guy Sanders, sole designer and senior sculptor and builder in the workforce of two. And when, as inevitably occurred if the maestro was not looking, a red bit came out grey, or a green bit blue, Helena enjoyed lively premonitions of the terrestrial wrath to come, now and then, during their married life. The finished stand was nearly destroyed by storms the night before the show opened, but the couple were able to apply sufficient first aid with hammers and nails to make it presentable for the early crowds.

Helena now thinks that hers must have been 'the weirdest courtship in the world'. They continued to meet after the show had been struck, she visiting his cottage at weekends, helping with fumbling fingers and frequently rapped knuckles in the manufacture of carnival masks, quietly cuckooing the too-often absent Marjory from the place in the nest she wanted to retain by remote control, steeling Guy, as she had tried once before to steel Gerhard, in the art of confronting a mother, sifting the good advice from the sentimental dross, and having the strength to accept the first and discard the second, and to differentiate as well between affectionate common sense and possessive hysteria.

'After several months we became engaged in his office at County Hall. The only possible date when we could get married was August Bank Holiday, 1959, because that was the only holiday he hadn't already mortgaged to his brass bands or his training with the RMVR.' Mrs Sanders had not, as we have seen, resigned herself to the marriage, but she had recognised, for the first time, a superior and well-marshalled force at work, restlessly, in her son's life. 'He still felt he had to ask her permission, even at the age of 45, although by now he bitterly resented her domineering ways. He told me it was very fortunate that she didn't actively do more to oppose his getting engaged, beyond making her disapproval clear.'

August Bank Holiday was hardly the easiest day on which to arrange a wedding at relatively short notice. Every hotel, hall and bar seemed to have been booked months before. 'In the end we got a large marquee and had it erected on the lawn at Tenderah. Apart from the cake that was made by a baker in Truro I did most of the preparations myself. Two people came down from the Industrial Christian Fellowship, ostensibly to help me get the wedding breakfast ready, but of course they had to be fed, looked after, and entertained, so they weren't a vast amount of use.

'We had two bands in church—Carharrack and Helston Town. Guy had played with both of them, appearing with Helston Town for sixteen successive years on Flora Day. The noise they made at the ceremony was absolutely deafening. When the service was over we put the aunts in our wedding car and walked up through the fields, past three kissing gates, from Helston to our reception at Tenderah.'

As the guests began to leave, a sturdy female figure in hiking gear with a rucksack and boots marched up through the grounds.

'Are you Miss Charles?'

August 1, 1959. Helena Charles marries Guy Sanders in Helston. 'Look,' said Guy, 'we really can't leave them to do all that clearing up.' So the couple turned back after setting off for their honeymoon, and helped to wash the dishes.

'Well I was, but I'm Mrs Sanders now.'

'I have been sent to represent Israel at your wedding.'

Helena had notified a number of contacts, former refugees among them, that she was about to get married, and a girl whose holiday plans were taking her to Cornwall had been deputed as official representative. It was a ceremonious ending, even if it was carried out in rather unusual livery. The new Mr and Mrs Sanders thanked the girl and climbed into Helena's little green van for the drive back to Guy's cottage near Truro.

'Look,' said Guy, after a few hundred yards, 'we really can't leave them to do all that clearing up.'

'No, you're absolutely right,' said Helena, realising perhaps that even on her day of glamour she was being asked to choose between Mary and Martha, and accepting the role that would now, as it had always done, leave her 'cumbered about much serving', and 'careful and troubled about many things'. So they stopped the car, and walked back, went in through the rear entrance, and helped the others to wash up the dirty crocks and glasses of a hundred wedding guests. 'We drove back in a state of almost complete exhaustion. Guy went up ahead of me, and when I arrived in the bedroom I found him snoring. I quickly learned that if anything happened to interfere with his bedtime, which was about nine o'clock, it was quite impossible to keep him awake for any reason whatever.'

The next day a builder who had failed to complete some alterations to Guy's cottage before the wedding turned up to continue his work. And was propelled from the premises at great speed by a series of caustic phrases. The honeymoon was not so languid as to allow a single morning's interruption. Guy was booked to take a youth band camp in just a couple of days.

* * *

Forty-eight hours later, Guy left the cottage to begin his Summer duties. He had been running the youth band camp in St Austell for a number of years, and had achieved such a success, and generated such loyalty, that his sense of duty prevailed over any sneaking desire to avoid the dislocation of his honeymoon by pleading a sudden illness. He had already told Helena that he would not be able to return at nights, and she decided to try to sustain at least the more prosaic of their new matrimonial relations by motoring over every day with his breakfast. The very first morning was unseasonably damp. The old van murmured asthmatically but refused to start. Helena applied the crank handle at first to the engine, and then, as each revolution protested itself back to silence, began to belabour the bonnet. Scarred paintwork relieved her anger—and was for years a souvenir of the occasion—but for all her noise and violent admonitions, the van remained speechless. So she set off on foot along the towpath to the nearest village, and managed to borrow a lift from a tame vicar.

By the time Guy came home from St Austell, Helena had her bags packed. She was off to Oxford to give the summary speech at an ICF conference. Her subject (maybe she had the van in mind) was the strike as a phenomenon in modern life. 'We are a prize pair,' Guy would remark, more than once, as they passed each other in the revolving doors of their various commitments.

Humour they both needed, because years of domestic solitude and more or less emotional self-determination had been a poor preparation for the time they were to spend together. 'I can't honestly say that the first few months of my marriage were particularly happy,' Helena confesses. 'For one thing, I was in the middle of an extremely bad menopause, and poor Guy, who was quite unprepared for and unaccustomed to such things, had to put up not just with fearful tantrums on my part, but hysteria as well, and hysteria is quite foreign to my nature; in fact, it frightened me as well. The other thing was that I had absolutely nothing to do. There was no telephone, I had no job, I had almost no contacts with educated people, and there was no one I knew locally who could stretch my mind at all.

'This wouldn't have been so bad if Guy hadn't been so terribly occupied with his various interests. The Brass Band Association kept him out rehearsing at least once, sometimes more often, every week, and there were concerts at the weekends as well. And for quite a while he used to spend two nights a week in Bristol with the Royal Marine Volunteer Reserve. On top of that he was tied up with a local garden society, so for me it really was a very difficult time indeed, left as I was to my own devices, particularly since I have to say that I've always loathed and detested housework.'

Over the years, however, the couple began to spend more time together, because many of Guy's local preoccupations fell away. It was not because of any growing apathy on his part. He was by nature a professional, and in all the cultural fields with which he involved himself, one of life's producers and directors, an inheritance, perhaps, from his mother. As he matured, he strove harder and harder for excellence, drilling the bands and moulding the garden societies to reach for ever more singular successes. Amateurs tend not to respond to the degree of professionalism which transforms their leader into a benign or occasionally an angry despot. His work with the bands ended in a row about the quality of their public presentations. The garden society decided to dispense with him after he quietly rearranged the programme of a visit by the Queen Mother to ensure that she would spend more time looking at flowers, and less shaking hands with Cornish dignitaries. 'Given Guy's awkward temper and perfectionism, it was almost inevitable that most of the associations that he formed would end in tears,' Helena concedes. He quit the RMVR for reasons that are now obscure, although without doubt they also hinged on some indissoluble point of principle.

After an overture that seethed with difficulties, the marriage grew more harmonious. The couple moved to a semi-detached house and discovered new affinities as they designed a new garden, Guy chopping down trees that obscured the view and pinstriping the lawns, Helena taking charge of the flower-beds. By 1962 they were on the move again. Aunt Ethel Charles had died, and left her niece £2,000. For that sum, not so very many years ago, you could buy a thatched cottage on the banks of the River Lemon, downstream from Truro. It was owned by the Duchy of Cornwall and had belonged to a farmer and his wife. Aunt Ethel's cash and some other legacies would enable Guy to give up his job at County Hall and concentrate full time on sculpture—with a brief interlude when he worked as the organiser of the local oyster fisheries. There was a room in the cottage that made an ideal studio, with an old Cornish range which Guy restored. Helena would prepare a casserole, and he would pop it in the oven mid-morning, and at lunch time he would move all the plaster casts to one side, take out the saucepan, and they lunched together, discussing the success or failure of his latest enterprise. Only one serious cause of dissension remained in the body of the house, which Guy's diligent conversions had changed into an open-plan establishment.

'He liked to go to bed at nine at night, and I liked to go to bed at one in the morning. He liked to get up and put the wireless on at half past six, and I disliked getting up before nine. He used to turn in at his usual time, and I would sit feeling totally frustrated, not able to listen to music or use my typewriter or the sewing machine, and finally I would go to bed in a bad temper, while in the morning the position was reversed, with Guy creeping around rather cross because he couldn't listen to his wireless programme unless he was willing to wake me up and risk being the victim of my sore head.'

Among their improvements to the cottage, the couple had rethatched an adjoining building, and made it into an agreeable little flat, with two rooms, a kitchen, and a bathroom. Now, after about two years of unsynchronised sleeping, it began to feature on Helena's mental agenda. I suppose if I said that I wanted to go and sleep there it wouldn't be very well received, she thought. Until one morning Guy looked sheepishly at her and said: 'I suppose you wouldn't think of moving into the flat?'

'And so I did, and that was that, and it resolved an awful lot of tension between us.'

The prize pair spent as much time as money and their duties allowed jaunting around Europe, travelling in one of their succession or vans, or by 'plane, or by boat and train. I can see them at stations, on quays, and in departure lounges, Guy struggling irritably with all the luggage, Helena trying to achieve invisibility as a valise tumbled to the deck, or one of the suitcases that they stuffed with papers burst to strew socially purposive confetti around their feet. One of their most enchanting travellers' tales, although its charm is not entirely intentional, finds them in Majorca, on a package tour, but really dedicating themselves to a quest for the local dancing which Guy had enjoyed on an earlier visit with the Royal Marine Volunteer Reserve.

'Do you want to see a bullfight?' shouts the lady courier enthusiastically as the bus pulls out of Majorca.

'No!' yell Guy and Helena in unison, becoming the archetypal couple in the back.

Comes the evening for the dancing, and the courier announces that she has arranged a fleet of taxis.

'We'll go by bus,' say Guy and Helena.

'There aren't any buses,' says the courier.

'We'll walk, then.'

'Please yourselves.'

'So,' Helena remembers, 'we set out to walk and immediately a bus came along which we took, and we arrived very early. By the time the courier came with the party from the hotel we'd been talking to all the people, and we were in the front row catching the eyes of the dancers, and the rest of them had to sit at the back. She was furious.'

The point-scoring continued until their departure, when the courier asked if they would mind taking some cigarettes home for her relatives. 'We were very surprised that she'd chosen us to ask, and in the 'plane going home I told Guy I was convinced there were drugs mixed with the tobacco. So I went to the 'plane's lavatory and opened the packet.' The fact that it contained ordinary cigarettes suggests that they might have been leaving a rather dry sense of humour behind them in Majorca.

But the story that I find most affecting, and most revealing of the quixotic humanity and determination of Mr and Mrs Guy Sanders, concerns a certain French family who brought their guinea pig with them on holiday to England. At the port of Plymouth, as they prepared to return home, the unfortunate animal was spotted and arrested by HM Customs. Father was flung in the brig, brought to court, and fined £90, while the guinea pig was sentenced to an indeterminate spell behind bars. Exit French family across the Channel, wiping their eyes with their sleeves. Case makes headlines in all the local papers.

'Guy said to me that unless I did something about that creature it would end up in a laboratory. At the time the propaganda about the dangers of importing animals into England and the threat of rabies was awfully poor. I had serious thoughts about getting Guy to make some fibre-glass sculptures of rabid dogs which we could fasten on top of the van. The plan was then to get a couple of veterinary students to accompany me as we drove through various French towns, where the students would put on the dogs' heads and run about while I did the talking. I hoped I might be able to get on to television and explain the problems, because at the time it really was impossible to expect that any ordinary person would stand and read the lengthy dissertation in small print that was fixed up at the ports. In the end I let the idea go, although I did write to the President of the French Republic and the Minister of Agriculture and urge them to do something about the inadequacy of the advertisements.

'Anyway, the guinea pig had been confiscated, and I did lots of telephoning and some telegraphing. We'd had a pretty poor holiday that year, so I suggested that we took the guinea pig and reunited it with the family in Marseilles. We were met at Plymouth airport by the vet with the guinea pig, and we put it in a canary cage and flew across to Paris where we caught the night train south. Finally we met the family, who were overjoyed, and on our way back visited Toulouse and Carcassone, and had a thoroughly pleasant time. Everybody wanted to know why we were carrying an empty canary cage, and that gave me an opportunity to explain about the guinea pig and the rabies laws, and not one person to whom we spoke had ever heard of the regulations. For example, there was a woman who said her dog would be all right, because he'd had an anti-rabies injection. And I had to explain all over again that he wouldn't be exempt, and if she took him to England he might be confiscated and killed.'

At home, as well as abroad, Helena's thoughts after her marriage gradually busied themselves with greater intensity on the matter of animal welfare. There were parallel interests. She worked for a while as the secretary of the Diocesan Adult Education Committee, but was told cryptically by a senior colleague that she was 'far too intellectual, and what is more, not intellectual enough.' Following the death of Guy's mother in 1962, when she had moved wardrobes of old clothes to the Oxfam centre in Oxford, Helena agreed to found a local branch of the charity in Truro. After two stints as chairman she wearied of 'the quarrels the devil always seems to sow when people of goodwill are trying to work together.'

But animals had always been close to the centre of her life, and sometimes, indeed, the most companionable and loyal members of her household. During the mid 'sixties the indignation which she had harnessed for years to alleviate the sufferings of fellow humans was organised in a new direction. She had always, of course, despised people who maltreated animals, and had intervened whenever she saw cruelty threatened. Now she began to contemplate the attitudes which connived at ill-treatment; the negligence, for example, of a local farmer who watched his cat breed twenty-six kittens and then proposed to shoot them all. She argued the gun out of his hand, and 'spent a dreary winter driving back and forth, setting the trap, and either finding homes for the cats or arranging for their humane destruction.' At home, her efforts led to the creation first of the Truro Cat Rescue Group, and then of the Cornwall Cat Rescue Group, and to the opening of a fund-raising shop. Scores of cats and kittens were rescued, spayed, and placed in good homes. And at

Mars and Neptune, the pagan gods this Christian city annexed as local deities, dominate the Scala dei Giganti in Venice. It was the thought of a Doge being decapitated here, and his head rolling down the staircase, that made Guy Sanders vow never to enter the Doges' Palace again.

home, even today, she continues to lobby Members of Parliament, Civil Servants, and the media in the cause of animal welfare.

Abroad, 1964 was the critical year. Helena and Guy holidayed in Italy, travelling first to Florence, and then to Venice. Both were profoundly affected by different aspects of human savagery portrayed in the Serene Republic. Guy vowed never to step inside the great Palace again. The image out of history of the head of a deposed Doge tumbling down the marble staircase was too vivid for him to support. And Helena?

'There were thousands upon thousands of emaciated cats. I'm not exaggerating. Thousands. It ruined the holiday for me completely. Some of them could hardly crawl. They were ill. They were in an appalling condition. Their eyes were running. Everywhere you looked you could see a cat dying. It never occurred to me at the time that I would be able to do anything about it all. I remember simply thinking what a horrible place Venice must be if nothing was being done to help all these sick animals. The attitude seemed to be one of complete indifference. They didn't notice the cats, they didn't seem to see a cat that couldn't even move because it was so starving and diseased.'

* * *

Guy and Helena returned home, dejected in different ways. She might, at the time, have felt both repulsed and impotent, but the spark had been kindled, and would shortly fire into an international campaign.

CHAPTER TEN

DINGO

Back to Tenderah, its secret melodies turned solemn, the magic garden now dishevelled. The year is 1967. Tennis court, walled garden, flower-beds and fig and apple trees are sorrowfully neglected. On hook and hanger, necklaced with shrinking pills of camphor, poplin flowers have been changing to sepia and grey. At the focal point of the Tenderah landscape, its margins encroached upon, now, by bungalows and holiday lets reaching out from Helston and in from the coast, there is just a solitary figure. Helena Sanders, executrix.

Two formidable women had died within 51 weeks of each other, complicating, by the way, a matter of death duties already nicely tangled by the unlikely event of two maiden aunts cohabiting for so many years in such an abundance of land and masonry. Aunt Gwen was the victim of a gangrened appendix. It caused her little pain—in fact, in her last weeks, dreams that were almost hallucinations were suffused with delicious phantom meals. Aunt Kit found her in an armchair one day and berated her for sitting about when she should be attending to the housework. There was no reply, because Aunt Gwen was dead. She was laid out by candlelight on the dining room table. The house remained much as it was when the spinsters' parents had it built in the nineteenth century. There were relatives who murmured that the paint and paper were still the same. Nothing, anyway, as disruptive of its tenebrous and Victorian reveries as electricity had ever been allowed to invade the premises. Under the neons of the inquest, Aunt Kit, in turn, was berated by the coroner for failing to summon a doctor when it must have been clear that her sister was declining. Helena Sanders got the message when, three seasons later, she saw Aunt Kit begin to fade.

'I'm sending for the doctor.'

'If you do, I'll cut you out of my will.'

'Very well, I'll send for a lawyer as well.'

Aunt Kit, with the negligence of self which was apparently a characteristic of the Tyacke sisters, had ignored an injury to her leg. It ulcerated, and the poison seeped into her system. Helena sat up with her in the same dining room while she died, swearing belligerently almost to the last. 'She made a point of disapproving of everything.'

Other members of the family inherited the house, but it was Helena's task to empty it. Over the years, Tenderah had become a sort of vault, a repository where unwanted furniture and chattels were sent when someone moved to a smaller property, or another Tyacke or Charles died with an overplus of goods. Every Tuesday for six months, Helena sorted through the contents. Chairs, tables, beds, stools, wardrobes, chests, pictures, prints, mirrors, creams, ointments and potions; antique silver dating from the reign of George II; a collection of dresses beginning in the late eighteenth century and stopping well short of the mid-twentieth. A cellar of wine and port, first laid down in the 1880s, in more or less undrinkable condition; vast quantities of books of the sort the Victorians used to buy: improving by intention, dry by nature, and deteriorating, now, in quality; cheque book stubs; petrol coupons from the Suez crisis, and assorted, unusable lengths of string.

I watch Helena in my imagination sweeping up the myriad fragments of the broken *hortus conclusus* of Tenderah, the valuable with the trivial, and even some of the trivial, surely, charged with a degree of significance. Wasn't it like conducting an autopsy on the roots of herself? 'I got hardened to it as the months went by.'

* * *

Invisibly, the seeds drift forward from the ruins of one era to flower in the next. By 1967, Helena was already committed to the campaign that proved to be the crowning achievement of her life. So here are the garments to Tenderah's aunts, dry-cleaned and pressed and turned out of their wardrobes to dress the thespians of Cornwall. The proceeds go to Dingo. There is Guy, legs braced, cheeks red and full of tentative breath, trying to govern twenty-foot or so of gondola as it swirls in the currents flowing northwards to Truro from the Carrick Roads. Fares, please, to the funds of the same charity. Here are two local helpers, Mrs Wilson announcing that she has second-hand silver to peddle (did anyone think to mention this to the police?) and Mrs Selzer, begging everyone for the equivalent of the price of a pint of milk (did anyone think they should call a social worker? Helena Sanders, perhaps?). All to raise money for an oversized, undernourished, brutalised and distempered colony of cats, living and dying beside a foreign lagoon.

Helena had turned away, on that first visit, disgusted but unaware that within a couple of years she would be rolling up her sleeves to clean out the

A colony of original Venetian tabbies lives around and under the Ponte dell' Accademia. Even friends must be approached with caution . . . when one is contemplating inveigling one's way into a place in the sun.

augean cattery. When I asked her once if there was any single word to link together the multiple branches of her career she replied, only too conscious of the pun, that I ought to describe her as a 'catalyst'.

The catalyst that led to the creation of Dingo was a parcel of Linguaphone records, lent to a friend, Marjorie Royston, who died in 1977. Helena wrote her obituary in Dingo's annual report for the same year.

> But for Marjorie Royston there would not be any Dingo, and her death has deprived us of a very loyal friend and support. She came to Wiltshire in the 1930s as a supply head teacher, and after the War she became Assistant County Youth Service Officer. It was in this capacity that I met her, many years ago, when I was secretary of the Cornwall Standing Conference of Voluntary Youth Organisations. We shared a common interest in Italian. I had a spare set of the old vulcanite Hugo's Linguaphone Records, which I lent to her, and she passed her 'O'-levels in Italian at the age of forty. The problem was how she

should get the records back to me. They were very brittle, and none of the County Youth Officers seemed to want to be responsible for their transport. So when my husband was in the Bath tattoo, Marjorie came to lunch with us, bringing the records. We were just about to go to Italy and stay for a short while in Venice. This was a year after I had been so distressed by the swarms of emaciated cats.

During lunch Majorie said: 'You're a catty person. When you get to Venice go to see Rafaella Pucci. She is very worried about the enormous number of starving cats that neither she nor the other Venetian animal lovers can cope with.' So I promised to do so, not seeing at all how I could help. When I met Rafaella Pucci, more to please her than because I could foresee anything coming from it, I promised to write an article. 'The Cats of Venice—An Appeal' eventually appeared in *The Cat*. It was read by Miss Mabel Raymonde Hawkins, who got in touch with me, and six months later we went back to Venice together. But for Marjorie Royston's concern and the problem of the Linguaphone records, none of this would have happened. We rarely recognise our climacteric moments.

Raymonde Hawkins, whose work at the Raystede Animal Centre in Sussex had made her something of a celebrity in British animal welfare circles, was a formidable ally, and her characteristic response was not to volunteer her own ingenuity and skill as the lynchpin of a campaign, relegating everyone else to the touchlines, but to conscript Helena and push her into the centre, offering to accompany her to Venice and provide some practical help as their work began. Their first trip was in October 1965, and contact was immediately made with the existing nucleus of sympathetic Italian women—not only Rafaella Pucci, but also Gina Scarpabolla, a painter who divided her love equally between art and animals. Rafaella and Gina were as anguished as their new English friends at the plight of the cats, but so far had lacked the support or knowledge to engage in anything more than the most superficial first-aid service, supporting the cat mothers, rescuing animals, whenever possible, from the slaughterhouse, and remonstrating with louts and vandals, whether of freelance or municipal affiliation. The story unfolds from a network of Dingo reports and documents almost as anfractuous as the canals and alleys of Venice.

'There was no first cat, there were just swarms. There were, however, a few cats that we would always recall. A dying cat, his eyes and nose bunged up with discharge from 'flu. He could neither see nor smell and was unaware that a plate of food was beside him. There were cats in the Rialto fish market eating the paper in which fish had been wrapped. There

Backstreet Venice: a carnival of ancient stone and crazy civil engineering.

was a colony of black cats near our hotel. They were in fairly good condition as they were all fed by the proprietor. One day they were all found dead. They'd been killed by the rat poison the authorities had put down in their territory.

'In consultation with animal lovers, Miss Raymonde Hawkins drew up a veterinary form which said, in Italian, "Please sterilise/give veterinary treatment/put down this cat." The forms had been printed in England, and were given to carefully selected, trustworthy cat-women. One in particular, Linda, was paid a hundred lire, then about one shilling and twopence, to catch sick and injured cats, a dangerous proceeding, and have them put down. Another, Maria, had two pensions, but she went out to work to get money to feed the cats. Every time she found an injured cat she took it home. She admitted to having forty in her house. We climbed up several flights of stairs in the dark. There was an overpowering stench of tomcat. At last we came to a room with a kitchen table and some wooden chairs. The only light was a low-powered and unshaded bulb, and the only other thing on the table was an enormous bottle of brandy of which we all partook . . .

'We interviewed an Italian vet, who agreed to spay, neuter, treat or destroy, for his usual fee, and then we came home. Our visit had caused little stir. We set about raising funds. The Headquarters of the Cats'

Protection League gave us £500. The International Society for the Protection of Animals gave us, I think, £50. I cajoled our local Cats' Protection League, of which I was then chairman, to give us £100. The money was sent to one of the cat women, Angelina, who agreed to pay the vets' bills as they came in. Very gradually the women started to take the cats to the vet. There was still a lot of feeling against spaying or castration, which were looked upon as a cruel mutilation, and some futile discussion about whether it was a sin to put newborn kitten to sleep. There was never, as far as I know, any discussion about the immorality of allowing unrestricted breeding, and the consequent starvation as the cats outstripped their food supply.

'Miss Raymonde Hawkins and I decided to go back in January when the cats were at their hungriest, because the hotels are closed. But before we left, we gave interviews to one of the English popular papers which gave great prominence to a completely distorted article, composed mostly of

Breakfast among the refuse in the Campo Sante Maria Nova . . .

. . . before setting forth on the day's business . . .

. . . across the Square of Miracles.

lies, which said we were going to hire a gondola and put a big cage in it, and go round paying the old women 100 lire to give us cats. The impression was given that we were going to arrange for the creatures to be burned alive, because we hated them.

'Fog meant that Miss Raymonde Hawkins and I and her photographer had to land at Milan and catch a train, and we didn't arrive in Venice until one in the morning. We were weighed down with our luggage, two cat traps, photographic equipment and other paraphernalia. The fog was still thick when we arrived at the Piazzale Roma, the road and rail entrance to Venice at the end of its causeway with the mainland, so we went to a nearby hotel for what was left of the night. Next morning we caught a water bus and went the entire length of the Grand Canal to another small hotel where our rooms were booked. A headline in the *Gazzetino* caught my eye: "The Whole City is Laughing at the Cat Safari". At the landing stage a posse of journalists was waiting for us. Italian reporters had been alerted by the English newspaper article. Their stories had been picked up in turn by journalists from other European countries.

'The authorities, frightened of the effect the story might have on tourism, had swooped on the worst of the cats before our arrival, lassoed them and killed them, it was said, "otherwise than by euthanasia". We saw fewer cats, and they seemed in better condition. The so-called Italian Animal Welfare Organisation, *Ente Nazionale per la Protezione degli Animale* (ENPA), was furious with us. Its Director—I never heard any animal lover say a good word for him—announced, untruly as it turned out, that he had mobilised all eighteen of the *Guardia Zoofili* (animal police) and that "if Mrs Sanders ill-treats one cat she'll have to face the full majesty of the Italian law." When we went out to try to do some shopping, it was impossible to walk because of the reporters and cameramen. They lay on the ground to photograph us, they held microphones to our lips as we were talking. One told Miss Raymonde Hawkins that if we went with him to the best café in Venice and told our story we would be left alone. I persuaded her to comply, but when we got there the café was shut. I asked the police to get rid of the mob, but they refused, saying, "You are celebrities." A picture of this conversation appeared in one of the West Country newspapers with the headline: "Truro Woman Arrested by Venice Police". There was also a cartoon of us in the *Corriere della Sera*, which had a leader article inset: "Dangerous Times for the Cats of Venice", saying that we were retreating in the face of opposition, that there would be no massacre, and Venetians would continue to "spoil and cosset" their cats.

'We weren't able to change before going to a party given for us in their palatial flat by a wealthy couple. All the animal lovers were assembled, and the idea was that we should talk about what to do. But this was impossible because Linda, who was among the guests, made an impassioned speech denouncing ENPA, shouting her head off and making any discussion impossible. Nevertheless, we met with nothing but kindness from the ordinary Venetians, and after a short while the tenor of our Press coverage began to waver, and then to change. A doctor from the hospital wrote a letter in our support, explaining what we were setting out to achieve. Our vet wrote another in a similar vein. The penny dropped. An article appeared in the *Gazzetino*: "*Sono Amici dei Gatti*—They Are Friends of the Cats—they do not want to kill them because they hate them, but to spare them suffering."

'Then one of our supporters made a scene in the street with the Director of ENPA, who complained to the police. We were summoned to appear before the head of the Aliens Department. For half an hour he shouted at us, and although I did not understand much of what he said, I gathered that he was inveighing loudly against the iniquity of *ca-stra-za-sione*—castration. He asked me: "Why do you come to this country to break the law?" To which I replied: "In which country is it illegal to take a sick animal to the vet?"

'I tried shouting back, but it had no effect. But after thirty minutes something must have got through, because he called in the Director of ENPA (his white hair was dyed blue), who kissed our hands, and we were dismissed. As soon as we were safely away from the police station we collapsed in helpless giggles, leaning against a wall. The next day we flew home.'

Their initial plan was to set up an efficient veterinary and propaganda machine, demonstrate how simply it could be kept in operation, and withdraw, leaving local supporters in sole command. Raymonde Hawkins was particularly anxious to turn her attention exclusively to the sanctuary she was establishing in Sussex for horses and ponies abandoned by travellers. At first, signals from the lagoonside were encouraging. Sick and injured cats were regularly being treated, a spaying system was successfully introduced, and favourable publicity continued, inevitably, if slowly, transforming social attitudes. But then a sequence of events occurred which demanded another infusion of that peculiarly British mixture of pragmatism and prayer with which the two women were endowed.

Helena called them 'the two horrors'. One was wrought by men, the other by nature. First, the local authority decided to spend £70,000 on phosphorous to poison rats and mice. Their motives have never been successfully unravelled, but the consequences were already clear—a limited experiment had wiped out an entire colony of cats, each of which had died in torture after eating the contaminated corpse of a rodent.

Helena and Raymonde Hawkins flew to Venice and began to beat a loud drum against the scheme, writing to every person of influence or authority, threatening a worldwide campaign to draw attention to the cruelty and subvert the city's image in the minds of potential visitors. 'What tourist will want to come, knowing that animals are dying in agony?' their letters asked. And then they waited and prayed. 'The day before we left, which was also the day before the poisoning was due to start, the council abandoned the project because it was too expensive.'

Almost as soon as the man-made horror had been averted, the natural one descended. Torrential rain inundated the river valleys of Italy and, as the lagoon rose, Venice was another victim of floods which caused devastation throughout the country. An extra three feet of water was enough to send the canals surging through the streets, and the basements and lower floors of buildings. Cat-women rescued animals wherever they could, but the rats and mice which had been spared from phosphorous now died in huge numbers, and the cats were beggared of their traditional larder. Back in Truro, Helena did what she could to moderate both human and animal suffering.

'I discovered that the Italian Red Cross desperately needed mattresses, bedding and clothing, so I toured Cornwall in my van with a trailer, in the dark and the pouring rain, collecting wherever I could. A farmer in Devon who'd just lost his wife volunteered to perform the same service for me there. Altogether we gathered together two tons of materials. A fruiterer provided lorries to take it to the docks. Farm industries gave me holed sacks, useless for grain, but ideal for packing mattresses. The Italian State Shipping Company gave me ten tons of free freight space, and Pedigree Pet Foods supplied 1,000 tins of cat food. I was able to give some of the space available to the Anglo-Italian Society for the Protection of Animals, who wanted to transport calf-food to the flooded Po Valley. The voyage took six weeks, and there was another delay when the whole consignment was held up by Italian customs because duty had to be paid on the foodstuffs. It was only released when the head of the shipping company financed the excise from his own funds.'

Without a doubt, Helena's dynamic reaction to 'the two horrors' deepened local confidence in the integrity of her ambitions for the animals of Venice, and wove her inextricably into each stage of their realisation. But she also had to contend with a level of intrigue and subterfuge which was quite foreign to her experience in England, where the opposition she encountered had always been outspoken and frontal. 'I was sitting on my balcony in Mestre, just opposite Venice, one lovely afternoon, drinking a beer, when the telephone rang. The message was to tell Mrs Sanders to get back inside the building—she could be seen. At first I didn't believe all this talk of spies and spying, but after a while I just had to accept it. When I telephoned friends in Venice from England I quite often got perplexing and non-committal replies, because whoever I was talking to was quite convinced someone was impersonating me to try to get information about Dingo's activities.'

Who was organising the espionage? Apparently the villains were members of *Ente Nazionale per la Protezione degli Animale* (ENPA), resolved by whatever means to protect their welfare monopoly. Stories of Dingo's sorry and often turbulent relations with this enigmatic organisation, which had been founded by Mussolini, are a regular fixture in the English group's animal reports.

Some Bad News from Venice

In our last report I wrote of the new, co-operative attitude that existed between us and the Venetian branch of ENPA. The new president, Professor Rizzoli, was giving us all the help he could, as well as trying to improve the conditions of the slaughter and transport of food animals, establish cat and dog shelters, control vivisection, find alternative methods of experiment, and, last but not least, 'to restore the dignity and efficiency of the society, with a minimum of centralisation, and a maximum of local autonomy . . . to make new contacts with Government, and to improve the efficiency of civic animal inspectors.'

But on November 20, 1972, he wrote: 'Dear Members, this is to tell you that I have today received news from the executive committee in Rome announcing that the Venice branch has been closed down, and that I have been relieved of the Presidency. This puts an end to the long battle that I have been waging, perhaps uselessly, on two fronts. Firstly, the front of centralised authority in Rome, and secondly, the local front which is tied in some ways to that central body, composed of petty interests, and little inclined to the regeneration of ENPA. Many things remain to be done—providing shelters for dogs and cats, stopping the use of live captive pigeons as shooting targets, controlling provincial slaughterhouses, and strengthening and reorganising the volunteer animal inspectors. None of this has been tackled by the council, in spite of all that I urged them to do.'

I spoke to Professor Rizzoli while I was in Venice, and he gave me permission to publish what I wished of this letter, telling us that we must act as if ENPA did not exist. In fact, it effectively does not exist in Venice. Dingo is the only animal welfare organisation in that city.

* * *

On the north side of the Ponte dell 'Accademia, Dingo advertises its aims and concerns and invites new contacts.

To try to improve our bad financial position, the committee is trying a new experiment. An advertisement has been inserted in the local paper: 'Let Dingo help you. We offer typing; dressmaking; knitting; nurse visits; translations; your fruit preserved; musical evenings (hi-fi); home-made bread and cakes, etc.'

Have any members of Dingo got talents that they could offer as fund raisers in their local paper? Baby sitting and boarding pets are possible further suggestions . . .

—from the Second Annual Report of Dingo, the Anglo-Venetian Group for the Protection of Stray Animals, October 1970.

* * *

Income and Expenditure Account
for the year ended October 31, 1972

Subscriptions and Donations	£506.06
Coffee Morning and Special Efforts	£46.88
Sale of Works of Art	£33.00

From the Chairman's Report, (Mrs H. Sanders)

The professional statement of accounts hides the fact that we have done some queer things to get money. We have found that coffee mornings and bazaars do not attract custom, although we were very

Gondolas moored just west of the Piazza San Marco.

glad to receive contributions from Mrs Warner's coffee mornings, and Miss Sindall's Sales of Work.

In Truro our efforts have taken some curious forms. In a past annual report we referred to Dingo Services—a series of advertisements offering musical evenings, typing, dressmaking, translations, and other skills. It received no response, although a local paper gave it middle page publicity. But I received a number of strange requests, including making two school dresses, translating a letter into more or less commercial Italian, and an SOS from Falmouth Police, who found my name on a twenty-year-old list of interpreters, long before I started to take Italian seriously, and begged me to come and interpret for three German seamen, accused of taking a boat. My only dictionary has tiny, illegible Gothic print, and I was never very good at reading.

I allowed myself to be persuaded. I got on quite well during the interrogation, and I charged and warned them. But as we were going into Court, a policeman said, 'Ask them if they accept the jurisdiction of this Court, or if they'd prefer to be tried by jury. Then I had to swear a terrifying interpreter's oath. However, all went well, except for one awful moment when nothing but Italian would come. I earned £9 for our funds.

My husband now has a gondola, the only genuine Venetian gondola afloat in Great Britain, and he is the only English gondolier. Last year, we spent a lot of money licensing it to ply for hire, in aid of Dingo; insurance, lifejackets and so forth came to £40. But no one was interested, and by bullying the local tourists we only got £30 of our money back. But it is a great attraction to photographers, and we also ask them to give to Dingo.

My husband has a collection of uniforms, and I have a collection of Victorian and Edwardian dresses. They are in demand for plays and fancy dress. We hire them out for Dingo. He is a sculptor, but because of the workings of the Inland Revenue, he cannot earn anything by the sale of his sculpture. So, Dingo benefits, either from the sale of his work, or by commissions from flower arrangers, some of whom win awards, using pieces he has made for their compositions.

All this is hidden under 'coffee mornings and special efforts'. I mention this, in case members have possessions, or talents, that they can employ in this way. Mrs Wilson sold some antique silver for us. Mrs Selzer asks her friends for the price of a pint of milk. Any more ideas . . . ?

—1972

* * *

Helena's frequent base in Venice was the American Hotel, in the Rio di San Vio, south of the Grand Canal. There is no particular reason why it should be called American, but then there is a Hotel Splendide near Mornington Crescent in London which is as French as boiled beef. Neither sumptuous nor Spartan, the American Hotel has a downstairs lobby where Helena would sit of an evening scribbling notes to remind herself of the next day's itinerary, and to remind others of duties so far neglected. Then she would make a few telephone calls from the front desk—you could hear her shout,

'Listen! Listen!' as she tried to punctuate a stream of Italian with her own remarks, or simply to slow it down to intelligibility—before putting her shoes back on (sometimes, after a hard day's trudging, a well worn pair of carpet slippers) and strolling the hundred yards or so between her hotel and the Trattoria Cugnai, a narrow, chaotic and delightful restaurant, well away from the main tourist arenas, which offers good food at prices that are, in Venetian terms, not unreasonable.

Sometimes for a change she would take the *vaporetto* to Lista di Spagna, at the other end of Venice, where an English friend and her Italian husband run their own trattoria. Before supper, they might walk a little way to visit a colony of cats so shy of human contact that the only evidence one ever saw of their existence was a paw flicked rapidly out from beneath a wooden warehouse gate to hook in a few morsels of food. Later, conversations over pasta, polenta and veal often turned on the delicacies of capture and castration, on new recruits and backsliders, willing vets and obstructive bureaucrats, crooks and charlatans who thought they could leach Dingo funds, and news from the frontier posts of their campaign—the sites where cat-women and other helpers voluntarily left food for strays, and risked abuse and violence.

Back in her hotel room, Helena fished in the mini-bar for her usual nightcap—a quarter bottle of red wine. Next day there would be more vets to see, more labyrinths of Venetian law and process to negotiate, and more conscripts to be bound so tightly into the organisation and so deftly and completely encumbered with jobs that a bolt for freedom became an impossibility. And although she said she had no time for sightseeing, as she roved the canals and alleys by waterbus and on foot, her eyes were always open, taking in the totality of Venice, savouring its changing moods, looking for the tiny details which would enable her to lift her cat crusade from the particular and the local, and broaden its context until it was woven into the very life of the city; the motto on the side of a church, perhaps—or three words daubed on the side of a building.

* * *

La Lotta Continua—The Fight Goes On!

> The communist slogan is scribbled all over the walls of Venice, but it might well be the motto of Dingo. Ever since we arrived in 1965, the state animal society has opposed us, with the exception of the brief period when Professor Rizzoli was the director. He was a staunch ally and fellow worker for the animals—a fighter and much too progressive for his colleagues. Perhaps he was also too honest. He was sacked.

Now the fight goes on, not only between us and them, but a free-for-all among the few animal lovers, who run each other down, and denigrate each other's work. It is very sad, and very silly, and a fearful waste of energy. A few years ago I ran into someone who had never been to Lazzaretto Vecchio, the island where we run our unofficial dog sanctuary. I had been the day before, and had seen the splendid condition of the dogs and their happy surroundings, but she assured me continuously for an hour that it was 'a disaster'.

ENPA decided that dogs were not to go to the island, and because of the ban many dogs were taken to the slaughterhouse by their owners or by municipal dog catchers, and were killed or sent to laboratories. But one day the Provincial Vets, very powerful people, paid a surprise visit to the island, saw the well cared for dogs, and arranged for the ban to be lifted.

—1973

* * *

The same issue of the annual report carried a translation of an article from the Venetian daily paper *Gazzetino*:

Stormy Waters at Venice Branch Meeting of ENPA

Tragi-comic scenes occurred with about 75 people collected outside the hall demanding loudly to be admitted. Accusations were exchanged, and strong opinions were expressed. Somebody was knocked down against a wall, and others threatened legal action: an unedifying babel for those involved, mostly elderly people and ladies. The meeting was called for 2.30 yesterday afternoon. It had already been the subject of dispute for fourteen days. Then, on September 16, a letter was sent to various high officials asking as a matter of urgency that the meeting should be banned, because eighty members of the society had been prevented from voting so as to obtain a big majority for the official candidates. Professor Rizzoli, the ex-President, said that to this end the notices had been sent out too late with the object of excluding certain members. And even worse, according to the Professor, some regular subscribers had not been invited. The atmosphere was white hot. At one point the police were called. The argument went on until the evening. It is not known where all this leads. Certainly it does not seem to do the animals much good. Stray cats and dogs have not got the right to speak.

* * *

One of the cat 'mothers' extends her generosity to encompass Venice's other notorious population of wild creatures.

There are people in Italy who are as deeply concerned with preventing unnecessary distress to animals as are those in other countries. Most of them have been members of ENPA and many have tried to integrate their own attempts to help animals with its local sections. Others have made suggestions to the Secretariat in Rome. Throughout most of the 1960s there seems to have been a feeling that ENPA was not making the best of the opportunities presented by this volunteer force because of certain internal deficiencies. In the last years such feelings have hardened into a belief that ENPA has become largely obsessed with bureaucratic concerns and has little interest in improving the welfare of animals. Rather than accepting competent help from those willing to give it, the accusation arises that those who are sufficiently concerned to take positive action are being gradually eliminated from local branches. During the last year or so some of the most patient and diplomatic of these volunteers have actually resigned in despair to protect their reputations.

The last ten years in particular have seen the establishment of a growing number of private organisations dedicated to special aspects of animal welfare. In the beginning they often sought to work in collaboration with ENPA. Their frustration has led them to criticise the state organisation openly, and finally to fight it . . .

With the expulsions and accusations of corruption now levelled against prominent ENPA officials in Rome, a purge has begun to spread through the branches. Signora Scarpabolla had been hoping to tell me of a final victory, but her latest letter makes it plain that an important trial is about to begin. Witnesses have been told to stand by. The law is even slower in Italy than in England . . .

The paper *Animalia* also has a depressing account of the killing of birds in Italy, in spite of the valiant efforts of the recently organised conservationists. This article refers to an astonishing law that permits the hunters to enter private property. The slaughter of small birds, many of them migrants from Britain, continues—with two million guns, netting, lime and decoys. In this sphere, too, *la lotta continua*. I mention these facts because sometimes we feel rather sorry for ourselves in Great Britain, since so little is done for conservation and there is so much cruelty. But the dedicated animal lovers and conservationists of Italy have a much harder struggle. Their courage and persistence, in Venice and all over the country, is beyond praise. One cheering piece of news is that there is a small group of young professional men who are prepared to co-operate to secure the continuation of the work started by our efforts . . .

—1976

* * *

This year the report is very late, for which I apologise, but the reason is that it has been impossible to get news out of Venice. I have written several times, and to several people, with no result at all. So finally I rang up. This is never a very satisfactory procedure, because the Venetians think it is a spy, and reply monosyllabically. And it's not easy to follow Signora Scarpabolla on the telephone. But at last I did ring her up, to be told that a tremendous fight was going on to save Lazzaretto Vecchio, and that the trial for corruption of the ex-ENPA chairman, who had always tried to harm Dingo, has not yet finished. This trial, which was promised for the summer of 1976 after a two-year delay, did start at the beginning of this year, but the hearings have not yet been completed.

Everyone to whom I spoke when I was last in Venice was waiting to see what would happen to ENPA, which seems a worthy child of its fascist founder. It has almost always opposed and hindered Dingo, as it has hindered and expelled true animal lovers in other parts of Italy. It was therefore on a list of useless societies that the Italian Government wanted to abolish. All the people to whom I spoke said they would prefer to see it reformed and purified, but a few months ago, the Government decided that ENPA was past saving, and it was wiped out, unlamented.

Everyone in Venice and Treviso is very worried about the abuse of animals in laboratories. In Italy there is not even the inadequate protection given to animals by our law of 1876. All stray dogs are liable to be sold to laboratories, or to medical students, and to be the victims of experiments performed without anaesthetics. I saw posters in every veterinary surgery asking people to sign a petition for the control of animal experiments, and the Venetians were most anxious that we should get the issue publicised in the British media. But I have had no success at all in this respect. It is a great scandal . . .

Meanwhile the cat work goes on, witnessed by the vets' forms I continue to receive, and the bills. Since the start of the year 193 cats have received veterinary treatment, 52 have been spayed, and 30 neutered, in the towns of Venice, Mestre, and Treviso. This has cost more than £1,000. The accounts for this year are not yet available, but you will see from the figures we have that costs are continually rising.

My visit to Venice during the February storms was very short, but I managed to get quite a lot done. I saw only 14 cats during my first day, and they all looked well fed. Then we went behind a hoarding, and saw a large colony. I was struck by the fact that there were no kittens, and asked the woman who took them food what she did with the young. She replied, rather defensively, 'I use your forms to have them put down by the vet. I should have hundreds if I allowed them all to live.' Then she added, 'Of course, all mine at home are spayed, but these are too wild.' That phrase 'of course' represents a major victory for our cause. It is difficult to realise the change in thinking that it represents.

—1978

* * *

One cat in ten years can have eighty-four million descendants. If only one tenth of one per cent survive, there will still be 84,000. The lucky ones die quickly.

—1972

* * *

The case against the former chairman of Venice ENPA (who did everything possible to hinder our work, tried to turn us off our island, and published defamatory statements about us) alleged peculation and abuse of power. It has now failed for lack of proof and lapse of time, but he was amnestied and not cleared. Meanwhile the state machinery has taken its course, and ENPA was unable to show that it had a useful function.

—1979

* * *

Helena herself had direct experience of the extent of corruption. She was summoned to give evidence against a young man accused of embezzling welfare funds and supplying maimed pigeons for illegally organised shoots. 'I was marched ceremonially into court to give my testimony. The accused wasn't there, but the intention was to put my deposition on record against the day when he was brought before the judge.' That case, as well, stammered and shuffled its way through a tortuous legal system until time limits expired, and the accused man escaped with an amnesty. On another occasion, Gina Scarpabolla and Helena were nearly inveigled out of £500. 'A Venetian businessman told us he would get all the vets together and bargain with them to give good terms for a sanctuary. We met him on the Lido, and he talked and talked and put the come-hither on us. But when I asked about stray animals he gave himself away. "I won't have strays near the place," he declared. The scales fell from our eyes and a pit opened at our feet, and together we shouted, "No!" He'd planned to use our money to pay a kennelman to look after his pedigree dogs. "Oh well," he said with a shrug, "you've had an interesting evening. Goodbye." I'm told

Getting down (in broad daylight, too) . . . to business.

that's typical of how some Venetians operate. They do their best to get the better of you, but if you see through them at the last moment they just laugh and chalk it up to experience.'

But a benign epidemic of Dingo idealism slowly permeated Venice, and those animal lovers who saw a function for a purged and reconstituted version of ENPA managed to revive the local organisation and impose upon it a very different structure of goals and working methods. The existence of the old society in a new and friendly incarnation provided an official cachet which was valuable when the welfare teams wanted to carry their work into more recalcitrant parts of the community. It was a kind of birthday present for Dingo, on an anniversary that Helena marked with a modicum of foreboding in her 1979 report.

> It was on November 1, 1969, that the work we began in 1965 was put on a permanent and regular footing. At a party in my St Clement cottage, the documents were signed that made us into a registered charity. A telephone call to Venice linked us with a little band of supporters, of whom, alas, all but the indefatigable Signora Scarpabolla have since melted away. An enormous amount has been achieved. An enormous amount remains to be done. One thing is certain. Dingo needs more and more members. The work is never-ending. Inflation is increasing. The faithful sixty who comprised the original group are now nearer ninety. But some have died. Few are young, and, most disquieting of all, there is as yet no one who can be seen with certainty as a successor to me. Whoever runs Dingo must have a good knowledge of Italian and the Italians, and such people are not easy to find. I am fourteen years older than I was in 1965, and in fourteen years' time I shall be eighty-two, if I'm living and spared, as we say in Cornwall. But for the moment, the urgent need is for more members. So, gentle reader, will you pass this report on to a friend, and try to recruit one more? If everyone did that, we should be nearer to two hundred, and the Dingo finances would be on a much surer foundation . . .
>
> Incidentally, for those who have not heard the story, Dingo was a stray dog rescued by Signora Scarpabolla. It was he who first made her think seriously about animals, and to a large extent, though not entirely, to sacrifice a distinguished career as a painter to the desperate needs of the animals of Venice.

New blood would eventually flow into the organisation, and indeed, the transfusion from Venice itself at last allowed Helena to liberate the Italian section from its English parents. But in the early days, Dingo was most remarkable for the support it attracted in Great Britain. One of its first presidents was Jonquil Anthony, author for eighteen years of the pioneering radio soap opera *Mrs Dale's Diary*. She was also the honorary secretary of the Anglo-Italian Society for the Protection of Animals. 'It was while she held that post that we made our second visit to Venice, the one that caused such a stir,' Helena recalls. 'At first she disapproved, because she thought we'd mismanaged the affair, but she joined the polemics in the *Daily Telegraph* with a letter about the appalling condition of animal pounds in some Italian towns. Later in a telephone conversation she remarked that Dingo was "a wonderful institution", so I immediately asked her to be our President.' It was a canny move, at once enlisting a passionate supporter and a voice which had learned how to engage the nation's attention with its intimate and colloquial style. In her first letter to Dingo members, published in 1971, Jonquil described how she shared with Helena the experience of being drawn ineluctably into the business of animal welfare by a chance encounter.

It's a curious thing, but whenever friends of mine have been to Venice, they don't seem to have seen stray cats and dogs. I'm sure it's a question of what you're looking for. Personally, I have this awful failing. I can't go to any country without all the strays being alerted at once and ready to queue up to meet me at the airfield or the quay. As it doesn't happen to most people (but most probably to Dingo and AISPA members and those of other animal societies like ours) I can only assume that ordinary people are blind to these things and if they see a stray they just mumble, 'Oh, there's a dog—or a cat—running around,' and think no more of it.

My connection with Italian animals began when my husband and I were in Rome. We were doing a bit of culture, and on our way to see Keats's grave in the English cemetery, we had to go through some Roman slums, and we must have walked part of the way. We saw a miserable grey object scuttling round in the traffic and, to cut a long story short, got ourselves introduced to 'Bella'. Various Italians were bribed to find her, which took three days. She was then brought to our hotel overnight. We rushed her upstairs, terrified that our proprietors would see her, and bathed her in the bidet. To our amazement, a sort of large, pure white fluffy Pom came out. We were then able to say that she was an English lady's dog we were taking home. Everyone was delighted with her, so we called her Bella, since that's what they kept saying about her. Unfortunately she bit people's feet, because she'd been kicked in the past, but she'd evidently once been a pet.

But what I am really saying is that we just didn't know what else to do with her. There was no Italian RSPCA we could find out about, and the only thing we were told to do was to take her to the pound and the gas chamber. We didn't. We just trailed her around for six weeks, appropriately enough to Assisi, among other places.

As I was writing *The Dales* then, I got some publicity when I returned home, because I had to stay in Calais since Bella's quarantine papers hadn't come through, and I was late with my scripts and someone else took over. Having heard the touching story of Jonquil's dog, she put the whole story into *The Dales*. I was appalled, but when I got back there were photographers to meet us, and then, when at the end of the quarantine we were practically broke, there were more photographers. It was because of their pictures in the daily papers that AISPA sucked me into their committee, and I've never stopped working since on behalf of Italy's animals . . .

By the mid 'seventies, senior clergymen and bishops were among Dingo's members and allies, and the organisation boasted two distinguished patrons, Beverley Nichols, and a man whose youth was famous not for the intrusion of any cats, but for his father's chronicles of its invasion by a bear, a piglet, an owl, a rabbit, a kanga, a roo, and sundry other stuffed companions whose adventures became part of the international mythology of childhood. Christopher Robin Milne wrote in his inaugural address that he took his seat beside Beverley Nichols 'a little nervously', adding:

> What dare I say in his company?
> That I too love cats and share my home with five? That I have loved Italy since I first set foot on her shores one early morning in September, thirty-four years ago? That once I knew Venice well enough to navigate her narrow streets without map or guide from the Piazzale Roma to the Piazza San Marco? That earlier this year Lesley, my wife, rang the bell of Signora Scarpabolla's apartment and was momentarily mistaken for another Milne, a more regular visitor, my cousin Barbara, who is secretary of AISPA?
> These are my credentials and I hope they qualify me for the honour you so flatteringly bestow upon me.

Helena, with her usual blend of impudence and enterprise, had trawled Christopher Milne into Dingo after hearing him profess his love of cats during an edition of *Desert Island Discs*. He turned out to be an indefatigable propagandist for the cause, writing in 1978: 'Nearly three hundred Venetian cats are saying thank you to their kind friends in Cornwall and elsewhere for all the help they gave last year. How many more cats will be holding out their paws this year? Please do not disappoint them. I don't suppose that cats—or indeed any other creatures—have a very high opinion of humans just now. Let us prove to them that a few of us can still be kind and generous and loving.'

The cruelty to which he alluded was the continuing use of live animals for vivisection and experiment. But by 1982, the vociferous protests of Dingo and AISPA began to penetrate the chambers of Italian Government. On April 6, the Minister of Health announced that he intended 'to review the present standards relating to experiments on animals for the purpose of limiting the use to cases of proven scientific necessity.' He added that he hoped 'to encourage by opportune and appropriate allocation of funds research into alternative methods of experiments, and to support initiatives for drawing up regulations in this direction, in talks at the level of the Parliamentary Assembly of the Council of Europe.' Public institutions were ordered to reduce 'substantially' their expenditure on vivisection, and to divert the money saved into a fund which would be devoted to research into projects which did not entail cruelty. It was a considerable triumph. Government measures were investing animals with existential rights that Italian society—and theology—had previously denied. Exemplary steps were bound to influence public opinion, and the International Association Against Painful Experiments on Animals, to which Dingo was naturally affiliated, began to urge the Italian government to encourage private institutions to submit voluntarily to the same codes of practice. Helena advised her colleagues to mingle celebration with caution. 'Italians themselves are very sceptical. They say, for example, that a protest in Padua by a very active animal worker has resulted in stricter regulations there, but horrible things are still being done in secret.

'Every time I mention our live export problem there are groans and sighs and mutterings about the hideous trade in live food animals from Yugoslavia to Italy, and the number of animals that die of heat in railway trucks. There is also the continuing scandal, despite improvements, of the trade by sea of horses from Greece to Southern Italy. It's a sad world, but at last these issues are being ventilated on an international scale by animal lovers everywhere.'

It was a curious series of middle courses that Dingo had to steer. On the one hand, there were cranks and sentimentalists too squeamish to accept that the organisation's work inevitably involved euthanasia as well as food and veterinary treatment. On the other, there were brutes who seized on the soft words of a Jonquil Anthony, a Christopher Milne, or a Beverley Nichols ('the world would be a pleasanter place if there were a few more purrs') and used them to denounce the members of Dingo as cranks and sentimentalists. And again, so many issues seemed to insist on attention that the group might be tempted to spread its resources too thinly, and vitiate the effectiveness of a campaign that had its nominal root in the story of a dog, but was principally concerned with the health and survival of cats in one particular city. The dogs, however, would not go away. They had a habit of turning up, tails wagging appealingly, or paws trailing affectingly, or of howling, piteously, from beyond the slaughterhouse wall. Helena, who had given both dogs and cats house-room throughout the travels and travails of her life, would not allow Dingo to limit the scope of its manifesto by introducing an anti-dog apartheid.

'Our articles of association mentioned "cats and other animals" because I foresaw that we might need to help dogs as well,' she wrote in 1985.

According to a local by-law, all dogs in Venice must be muzzled. Any dog without a muzzle could be seized by dog catchers and taken to the slaughterhouse. If it was not claimed within three days, it was shot, or sent to the laboratories in Padua.

For fourteen years Dingo supported dog rescue because no one else was interested. AISPA paid the warden on Lazzaretto Vecchio a small salary, but apart from that, Gina Scarpabolla and a pensioner ran the refuge on a shoestring, with whatever help Dingo could give. On one occasion a supporter sent £250 to repair wire netting which had rotted in the salt air. It was all spent on food. In the ten years from 1970 to 1980 Gina rescued and homed 1,000 dogs. In 1980 Dingo handed the island refuge over to the Italian Dog League but foolishly continued to pay for veterinary treatment, a fact that contributed to our running out of funds. The two organisations are now entirely separate, and Dingo has reverted to cats, its original concern.

Helena's annual reports show that despite its widening circle of renown and support, Dingo was forever being threatened by cash crises.

Unfortunately we were only able to send £200 to Venice for the dogs during the year under review, and because of financial stringency, even this will have to be cut during the current year. A few, a very few generous Venetians spend a great deal of their own money, as well as a lot of time and energy, on the welfare of the city's animals. Many people feed the cats, some of them at great personal cost. Many people use our forms and take cats to the vets. And without the energy and devotion of Signora Scarpabolla, organised work in Venice would come to an end.

During the year the number of cats spayed rose from 29 to 63. During the same period, 114 were put to sleep, 12 males were castrated, and 60 received veterinary treatment. But spaying is expensive, and although Doctor Valetti does it for half price at 5,000 lira (about £3.30) we ended the year in debt, and quickly acquired more debts. I have had to lend the group more than £200 to pay vets' bills. We have spent all the donations that we received at the time of our inception, and subscriptions are not coming in quickly enough to replace them. Please try to make our work better known, and try to get us more members. Please remember the Anglo-Venetian group in your will . . .

—1971

* * *

The vets' bills came to over £1,000 during the year under review, and at the same time there was a very serious drop in our income from subscriptions. It is all the more serious because, unlike most charities, which are contracting under the strain of inflation, Dingo is expanding. It is mad, but there it is. We were asked to extend our veterinary work to a town called Treviso, about twenty miles from Venice, where there was a serious stray cat problem. What could we do . . . ?

—1977

* * *

Dingo is facing the most serious challenge of its career. Paradoxically it is threatened by its own success and its growing importance. We have about a hundred members. All are generous and some are exceptionally so. None can be asked to give more. There is a possibility that Dingo's growth and importance may put it out of business.

In 1982–83 our work doubled, and the veterinary treatments cost nearly £7,000. This was made possible as in addition to income from subscriptions and covenants we had a legacy of £1,000 and two generous donations amounting to £2,000. Alas, it all went on vets' bills, and even so, I was obliged to appeal to AISPA, who had promised us help. They came to our aid with £2,000. The money soon went. My husband gave the whole of the payment in advance for a large sculpture that had been commissioned, and there were other benefactors. AISPA gave another £700, and just as that was exhausted £5,000 of capital, a legacy from my aunts which had been invested with Cornwall County Council, matured and was paid into Dingo's account. Half of that has gone already. What happens when it's all gone?

Venetian animal lovers have come to rely on our forms as the basis of their work. Unfortunately there is no power on earth that can prevent the needy and responsible women to whom the forms are giving from passing on 'just a few' to richer friends. I am telling our vets that it is most important that the forms are only used for ownerless cats and the animals of the poor. Well dressed and obviously well-to-do people who present a form must be firmly told that they must pay for their own pet. Dingo's funds are not for that. I have also drafted a letter for all vets saying that we cannot spend more than £17.50 on spaying, or a little more if the cat is pregnant. In cases of complicated operations such as piometria or uterine tumours, which can cost as much as £35, the cat must be put down unless someone is willing to share the cost. Even so, 284 spays at £17.50 a time would cost us £3,622 . . .

—1984

Within a few weeks of the 1984 report reaching Dingo's members, the organisation was on the edge of bankruptcy, and Helena began to take steps to salvage what she could from a collapse she thought was inevitable. Vets were told to suspend the treatments they had been performing: there was no money left to pay their bills. Ironically, the emergency was the spur that Venice needed to discover its own muscle and achieve independence. Bewilderment and distress turned to resolution. The members of the newly formed Cat Committee of the Venetian Dog League sought out Gina Scarpabolla and asked why the veterinary service on which local animal lovers had begun to depend—many without too much curiosity about the funds that sustained it—had suddenly ceased operations. Gina explained, and very shortly, Venetian Dingo was formed. 'My most thrilling moment in Venice came when I put my signature to a document in a lawyer's office transferring responsibility to the local group,' says Helena. 'Now they can legally collect money and sue in cases of cruelty to cats.'

By now, she was used to the intervention of what appeared to be the miraculous, or at least the providential, in Dingo's affairs. Once she had authorised an exorbitant round of spaying when there was absolutely no money in the bank to meet the bills. 'I remembered the promise that, if we had faith, we could move mountains and uproot trees. In fear and trembling, I decided to act on this premise. "Yes, go ahead, spay them all."

'The money began to trickle in. But as the days went by, and my visit to Venice got nearer and nearer, there was still not enough. A week before I was due to leave, we were £100 down. I was leaving on the Sunday night. The Monday before, a cheque for £100 arrived in the post . . .

'The availability of money to meet our needs seemed little short of miraculous. I once prayed for £1,000 and received two cheques for that sum. On one occasion, when we were short of money to pay a vet's bill, a man arrived at our house in search of plaques to decorate a house. Some long forgotten work by my husband turned out to be just what he wanted. The price—the vet's fee . . .

'Gina has many problems, not least her own health, and the necessity of feeding up to a hundred strays at any one time. In order to economise, she burns wood rather than gas to cook their food. Once we were visiting the State Archivist, a young man whose goodness and kindness are as great as his intellect. We were trying to plan the future with him, and Gina mentioned her need for wood. "Wood, did you say? I beg you, I beseech you, I supplicate you, come along with me.'' Then he led the way through a maze of buildings, vault after cathedral-like vault, stretching up to the sky, lined with tome after tome of papers, the history of the city of Venice, surely since written records began. On we went, and the mouldering vaults seemed endless. They are prone to mice, and a well-fed and much-loved army of cats is maintained to keep them down. At last we came to a ruined cloister, and there in the middle was a pile of wood as big as a house. ''Please take it away,'' he begged. I was wondering how we could get it back along all the corridors, but he opened a door on to a square, near which ran a canal. In a nearby garden there was almost as big a pile. We had wood for life.'

Pragmatism and prayer. There are sanctuaries now in Venice, for both cats and dogs. 'It is most encouraging to see the amount of time and money Venetian animal lovers are prepared to spend. I visited the house of a woman on the Lido who is not only supplying gravel for the kennels, but arranges the spaying of all the cats in her neighbourhood. When we first went to Venice, spaying was almost unknown, and on the rare occasions when it was mentioned, the mood was of disapproval. I have the feeling now that we didn't so much start a movement as catch a tide.'

In 1984, the Venetians announced that they proposed to bestow on Helena Sanders *un onore ed un onere*—an honour and a burden. She was to join the select company of the Knights of St Mark. Her investiture took place in April the following year.

'We assembled outside the church of San Moise at 9.30 in the morning. There were several knights wearing their chains and the bifurcated cross of St Mark. We went in, and I was introduced to the Venetian lady knight who was to present me. The new Cavalieri sat in two rows of five at the front of the church—nine Italian men, with me at the end of the row. First of all there was an announcement about a death, and I did not immediately understand that the person who had died was the wife of the Doge, the head of the order. But with great fortitude he performed his duties.

'My presenter called me out. I told her that I didn't know what to do, that if I knelt down I would be unable to get up again. She reassured me and took me to face the congregation. A list of my supposed virtues was read out, mentioning work for Jewish refugees and ending with a reference to the founding of Dingo. All the men were then invested in turn, and my sponsor took me again before the Doge. He placed the chain with the cross around my neck, saying, ''I admit you in the name of our Holy Patron. Be a good citizen.'' I can't remember now if he spoke in Italian or Latin. The lady pinned on a small buttonhole with the miniature badge, and put her white cloak around my shoulders, symbolising, I suppose, that ''you are one of us''.

'Un onore ed un onere'. Helena newly installed as a Knight of St Mark in 1985. 'My almost new shoes were killing me. I hobbled back to the hotel and kicked them off . . .'

'There was a Mass and a sermon, and we all had our photographs taken. After that we went into the church hall for wine and cocktail dainties. The first person I met told me he'd been in Dachau for 23 months. Then some people sang 'It's a Long Way to Tipperary' with me. My feet had swollen up on the plane and, because of the heat, my almost-new shoes were killing me. I hobbled back to the hotel and kicked them off. After that I wandered around Venice in awful bedroom slippers with a hole in them.'

It had certainly been a long journey from the confusion of a caption announcing, 'Truro Woman Arrested by Venice Police', to reports in British newspapers describing how an Englishwoman had received one of the highest honours the citizens of Venice had in their gift. There were still some modestly abusive letters to contend with from myopic individuals who wanted to know what was so special about Italian animals; weren't there suffering creatures on the right side of the Channel that deserved her care? To coin a phrase, as bigots always do when they wear a proverb into a cliché in the service of their prejudices, charity begins at home, you know. To which Helena could succinctly reply that her long-distance crusade had been conducted in parallel with an uninterrupted rescue mission among the unwanted and neglected cats of Cornwall.

And there were others who wrote to say, as a man said to me at lunch in a restaurant today, why animals, eh? I mean, all your soft-headed and soft-hearted animals lovers are wasting valuable time and money that ought to be spent on humans, aren't they? And Helena could look back on a lifetime's dedication to the needs of the underprivileged and the rights of human victims of human aggression, and wonder, perhaps, about that bizarre mentality which supposes that the charitable impulse must discriminate and exclude, rather than encompass and expand and embrace.

For Helena, the transitions between the homeless, and the unemployed, and the refugees, and the sick or abused cats, dogs and pigeons of Venice were seamless. Her mind moved always towards unity, and the force that held the disparate limbs together was faith: profound, apparently unshaken by any adversity, constantly renewing and refreshing itself in each of the phases of her career; and willing to explore whatever realms of heterodoxy might further stock the arsenal to defend and advance the cause in hand. In 1973, she pillaged the bulletin of the Anglican Society for Animal Welfare to grasp and reprint this helpful paragraph from 'The Apocryphal Gospel of the Holy Twelve', dating, according to scriptural authorities, from the fourth century:

> . . . And as Jesus entered into a certain village he saw a young cat who had none to care for her, and she was hungry and cried unto him,

The hidden Venice: 'alleys that with one twist discard the crowds'.

and he took her up and put her inside his garments and she lay in his bosom. And when he came to the village he set food and drink before her and she ate and drank and gave thanks unto him. And he gave her unto one of his disciples whose name was Lorentia, and she took care of her. And some of the people said, 'This man careth for all creatures. Are they his brothers and sisters that he should love them?' And he said unto them, 'Verily, these are your fellow creatures of the great household of God: yea, they are your brothers and sisters, having the same breath of life in the Eternal. And whosoever careth for one of the least of these, and giveth it to eat and drink in its need, the same does it unto me, and whosoever suffereth one of these to be in want and defendeth it not when evilly treated suffereth the evil as done unto me: and as ye have done in this life, so shall it be done unto you in the life to come . . .'

It was a text which Helena Sanders would quite happily have stitched into the main body of her Bible.

CHAPTER ELEVEN

GUY

Twenty years, it took, to reduce the cats of Venice from a miserable and sickly multitude numbering 68,000 or so to a stable and healthy population of around 6,000. Guy Sanders, although he was the sort of chap who would devise a census method smart enough to obviate the need for 'around' and 'or so', found 'this cat business' a bit of a bore, despite the fact that he was more than happy to share his home in Cornwall with two goats, two geese, two peafowl and a feline contingent that usually averaged eight. He began to cast around for ways to pass the time while his wife was engaged on her errands for Dingo, and quickly made friends with another cat widower, Francesco Scarpabolla, Gina's husband, who was a notable Venetian sculptor. Guy was too overawed by the quality of Francesco's work to offer his designs for the older man's appreciation or criticism. 'Professor Scarpabolla is so brilliant and so good that I just dare not try to emulate him,' he once explained. 'I'll ruin the little skill that I have if I try to be more skilled than I can be. Actually there's nothing in Venice that I feel I can use as inspiration, because if I wanted to take anything it would be his work, and I really can't go near it. I've got to fight my own battle.' But the two men talked endlessly about form and expression, and Guy lodged in the Professor's studio whenever he could. Francesco Scarpabolla paid his English disciple an artist's compliment when he said to Helena: 'I don't know if Guy is a good sculptor or not, but he understands.'

In 1965, Guy and Helena travelled to Florence, and both were enthralled by the quality of craftsmanship in an ancient silk factory they discovered there. They bought an altar cloth for the church of St Clement. The next year, when Helena was dealing with the devastation caused by Italy's floods in Venice and the Po Valley, Guy asked her to phone the silk factory to find out if they needed his help. It transpired that water had flooded the building to a depth of nine feet. Fragile patterns that dated from the Renaissance needed salvaging and restoration. Wooden looms and instruments were buried deep in mud. The factory had become a swamp, and the heritage of centuries of skill and invention was on the brink of oblivion. Guy rang his bank manager—it was a Sunday—and organised some funds. By the Monday afternoon he was in Florence, and he stayed there for a month, helping to excavate the equipment, and to transport bolts of silk and brocade out of danger and away to a place where they could be carefully dried and repaired. In the year that followed, he made a sculpture to commemorate the rescue. Mounted on a plinth of Cornish slate, it depicted a series of hands, first grubbing frantically in mud, then retrieving the looms, and finally draped in lengths of material. He drove the piece to Florence and presented it to the factory proprietor, who announced that his first reaction to the flood had been despair. He believed he had no choice but to close the works and make his twelve craftsmen redundant. 'But since an Englishman felt our enterprise was so important that he gave us a month of his life, and then designed this beautiful sculpture, we will stay open and keep our traditions alive.'

Many of Guy's sculptures, as we have already seen, were sold in aid of Dingo. But what of the gondola on the River Lemon, into which hesitant tourists were enticed in exchange for fares that also helped to advance the cat crusade? That was another spin-off from a bored husband's daily voyages around a watery city. You have to imagine him, I think, on the fifth or sixth visit. By now he has by heart the lore and detail which would give him such an impressive guide-book patter when he was fortunate enough to team up with English novices adrift in Venice. But on this occasion he is alone, resisting the temptation to tread on the tail of a cat that symbolises his wife's distractions. Moodily, an ex-Royal Marine marooned on dry land, he eyes a nearby gondolier. Then plucks up the nerve to speak in gruff Anglo-Italian.

'Look here. I'd like to learn to row a gondola.'

'What?' There tends to be a shortage of tactful phrasing in any boatman's vocabulary. 'Don't be absurd. No one but a Venetian could ever master a gondola.' A pause as he shifts the tapering craft demonstratively under his feet. 'Certainly not an Englishman.'

Which was enough, of course, to doom an Englishman like Guy Sanders to become a solitary and voluntary galley slave. There is a sort of skiff that the Venetians use to train themselves for the more complex manoeuvrings of a gondola. You progress from two paddles to the long, familiar oar. Guy took himself off to the outer islands and skiffed himself about with stumbling determination. Then he found an old crock among the gondolas in a repair yard. He jabbed it with his penknife to make sure it was not terminally decayed, and haggled a bargain price with the owner. The vessel was dismantled, packed in a railway carriage and transported back to England, where the receiving station staff, on opening the doors, were nearly suffocated by mingled odours of fishbones, mud, and sundry droppings. Once she had been scrubbed and reassembled, the gondola took her owner on a maiden circuit of the River Lemon.

'Circuit' is the right word, for the skiff turned out to have been inadequate preparation. 'I really hadn't got a clue how to row it at first,' Guy admitted once, when he had just navigated a smooth passage down the Rio della Madonna dell'Orto without raising a derisive or even an inquisitive glance from the surrounding Venetians. 'We had a fight which lasted seven days. Even though I'd been working in boats for years, this was one that seemed to have a mind of her own. You've got the oar on one side, and of course, she used to go round and round in circles, and I just didn't know how to get her back on course. But then I discovered that if I pushed in a certain direction I'd compensate for the natural bias, and eventually I got her straight and she began to go where I wanted instead of where she wanted to go. For six days she did it her way, but on the seventh I won the battle. But the trouble with this old gondola was that she was rather down in the nose, and her lines weren't what they had been, and often she wanted to behave more like a submarine than a gondola.'

A few more months pass by, and Guy is once again in Venice. He sees a beautifully maintained gondola. Recent heavy rains have left an inch or so of water in her. 'I thought to myself, this man obviously loves his craft. He'll be here before long to bale her out.' And within half an hour or so, the man was there and had begun baling.

'Good morning.'

'Good morning.'

'Where's this, do you think?'

The gondolier examines the proffered photograph, lifts his cap, and scratches his head with the edge of his baling can. 'Wide waters. Out beyond San Giorgio Maggiore, perhaps?'

'No.'

'Torcello?'

'No.'

'Don't recognise it at all.'

'England. Cornwall, to be more precise. To the west of the country.'

'England? Who's the gondolier?'

'Me.'

'You?' The gondolier reacts with laughter that's full of admiration, and not contempt. From that moment, Mario and his fellows were among Guy's closest friends in Venice. By day, when they had the time, they taught him to perfect his oarsmanship, and by night, while Helena attended her meetings and ruffled civic and social feathers, he joined them at their favourite cafés and discussed, well, gondoliering, naturally, and any other subject that occurred, with the possible exception of cats.

Guy was never allowed to carry passengers, because Venetian statutes require gondoliers who ply for hire to pass an official test and hold a licence. But he did become an honorary or assistant member of their company, and they used him, affectionately, one hopes, to save both their legs and their dignity. While the excursion gondola is a rather exorbitantly priced vehicle from which to view the sights, the craft have a more humble and inexpensive function ferrying people across the Grand Canal at various stations—known as *traghetti*—between the three bridges. Like most commercial and commuter traffic, the flow at certain times of the day is entirely in one direction. So the gondoliers would whistle up Guy Sanders, announce that their trade for the time being was between *traghetto* A and *traghetto* B, and he would keep fit and practise his rowing and steering by racing along alleys and across bridges to *traghetto* B, then taking an empty gondola back to *traghetto* A.

His efforts were crowned one afternoon when he accompanied two gondoliers who were using a limousine among gondolas as the official carriage for a wedding. 'When we got to the *pensione* where the reception was being held, they went inside and asked me to look after their gondola. It was a beautiful craft, decorated with gold, and I stayed with it and when the tourists came along I tried to answer their questions as best I could either in Italian or in English, which caused something of a surprise, since I was dressed in a proper gondolier's uniform. Eventually, hours later, it seemed, two very inebriated gondoliers staggered out of the reception and yelled, "Bring the boat over here." So I said, "What, me?" And they said, "Yes, bring the boat over here." So I took it over and they more or less fell into it, each clutching a little gift they'd been given at the wedding, and they told me to take them home. I had no choice. The President of the Republic happened to be reviewing a parade in St Mark's Square and it seemed the whole of Venice was watching, but somehow I got the damned thing along the Grand Canal. Everybody was waving and getting out of our way because they assumed my tipsy gondoliers were the bride and groom, and I was taking them to their wedding.

'Just when I thought I'd got them safely back to base they yelled at me to turn left, which I did at great speed, narrowly missing a *vaporetto*, and I discovered that they'd tipped off all their friends that I'd be bringing them home, and I had to row ceremonially along this narrow canal with people lining the sides cheering and shouting, "Long live the English Gondolier!" It was extremely embarrassing.'

When Mario died of cancer a couple of years later, he left instructions that Guy Sanders, who had proved he was 'a passionate artist of the gondola' should have first refusal of his craft. So the old crock with submarine pretensions was replaced by a new gondola, chased with gold and equipped with traditional ornament, which Guy displayed not only in the rivers and estuaries around Truro, but also, one year, at Henley. It is now on exhibition at Exeter's Maritime Museum.

At home, as well as abroad, Guy seemed in the mid-seventies to be at the zenith of creativity. His work among the oyster fishermen had saved an ancient industry from destructive commercial pressures. The practices he restored were economically sound and aesthetically pleasing. Once again, the men were fishing under sail instead of motor, and young oysters were left to develop undisturbed. As a sculptor he was also commanding interest. He experimented with mosaic tiles, brought home from journeys to France and Italy, and received two important commissions. A nine-foot relief of Christ the King was fashioned for St Mary's Church, Edmonton, and, nearer home, in 1976 he made a figure of Temperance and a bust of Kenstek, a Celtic Bishop of Cornwall in the ninth century, for the porch of Truro Cornwall. Cold tea from the bottom of his studio thermos flask stained the freshly carved stone so that it merged into the surrounding façade. Guy was then invited to add further decorations to the reredos, and designed a set of angels blowing trumpets. He had advanced the project well beyond preliminary sketches, constantly conferring with Dean and architect, when, through some internal confusion, it was discovered that permission had yet to be granted by the Cathedral Chapter—and when it was sought, the sculptures were rejected on grounds of principle, not of quality. It was, says Helena, 'a crushing blow' with traumatising effects on his self-confidence.

'He wrote to ask if, instead, he might make some more figures for the niches outside, and never received a reply. Guy always said to me that his sculpture was his worship. His designs for another Royal Cornwall Show display were also rejected, and he never set foot in a church again. Even when we were on holiday in France, and we stopped to look at a church, he would not go inside. One day I heard him talking to a friend on the telephone and he said, "I don't go to church any more. I was turned out." '

He would, however, invent and execute one more bravura design on a religious theme, not for the Church of England, but on behalf of Cornwall's Methodists: at Gwennap Pit, the ancient earthwork where John Wesley preached eighteen times between 1762 and 1789, and where Helena had produced her extract from a Cornish mystery play nearly thirty years before. Guy's brief was to create a series of panels expressing the origins and beliefs of Wesleyan Methodism, and its circulation through the world. Three mosaics, surrounded by carved texts, are the principal features of the display. One simply offers a polychrome 'welcome'; a second shows the globe of the world, swirling with colour and light, and

Guy Sanders with the mosaic globe he designed and made for his Wesley memorial at Gwennap Pit in Cornwall.

the third depicts Wesley himself, his arm raised to a miniature congregation of sculpted figures whose costumes and features betray their descent from each class and generation since the eighteenth century, and from the nations of all continents. Guy described them as uncharacterised sketches, explaining that 'this was a wise decision because I possess an impish flair for caricature which ought not to be indulged in such sober surroundings.'

He was surprised that they excited such attention from visitors. 'I regarded them as throw-away material.' The care which he had applied to their devising belies the tone of self-deprecation. Each group of figures was carefully planned and executed to capture social styles and manners, and a self-portrait was included by way of signature. If you go to Gwennap Pit, you will find a dwarf Guy Sanders supporting the figure of Charles Wesley, the preacher's brother.

There were, though, fraught times in the early stages of the composition. Months intervened between the commission and the arrival of architect's plans, and Helena feared that if the project failed through neglect, Guy's might once again succumb to despondency. Secretly, she telephoned and berated the people who seemed to be responsible for the delays. At one point she received a six-page amalgam of excuses, apologies, and complaints. Afraid that his plans were being misinterpreted, threatening another reason for the whole enterprise to collapse, Guy eventually added the role of labourer to his other functions. Commissioned in 1983, the panels were finally complete and open to the public two years later.

In the meantime, Guy and Helena were approaching another climacteric year. The couple went to Gwennap Pit during the Whitsun Holiday of 1984, partly to worship, and partly to mingle with pilgrims who had travelled from all over the country to join a Methodist festival, and who were the first strangers to see work in progress on Guy's displays. The weather was atrocious, and very shortly afterwards, Helena was prostrated with influenza. After several weeks in bed, still more an invalid than a convalescent, she left St Clement with Guy on a journey to Andover, where members of her family had arranged a party to celebrate the couple's silver wedding. 'I was lurching about when I first got up from the 'flu, and even when I reached Andover I couldn't walk straight, and although we were very moderate with the wine, Guy thought I must be drunk, and so, I'm sure, did many other people there.'

From Andover they went to San Gimignano in Italy, where Helena began to recuperate slowly on a self-imposed prescription of 'gentle walking, drinking Chianti, sleeping, and, one warm evening, listening to a cellist playing in a square among the towers.' Guy had always regarded the Tuscan town as his *hortus conclusus*, and that year's holiday was their sweetest and one of their last together. He returned to Cornwall, and she moved on to Venice for a few days. 'When I got back I was still very unsteady on my feet, so I went to see the doctor, and he discovered that I'd suffered a mild stroke.' She permitted herself as much rest as her temperament allowed, and by early the following year was ready for her installation as a Knight of St Mark, and a happy return to England.

It would be absurd at this distance in time and space to attempt to arbitrate the hostilities that seethe among the herbaceous borders and beneath the thatch of charming villages. By and large, one may remark, the residents of these aesthetic gintraps divide into two camps. The longer established incline to be relaxed about change, and even languidly innovative in their attitudes. More ultra-montane are the recent arrivals, who would resist, one suspects, the advent of main drainage and electricity were these absent when they exchanged their contracts. One can state for a certain fact that St Clement had evolved over two decades or so from a remote hamlet over whose welfare and maintenance the stewards of its landlord, the Duke of Cornwall, mostly nodded, to a jealously desired conservation area whose property prices were already on the launch pad to astronomy before motorways and high speed trains scooped the far West Country into London's hinterland. And within the community, there were undertows of contending allegiance almost as deep and strong as the nearby tides.

Helena and Guy were partly responsible for the declaration of the village as a conservation area, because in the 1960s they had successfully fought to prevent the Duchy from replacing thatch with slate on a group of cottages in the square. But there had been mutterings, letters, and petitions about some of their own restorations and additions at Condurrow Cottage. And the yells of the peacocks had provoked howls of complaint from the sort of newcomers who believe the countryside should have the acoustic of a museum, and Guy had at last capitulated thoroughly—or charitably, if you prefer—and carted cocks and fowls off to a deserted farm, where he kept foxes at bay by camping with the birds overnight and keeping a monastic vigil himself while they screamed and explored their lusts during the few weeks of the mating season.

Another dispute erupted over an elderly and infirm couple, living just outside the conservation area, who wanted to sell their over-large house and build themselves a more manageable home in its grounds. But 'the clique went into action', and after antagonistic pieces had appeared in one of Cornwall's weekly newspapers, local councillors turned down the planning application. Helena intervened with the Department of the Environment, and the ruling was reversed in July 1985. The dates are important, because by this time numbers of villagers in St

Clement—our principals included—had ceased to talk to each other, and there was mounting tension in the atmosphere.

* * *

At the beginning of September, Guy Sanders, as usual, rose shortly after first light, put on the radio, and began to make some tea. Of all the cats at Condurrow Cottage, one was his particular favourite. He was called Tufty, and part of the morning ritual was to him send out for a stroll before breakfast. Fifteen minutes later Helena was woken in her room by her husband's cry. 'I can still hear those words,' she says. '"Something terrible has happened. Somebody has killed Tufty."'

The cat had dragged himself back across the threshold, a knife buried in his side. Guy and Helena thought they saw a youth slipping away across a nearby car park. They called the police. There was a friendly constable at the local station whom they always contacted in cases of animal cruelty, but now, when that cruelty came for the first time into their own home, the laws of irony arranged for the officer to have been called away to cope with a traffic accident. By the time other policemen had arrived, it was fruitless to organise a search for the mysterious boy.

'The police instituted inquiries and called at most of the houses in St Clement, but could find no trace of him,' Helena recalls. 'Then, after a week or more, I heard an old man who loved Tufty talking to a local woman about the case. She was saying it would be a good idea if he went to the police and accused five boys from a local housing estate who used to come to play in the village. They were probably as naughty as most boys of fourteen. They used to throw stones at the boats sometimes, and their most heinous crime in other people's eyes was that they actually ate the sloes from the blackthorns. But we liked them. I used to tease them, and they helped me to put the goats to bed—five boys to one goat. I didn't think they were responsible.

'When the woman had gone, the old man told me that her recent holiday tenant, a young man, had been a sadist. He tore the fins off her goldfish and scattered crumbs for her ducks and then tried to cut their legs off with sharp stones. When she'd seen a description in the local paper of the youth wanted for police interview, she'd said, "Oh, it was him," but she hadn't been to the police because she said she didn't want to be involved. In the meantime, he'd gone home to the north, and was never, in the absence of witnesses, interviewed or tried.'

* * *

In the living room of her cottage at St Clement, near Truro. Helena and two of her cats shortly before Guy's death and her departure to Cambridgeshire. *Photo: The Western Morning News*

Tufty's death had a devastating effect on Guy. His fits of depression, always intermittent, seemed to merge into a permanent melancholy, and his feelings for St Clement were poisoned. 'He stopped reading the newspaper or doing his crossword, and had no desire even to see people whom he liked. We used to sit in silence in the darkness until it was time to go to bed. He couldn't bear any reference to Tufty, and on one occasion I remember, when I foolishly said that he couldn't have suffered much, Guy started to cry. I still weep myself occasionally when I think of what happened.'

There was a brief and happy interlude at the end of October, when the Wesley Memorial at Gwennap Pit was officially opened. 'Many misunderstandings were cleared up, and the Methodists confessed that at the outset they hadn't understood what Guy was talking about. They didn't know, for example, when he described how he was going to achieve an effect with tesserae, that these were the component parts of a mosaic. People came from everywhere to see the panels, and were thrilled by them. Guy was given a gratuity and thoroughly enjoyed himself ordering a new wardrobe of rather extravagant and fun clothes.'

On a Sunday, not very many days later, Guy and Helena arranged a lunch party. Their guest was a venerable old gentleman, an engineer of considerable repute. When his daughter was away, Guy would occasionally go to stay with him to provide company and help with domestic chores. Helena went to fetch him, while her husband laid a fire and set the table. 'When we arrived back from Truro, Guy was dead on the sofa. I telephoned for a doctor, but of course it was too late. There was a post-mortem, which diagnosed hardened arteries and a massive heart attack. He'd appeared to be in excellent health, and had been working very hard taking solidified tar from our recently repaired flat roof to the orchard, where he'd kept a bonfire going for a week. His own doctor, who'd been away at the time, telephoned me later and said he was astonished. He'd only recently examined Guy, and thought he was more like a sixty- than a seventy-year-old.'

Helena has no doubt that the death of his cat and the mounting aggravations of life in St Clement conspired to add a lethal injection of stress to a constitution weakened by old age and deteriorating arteries. The burden of all she has written and spoken on the subject suggests a belief that the couple might have enjoyed a little more time together —perhaps a few months, perhaps a couple of years—if she had pressed more strongly nine years or so before, when he was, in his own phrase, 'turned out' by the Cathedral, the case she was then making for a move away from Cornwall and back to the South East.

As it was, twenty-six years and two months after marriage had ended a spinsterhood which looked like becoming her natural condition of life, Helena was by herself again. 'It was a most dreary and depressing period. I had not only to cope with the loneliness of suddenly losing my companion of more than a quarter of a century, but also with disposing of all his treasured possessions—his hi-fi, his collection of uniforms, his clothes and gondola, and the contents of his studio.' Among the artefacts to be sorted and allocated to friends of her husband's or admirers of his talent was a mosaic of Christ's empty tomb with one solitary figure depicted: Mary, with the shroud over her shoulder.

'And all the while the vultures were hovering and quarrelling among themselves. At least avian vultures have a place in nature's chain as scavengers . . .' Here was a woman of 74, bewildered and distressed at the sudden loss of her husband. One wound too many had temporarily paralysed her formidable duelling skills. Would she stay in St Clement? No. She had had enough of the place and decided to move nearer her relatives in East Anglia. She had a prime residential property for sale, in a much sought-after area of Cornwall, a period cottage renovated with care and taste, commanding extensive estuarial and country views. She was advised to put it on the market for £52,000, and accepted an offer of £51,000. Two years later it was on the market again at £145,000.

It was from an armchair in her new cottage that she reached for a cassette recorder and set down the memories that are occasionally interrupted by a snuffle or a mew or the dab of a paw at a microphone, by a whispered 'get down!' or a memo to herself ('I'm saying "you know" too much. It's an irritating habit which I despise in other people. I must try to stop it'). The relaxed and reflective stream of thought is occasionally fractured by an unexpected pause in the tape, when one imagines the kettle going on, or a tin of cat food being opened to placate an impatient audience, or maybe just a stroll among the rampant Japanese anemones which symbolise, only for the gardener, the magic acres of Tenderah, wholly translated to Cambridgeshire after St Clement splintered the Cornish spell. Indoors again, to set down another passage, fruit of a couple of turns between the flower-beds. 'I find Haddenham a much healthier, saner, and better place, with kind and interesting people. St Clement, beautiful as it is, will always be tainted with evil for me. I shall never go back.'

CHAPTER TWELVE

A KINDLY, FRIENDLY PLACE

Haddenham, May 4

Dear Frank,

I hope you had a pleasant and successful trip to Venice. I have been expecting you to ask about the vultures and the evil in St Clement, and wondering how I would answer. Neighbours' quarrels are very tedious, and lengthy disputes between the buyers and sellers of houses are equally squalid and boring. There is also the fact that was emphasised by an old man I met yesterday in The Three Kings. He is a retired welder, and it transpired that he knew the friend who was with me when I went back to the house and found Guy dead. The old man is known as Bronco, and we had a wide-ranging conversation which lasted until closing time, during which he made a remark that stayed in my mind. He said that if Christ really existed, the truest statement he ever made was, 'they know not what they do.' That was a principle we always tried to keep in mind in the face of our enemies.

If I'd known you were going to Venice, I would have asked you to try to get hold of Gina's portrait of Dingo, the stray dog she rescued whose name became the title of our organisation. Gina takes very little part in things now. She is far from well, and has got to get out of the two-storey flat she shares with her husband as the building is to be sold. I sometimes hear about her. At the moment (have I told you about this?) I am extremely concerned about a young man in the South of Italy who has rescued thirty-two cats, seventeen of them females, and has abandoned plans to have them spayed, despite my offer to pay. As far as I can see his reasons are entirely specious. I grieve for the as yet unborn and unwanted hordes of kittens who will breed from the females in rapid geometrical progression. It is a measure of my reformed character that I've decided not to bother to write back to the man concerned. There was a time when I would have massacred him by letter for chickening out. I rang up the Dingo member who first brought the matter to my attention and she was very upset as well, but she adjured me not to have another stroke by getting myself too agitated about his defection. I may say that I am not unaware of how little all this matters in the context of world events. But there is nothing I can do about South Africa, Northern Ireland, or the Lebanon or Israel, and money given to charities seems to do little to alleviate the famines in Africa. But I can do something about Italian cats, and it infuriates me when sentimental people create obstacles . . .

I spent part of my 77th birthday at the Woodgreen Refuge Animal Blessing Service in Ely Cathedral. The enormous congregation included a pig, a swan, and some stick insects. Outside were various large animals, including a heavy horse and one of those adorable miniature ponies, no taller than a labrador. The whole point of these services is to give thanks for the beauty and variety of God's creation, make penitence for our abuse of that creation, and to pray for compassion.

* * *

A tiny cottage with a tiny garden, and that festooned with so much chicken wire that it resembles a tiny concentration camp. In fact, the garden at Haddenham has been enclosed to allow several cats the freedom to cavort or relax *al fresco* or to annoy each other and the anemones, but not to stray onto an adjacent main road. Her move from the far west to the far east of England took Helena within a few miles of the half-sister for whose infant safety she had, decades before, grudgingly sacrificed a cat. No similar pressures complicated their reunion. Bast, Minnie, Ronnie, Purrkins, Blackie, Jenny and Fatty all travelled in the car from Cornwall to Haddenham on May 1, 1986. Jenny, Blackie, and Fatty were moved into a shed, where they were comforted during the coming cold winter by the loan of Guy's old stone hot water bottle. Bast, Minnie, Purrkins and Ronnie were allowed to use the amenities of the cottage.

Once Helena's neighbours had worked out that the wire contraptions portended not an aviary but a private cattery, she was quickly conscripted into the local community as an unofficial and unpaid consultant on feline affairs. 'Soon after my arrival,' she recalls, 'there was a ring at my door. Outside there were five people: three generations—grandmother, mother, teenage daughter, little boy, toddler, and a cat they had found in the lethal traffic.' Helena located its owners and restored their pet. Soon she had become a regular clearing house for displaced animals. 'There was a lot of anxiety caused by a very thin ginger and white cat, sometimes seen wandering near a house which had been empty in Haddenham High

Street. I saw him ejected from a parked car, and trying to get into the house again. Someone had bought him a pound of liver, which he demolished. I tried to persuade him to follow me home, and in view of the amount of concern about him I seriously thought about kidnapping him. I decided to call on some newcomers to the village. When they let me in I saw several healthy cats and the thin cat lolling in a chair. "How many of your cats have been neutered," I demanded to know. "All of them," they replied. The thin cat turned out to be a much loved pet, very old and under the vet. He was on a low-protein diet and the kindly meant pound of liver had made him ill.

'Besides this old cat I fostered two almost identical black and white kittens which were found wandering. The first, a female, was quickly found by a friend of her owner, who knew she had been missing for several days and was astonished when, in response to my card on the gate, she came in and found the lost kitten so far from home. The second walked into The Three Kings. She was also about three months old. It was another two months before she went to a lovely home.

'Haddenham is a singularly well balanced village—a kindly, friendly place. On my first day both immediate neighbours offered me lunch as I was waiting for the furniture to arrive. As I am obviously geriatric, I have been urged by all my neighbours, including The Three Kings, where I have lunch, to ring up if I have any problems. I take my laundry to the ironmongers, and I cash cheques at the post office, which is also a stationer and haberdasher. And I cannot escape from cats. The vicar said to me, "When you get to Heaven your cats will come leaping down to meet you." I replied, "I hope there will be forty-one, my own forty cats and one representative from the Venice cats. Perhaps there will be forty-two, to include one rescued Cornish cat. If they all came, there'll be too many cats, even for me."'

* * *

As I was writing these concluding pages of Helena's story, I received the latest annual report from the Anglo-Venetian Group for the Protection of Stray Animals. How fares Dingo? According to the balance sheet, at the end of 1986 it possessed assets of just £872. But one year later, the society's wealth had risen to £75,162. A sudden influx of new and prosperous members? A series of dizzily successful street collections in England and canal collections in Venice? As a matter of fact the excess of income over expenditure had risen from £442 to £2,664, but the most revealing entry in the ledger read as follows: 'Investments transferred from Mrs H. Sanders: £70,819.'

Inside the annual report, *la lotta continua*. Now Dingo is viced in a conflict between the Venetian Council and regional government officials who are questioning the validity of local agreements which would have allowed a cat clinic to be established in the Island of San Clemente. Cat lovers in Venice have already spent thousands of pounds on restorations and conversations, and it looks as if they may have to whistle for the grants that were promised to cover their costs. But there is good news of dynamic achievements by colleagues in Trento and Vicenza, and this from Milan:

> On Friday, April 29, 1987, at 21 Via Panfilo Castaldi, a cat was thrown from a fourth-floor window and brutally killed. Several people heard its terrible cries of pain. The body of the poor animal was thrown into a dustbin.
>
> As well as expressing our pity for this animal, a victim of human cruelty, we wish to underline certain facts.
>
> Whoever perpetrated this act showed himself to be uncivilised and lacking in finer feeling. Cats have the right, recognised by the national veterinary rules, to live and wander freely.
>
> Ill-treating an animal is punishable under Article 727 of the Penal Code.
>
> We hope that this horrible act will not be repeated and we shall fight to increase respect for nature, animals, and plants.

The statement was made into a poster and displayed throughout Milan. Its signatories included Mondo Gatto, the Friends of the Earth, the Ornithological Group of Lombardy, the League for the Abolition of

Shooting, and the Anti-Vivisection League. As Helena added in her report: 'This is an example of a flowing tide in Italy that might well overtake and engulf our claim to be the world's leading animal-loving country.'

Helena Sanders, after so many years of grappling with so many issues, with varying success and no little price to pay in personal grief or exhaustion, has managed to turn a tide, and she did so by her unswerving adherence to a philosophy which embraced life from the minute to the monumental, which tolerated no exemptions, never blinked, and never faltered.

* * *

Charles, Helena Trevelyan Edmonstone: *They Can't All Be Right*. The Industrial Christian Fellowship, London, 1946.

> If you meet a friend whom you are pleased to see, you show your joy by smiling, shaking hands, or kissing the person. If you meet someone you dislike, you may be tempted to scowl at them, and even hit them on the nose. A soldier salutes the colours of his regiment; a crowd cheers, hisses, throws flowers or stones, if it wants to express joy, anger, gratitude or hate. In each of these cases something material—face, hands, cloth, flowers, stones—is being used to express something spiritual—love, loyalty, or hate. Things like love or hate, generosity or greed, spiritual things that cannot be touched or measured, can only be expressed through material things, such as food, money, machinery and armaments, that can be seen and handled. This principle goes right through life.
>
> So a factory, an industry, the whole industrial system, not only can, but always does express something spiritual, either the glory of God, or the glory of mammon. The Sacraments of the Church sum up this principle. Things which can be seen and weighed—bread, wine, water—express things that cannot be seen—the presence of Christ, or the rebirth of Christ.
>
> We cannot abolish this principle, we can only ignore it. If we do, it will not cease to operate. Material things—machinery, coal, slums—will express evil spiritual things. The same machines, coal, bricks and mortar could be so used that, like the Heavens, they will declare the glory of God. There is no part of life for which Christianity has not got a message . . .